HISTORY'S SHADOW

History's Shadow

NATIVE AMERICANS AND HISTORICAL CONSCIOUSNESS
IN THE NINETEENTH CENTURY

Steven Conn

The University of Chicago Press
Chicago and London

Steven Conn is associate professor of history at Ohio State University. He is author of
Museums and American Intellectual Life, 1876–1926 (1998), also published by the
University of Chicago Press.

The University of Chicago Press, Chicago 60637
The University of Chicago Press, Ltd., London
© 2004 by The University of Chicago
All rights reserved. Published 2004
Printed in the United States of America

13 12 11 10 09 08 07 06 05 04   1 2 3 4 5

ISBN: 0-226-11494-5 (cloth)

Library of Congress Cataloging-in-Publication Data

Conn, Steven.
   History's shadow : Native Americans and historical consciousness in the nineteenth
century / Steven Conn.
      p.   cm.
   Includes bibliographical references and index.
   ISBN 0-226-11494-5 (cloth : alk. paper)
      1. Indians of North America—History—19th century. 2. United States—
Civilization—Indian influences. 3. Ethnology—United States. I. Title.

E77.C75 2004
973.04´97—dc22

                                                                2003022756

♾ The paper used in this publication meets the minimum requirements of the American
National Standard for Information Sciences—Permanence of Paper for Printed Library
Materials, ANSI Z39.48-1992.

FOR ANGELA

When I say that I wish you happiness, I mean that I hope as you grow older you will become more intensely alive.

—LEWIS MUMFORD TO SOPHIA WITTENBERG

CONTENTS

ACKNOWLEDGMENTS

Accruing debts both personal and professional is in many ways the most enjoyable part of any scholarly project. My ledger for this book is heavy with such debts, and so let me try to balance those accounts at least a little now.

This project began, in quite another guise, in the exceptionally pleasant library and archives at the American Philosophical Society. The Mellon grant I received from the APS made it possible to work with their remarkable collection, but also to benefit from the expertise of Roy Goodman and Rob Cox. The book took further shape several blocks away at the Library Company of Philadelphia, where I was also fortunate to receive a Mellon grant. As anyone who has worked there knows, the Library Company is a scholar's heaven, and I surely took advantage of the help and good advice offered by Connie King, Wendy Woloson, and Jim Green. Finally, I must thank the American Council of Learned Societies for a year-long fellowship which allowed me to complete the research and most of the writing. Without that, this book would still largely be a collection of fragments strewn across my desk.

I visited several other archives and libraries, often not quite sure what I was looking for, and was met with patience and good humor wherever I went. In Cambridge, my thanks go to the staff at the Harvard University Archives and at the Peabody Museum Archives. In Washington, I made good use of the collections and staff at both the archive of the Smithsonian Institution and the newly reopened National Anthropological Archive. In New York, I found some very interesting things with the help of the staff at both the American Museum of Natural History and New York Historical Society. The Benjamin West collection at the Historical Society of Pennsylvania proved very useful. The Newberry Library is a wonderful place to work, especially during a cold January, and more so because Jim Grossman was so hospitable to me during my visit. Thanks too to the staff at the Beloit College Library and to John Weeks at the Anthropology library at the University of Pennsylvania Museum who helped me navigate through their Brinton Collection.

This project necessarily forced me to cross several disciplinary terrains, and I got good guidance through these undiscovered countries from friends and colleagues in several different fields. Bob Berkhofer offered much encouragement early on, as did Dorothy Ross. Dell Hymes brought his vast anthropological experience to bear on the manuscript at different junctures. Bruce Grant and Lee Baker offered smart critiques of my reading of the history of anthropology and shared some of their good ideas with me. Bruce Trigger helped make sure I got my history of archaeology right. Chapter 2 would be considerably more confused (and would, incidentally, be Chapter 5) were it not for the close reading it got from Steve Hunt, Nora Kilbane, Catherine Spaeth, Aida Stanish, and Melissa Wolfe, all students in Barbara Groseclose's dissertation-writing workshop. I also called upon Andrew Walker yet again for help with matters art historical.

Bruce Kuklick has continued to function as my advisor long after he thought he was done with that job. In the eleventh hour, my father Peter and my friend and colleague Susan Schulten gave this book readings that improved it immensely. Doug Mitchell at the University of Chicago Press served both as editor and as cheerleader, and Jay Boggis and Leslie Keros did a remarkable editing job on this manuscript.

This project is older than either my daughter Olivia or my son Zachary. They both arrived in the midst of all this and proceeded to interrupt it (and everything else) in every conceivable way. Far from slowing it up, however, they only prompted me to finish this book more quickly so that I could get back to doing the things with them that were and are inevitably more fun in the first place.

In the end, all of the above dissolves into the realm of the trivial when compared to that which I owe Angela Brintlinger. In between all the other demands on her, she found the time over and over to make this book better. More than that, she brings beauty and warmth into our lives every day. This book belongs to her.

1

NATIVE AMERICANS AND THE PROBLEM OF HISTORY, PART I

I regret with you, the want of zeal *among* our countrymen for collecting materials concerning the history of these people.

BENJAMIN SMITH BARTON, 1797

In 1903, W. E. B. DuBois wrote, "The problem of the twentieth century is the problem of the color line," and thus penned perhaps the most enduring pronouncement on the state of America ever made. By the time DuBois wrote, America's racial "problem" had become, on a host of levels, a matter of black and white. The color line, in DuBois's view, separated white from black. The contours of that line shaped the very essence of what America was in its soul, and the erasure of that line became DuBois's life work.

DuBois's famous statement needs to be seen as a prophecy—a remarkably prescient one at that—and as a summing up. We have become so accustomed to thinking of DuBois as a prophet of the key issues surrounding race in the twentieth century that it has been easy to forget that he came to maturity as much in the twilight of the nineteenth century as in the dawn of the twentieth. Among the developments he witnessed in the waning of Victorian America was the disappearance of a third race from the national consciousness. DuBois may have seen the world in black and white when he wrote in 1903, but when he was born in 1868, the nation's racial dynamic came in three colors: black, white, and red.

By the turn of the twentieth century, DuBois was already the nation's most profound thinker on matters of race. Yet it is not at all clear that he spent much time thinking about that third race. As his biographer David Levering Lewis remarks, DuBois recognized that in the United States there formally existed only two races—Asians had been "excluded" while Native Americans had become "invisible."[1] Invisible because by the time DuBois made his prediction about the color line the frontier had been "closed" for thirteen years, and the massacre at Wounded Knee had effectively ended a generation of continuous warfare between the federal government and native groups. Noting that most young people had never even seen an Indian, the author of an 1885 children's book about Indians pronounced: "With the exception of a few roving bands of Apaches and other wild tribes of the plains, the Indian pictured in these pages no longer exists."[2] The color line between black and white might well have become the "problem" of the twentieth century, but only because for most Americans the "problem" of the Indian had been finally "solved."

In this outlook, DuBois was no different from most Americans, black or white, early in the twentieth century. My purpose is not to chide DuBois for his oversight. Rather, his relative silence on the question of Native Americans at the turn of the twentieth century underscores how thoroughly they had disappeared from Euro- and even African-American consciousness.

Three generations earlier such invisibility would have seemed nearly impossible. In a speech given to a New York City church congregation, Thomas McKenney, the first Superintendent of the Bureau of Indian Affairs (1824–1830), quoted a "distinguished citizen of Virginia" reminding his listeners of the nation's two part problem: "one of these relates to the black population which we carry in our bosom; the other to the red population which we carry on our back." In his *Notions of the Americans,* a collection of letters to Europeans about the United States James Fenimore Cooper published in 1827 as his version of Jefferson's *Notes on the State of Virginia,* Cooper put his comments about Native Americans immediately after his comments about slavery.

Alexis de Tocqueville, as astute an observer of antebellum society as DuBois was of the Gilded Age, certainly saw the United States as tri-colored. He paired Indians and African slaves almost metaphorically as polar opposites: "The Negro," he wrote in his classic *Democracy in America,* "has reached the ultimate limits of slavery, whereas the Indian lives on the extreme edge of freedom." Although they shared nothing of "birth, physique, language, nor mores," they did share "their misfortunes." The effects of slavery on Africans proved "not more fatal" than the effects of too much "independence" on Native Americans.[3]

For citizens of the United States in the late eighteenth and early nineteenth centuries, Indians were everywhere. They lived in a world, as Anthony Wallace put it recently, "in which Indians themselves were a constant presence."[4]

A presence and, as we have already hinted, a problem.

The diplomatic struggles and military encounters that characterized

Euro-Native relations during the Revolutionary period are well known. American colonists found themselves fighting against Indians allied with the French, and then once more when other Indian groups became allies of the British during the Revolutionary War. Beyond the formalized violence of war, Euro-Americans clashed with Indians on numberless occasions, most often when tensions over land on the ever-expanding frontier came to a boil. When the revolutionaries established an independent republic, Indians may well have been a near-constant physical presence, but they now found themselves in, but not of, the new nation. In Wallace's words, "native Americans fell outside the pole of the Jeffersonian republic, but inside the arena of Jeffersonian geo-politics."[5]

It makes sense to begin our considerations with Jefferson. Jefferson, in fact, was DuBois' predecessor as a philosopher of the nation's racial dilemma. None of the other founders spent as much time or intellectual energy thinking about Native Americans. Likewise, none of the others shaped policies that would prove so fateful to Native Americans. More than any other member of his circle, Jefferson recognized the increasingly intractable nature of relations between Euro-Americans and Indians. Writing to Benjamin Hawkins, Jefferson first commended him for "the attention which you pay to their rights . . . the want of which is a principle source of dishonor to the American character." But then he turned more despairing: "the two principles on which our Conduct towards the Indians should be founded, are justice and fear. After the injuries we have done them they cannot love us, which leaves us no alternative but that of fear to keep them from attacking us, but justice is what we should never lose sight of."[6] Jefferson did not describe the relationship between white Americans and Indians with the famous metaphor he used to describe the institution of slavery, but he might as well have. Native Americans represented another wolf held by its ears.

Yet, as Anthony Wallace has portrayed him, Jefferson, much as he struggled with the issue, could simply not envision a future for the United States that included a place for "Indians as Indians." As president, Jefferson tried to design an Indian policy that would humanely assimilate Native Americans into the new republic, but his vision of national expansion turned out not to have any room for Native Americans. Whatever uneasiness Jefferson felt about centralized power he lost to his "desire to obtain Indian land, at almost any cost." The buffer zone Jefferson tried to create between settlers and natives during his administration failed to prevent abuse of the latter by the Euro-Americans. By 1816, the policy was a "nullity, in Wallace's estimation."[7]

Most significantly, Jefferson's purchase of the Louisiana Territory in 1803 set in motion a sequence of events and forces that reached its antebellum conclusion in the Indian Removal Act of 1830. Jefferson's desultory policy of civilization and assimilation culminated, ironically but perhaps predictably, in Andrew Jackson's Trail of Tears. By the mid-nineteenth century, Indians remained a problem of national "geopolitics," but they no longer constituted the kind of presence they had been a scant fifty years earlier.

FOR JEFFERSON, Native Americans represented another kind of dilemma as well. Whatever agonizing he did over questions of geopolitics, Jefferson found in Native Americans an irresistible set of intellectual problems. As discussed in subsequent chapters, Jefferson the scholar pursued and encouraged the study of Native Americans with real enthusiasm and vigor. In his work emerge the beginnings of American linguistics, archaeology, and ethnology. In this respect, Jefferson was exemplary, but he was by no means alone. In the nineteenth century, Indians were the subjects and objects of all kinds of speculation, research, polemic, and jeremiad in the worlds of science and letters. By 1841, the anonymous author of *Events in Indian History* anticipated a certain weariness and impatience from the reading public when he began his short volume this way: "Another book upon the Aborigines of North America! Have we not volume upon volume of works on the Indians of this continent?"[8]

I should be clear at the outset that my book does not add to the "volume upon volume of works" written about Native Americans. Strictly speaking, this study is not really about Native Americans at all, and I am certainly no historian of Native America. The challenge of writing the history of Native Americans has been taken up by historians and anthropologists, both Native and non-Native, including Anthony Wallace, Vine Deloria, Richard White, Daniel Richter, and Lucy Murphy, to name a few whose works stare down at me from my shelves. (Recently, historian Ellen Fitzpatrick has provided an excellent account of the rise of Native American historiography in the twentieth century.)[9] This book, I trust, would not cause further grimaces from the acerbic R. S. H. who wrote in 1848: "So much has of late been written upon the Indians that I tremble in approaching them.... [T]hey have suffered [at] innumerable hands, been bemoaned in lamentable prose, and wept over in most imaginative poetry: their fate has certainly been a hard one."[10]

Nor does this book belong exactly with those by scholars—most notably Robert Berkhofer, Anthony Pagden, Roy Harvey Pearce, and Bernard Sheehan—who have addressed the ways in which Europeans and Euro-

Americans have imagined the American Indian. Berkhofer's landmark book *The White Man's Indian,* for example, demonstrated how the ways in which Native Americans were portrayed in popular culture served as blank screens upon which Euro-Americans could project their own fantasies and desires.

Rather this is a study of the volumes upon volumes of books like *Events in Indian History,* and of their authors. It examines Native Americans as objects of study and as subjects of intellectual discourse in the nineteenth century. This study amounts to an intellectual history whose major actors are the Euro-American men (and occasionally women) who, for a variety of reasons and with a variety of motivations, took it upon themselves to study, record, and write about Native Americans. Neither intellectual historians nor historians of Native Americans have really considered fully how the curiosity that Indians aroused—and the ways that curiosity was pursued—shaped the nineteenth-century American mind. Studying Indians, I will assert, constituted a central, if now largely forgotten, part of the nation's intellectual discourse, defining American science and social science, and shaping conceptions of the nation's history. That is the story I have attempted to tell here.

In examining the study of Native Americans as a chapter in the nation's intellectual life, I make three, interrelated claims. First, the very existence of Native Americans posed fundamental challenges to the way Euro-Americans understood the world. They found themselves unable to answer basic questions: Who are these people, and where did they come from? How are they related to other human groups, past and present? Have they demonstrated historical progress, or are they doomed to extinction? Attempts to answer such questions lay at the heart of the way several intellectual genres developed in this country.

Second, as they attempted to answer these basic and fundamental questions, Euro-Americans relied first on the only explanatory apparatus they had available: biblical and classical texts. As the nineteenth century wore on, however, and more research accumulated, it became increasingly clear that Indians were descended neither from a lost tribe of Israel nor from any colony of displaced Etruscans—to name two of the more popular theories that circulated in the antebellum period. I suggest that the failure of biblical and classical texts to explain the questions posed by Native American language, culture, and history—along with more familiar phenomena like the arrival of German criticism and Darwinian natural science—shaped the transition from a sacred world view to a secular one. Although that shift occurred on both sides of the Atlantic, I suggest that the

American intellectual encounters with Native Americans gave a particular cast to the way it happened here. As Samuel Drake put it in his 1851 *Biography and History of the Indians of North America*, "if we are to attribute everything to miracles, wherefore the necessity of investigation?"[11]

Finally, though, what troubled Euro-American scholars the most about Native Americans was their relationship to history. While people at all points in the past and at all points of the compass have had an interest in their own history, it is surely the case that history as a formalized practice and as an organized discipline only emerged during the course of the nineteenth century. That emergence had two components, each bound tightly to the other. On the one hand, the practice of history developed its own methodology during the nineteenth century, based on a set of rules that governed what historical questions should be asked, what constituted historical evidence, and in what form history should be written. On the other hand, Americans developed a new historical consciousness during the nineteenth century—a rough consensus shared by many about how the mechanisms of history worked, the exceptional place of the United States in the flow of history, and a sense, both reassuring and disquieting, that the distance that separated the present from the past grew almost daily. Method and consciousness reinforced each other, thereby drawing the boundaries of what constituted history.

This book argues that the attempts to study and understand Native Americans figured centrally in that process of definition. Trying to answer questions posed by the very presence of American Indians and the astonishing variety of their cultures forced Americans to confront the meaning of history, both their own history and the history of the Native Americans: How should history be studied? What drove its processes? Where might it ultimately lead? The change of American historical consciousness across the stretch of the nineteenth century meshed with attempts to figure out exactly where and how Indians fit into "history," as it was pursued and understood. Did Native Americans have a history? If so, how should it be recovered? More importantly, could "their" history be seen as part of "ours"? My sense is that the intellectual encounters with Native Americans made it possible for Euro-Americans to define history apart from myth, history apart from culture, and the realm of history as something quite different from the realm of the past. By the 1890s, Native Americans could very well have a past, but they did not, by and large, have a history. In this sense, Native Americans constituted history's shadow.

To get at this intellectual history, I have relied heavily on the discourse surrounding Indians that appeared in print during the nineteenth century.

Vast as this literature is—the anonymous author of *Events in Indian History* did not exaggerate!—it comes as no surprise that it varies widely in a host of ways. Some of this variation stems from the wide variety of writers who turned their attention to Indians—from presidents and diplomats, to scholars and scientists, to ministers and poets. Then too, this immense body of writing, appearing in the form of books, magazine and journal articles, pamphlets, and lectures, was read by very different audiences as well. Writings about Native Americans in the nineteenth century traversed the full spectrum from the serious and learned, to the silly and laughable.

My purpose is not to sort out the serious from the trivial, to separate the scientific and scholarly wheat from the popularized, fantastical chaff, although some winnowing inevitably happens here. Rather, by treating these publications more or less as a single body I am attempting to demonstrate how pervasive Indians were in the intellectual life of nineteenth-century America. Further, I am arguing that the sheer volume and variety of this published material can reveal important things—not necessarily about the Indians themselves, but about the Euro-American culture that produced and read it.

Some years ago, when writing about the American 1930s, Warren Susman made a similar claim. One doesn't have to insist, he argued, that Superman comics are better than Shakespeare's plays to recognize that Superman might reveal a great deal about the culture of the 1930s. So it is here. Much of what got written, published, and read about Indians in the nineteenth century has been roundly and decisively dismissed by anthropologists, linguists, archaeologists, and others as useful or even legitimate science. After all, few among us take seriously the theory of the lost civilization of Atlantis, despite the currency it had in the mid-nineteenth century. Nonetheless, these writings remain important fragments of our intellectual and cultural history. In 1833, for example, Josiah Priest gave the reading public a ripping tale of the ancient and vanished races that once populated the American West. Not a word of his *American Antiquities and Discoveries in the West* is probably taken seriously today. By 1835, however, the book had sold 22,000 copies: serious sales even by today's standard. This book, and others like it, ought to command serious historical attention.

Yet at the same time, however, the trajectory I trace here describes the way in which discourse about Native Americans became increasingly professionalized. As in all other fields of intellectual life, the lines separating professional and respectable scholarship from mere popularizing were being drawn more sharply. The development of America's nineteenth-century intellectual life in many ways mirrors the delineations between "highbrow" and "lowbrow" that Lawrence Levine has charted in other areas of American culture. These realms interacted, to be sure, and the differences between the serious and the popular were never as sharp as many late nineteenth-century scientists and intellectuals insisted they were. One has only to think of the Barnumesque displays of Native Americans at the 1876 Centennial and at the 1893 World's Columbian Exposition—the former sponsored by the United States National Museum, the latter by the fair's department of anthropology—to remember that highbrow and lowbrow continued to intersect well into the last quarter of the nineteenth century. Nevertheless, the nature of intellectual discourse did change across the century. My concerns lie with how the study of Indians shaped what came to be considered the serious side of American intellectual life.

The next chapter begins by looking, in a literal sense, at these developments. In the nineteenth century, Native Americans filled the nation's visual culture in virtually every conceivable genre—from painting, to lithographs and mass-produced illustrations, to cigar store figures, and eventually to photographs. I make no attempt in the chapter at a full or complete evaluation of how Indians were represented visually. Instead, I want to focus on a few painters and photographers, to examine how their work was a historical documentation of Indians. We start with Benjamin West, arguably the first American to paint historical subjects in the grand manner. By the Civil War, history painting in the grand manner, once the apex of painterly achievement, had faded as a vital genre in both the United States and in Europe. I suggest, however, that the historical impulse did not disappear from American art, for American images of Indians, both on canvas and in photographs, created new conventions of how history could be represented. The shifting portrayal of Native Americans first in landscape paintings and finally in portraiture—both in paint and in photographs—charts the change from seeing Native Americans as part of a didactic and moral history to seeing them as part of an anthropology rooted in natural history. In this sense, the images examined in chapter 2 encapsulate our larger project. How did Euro-Americans construct a past for Indians? How did Euro-Americans construct a consciousness of their own history? And how did the two evolve quite apart from each other?

In chapter 3, we turn our attention to the study of Indian languages. In the early republic, the study of American Indian languages, by missionaries and others, was a thriving enterprise. Investigators compiled lengthy vocabularies, deciphered rules of grammar, and remarked on the rich, poetic and metaphorical quality of Indian speech. "Eloquent" was a commonplace description of how Indians used their language. Thomas Jefferson, in his

Notes on the State Virginia, was only one of many writers who pointed to Chief Logan's speech to Lord Dunmore as evidence of the admirable quality of Indian eloquence.

Students of Indian languages believed their research would be the foundation for the new, scientific study of language, and therefore a field in which American scholars could out-do their European counterparts. They also believed that language was the key to understanding history—not just Indian history, but all human history—and that through the comparative study of languages, genealogical relationships between human groups could be established. The study of Indian languages, which had begun in the seventeenth century as part of the missionary impulse, had become a historical project by the turn of the nineteenth century.

By the end of the nineteenth century, however, the field of American Indian linguistics had not developed as those early nineteenth-century pioneers had envisioned. Instead, the study of Indian languages became one of several subfields of American anthropology. Language study developed as an essential part of the anthropological method, but not necessarily as a field unto itself and not necessarily with the same concerns about the relationship between language and history. The more autonomous work of philology and linguistics was still done primarily by the Europeans, and mostly on the dead and ancient languages being uncovered by archaeologists. When William Dwight Whitney, himself a professor of Sanskrit at Yale, wrote *The Life and Growth of Language* in 1875, he generalized Native American language as "cumbrous and time-wasting in its immense polysyllabism." What had once been seen as the key to understanding Indian history was now used primarily to create a system to classify Indian groups.

Whether or not American archaeology began with Jefferson when he sponsored excavations of Indian mounds, it is certainly true that archaeology in America began with investigations in American Indian sites. Chapter 4 explores the history of American archaeology and its relationship to the study of Indian history. By the middle of the nineteenth century, as the Ohio and Mississippi River valleys filled with settlers, Americans searched for Native American history by digging up what had been buried by past generations. These excavations, and their discoveries, were reported widely in both the American and English press.

The turn toward archaeology represented two important shifts in how American Indians were studied. The first was a new reliance on objects as the place where knowledge inhered. What I have called elsewhere an "object-based epistemology" defined the intellectual mission of excavators who dug for, collected, and classified American Indian objects.[12] Related to this was the conviction that objects constituted a permanent record of Native American history, while language disappeared with the speakers, and that by the middle of the nineteenth century, those speakers did indeed seem doomed to disappear.

This chapter examines how the field of American archaeology developed, how archaeologists defined their questions, and how ideas about archaeology intersected with ideas about history. As with the study of languages, by the end of the century American archaeology had assumed a secondary importance to the work going on in the Old World. As Bruce Kuklick has described in his book *Puritans in Babylon,* American excavations, especially in the Near East, made spectacular finds. Even more important, archaeologists were driven by a desire to prove the legitimacy of the Bible as an historical source. Ironically, questions that had been asked first and been left unanswered about American Indians were now being asked halfway round the world.

By the end of the nineteenth century, nearly all the serious study of Native Americans fell within the purview of the newly emergent discipline of anthropology. This new field included four constituent parts: linguistics, archaeology, physical anthropology, and ethnology. Chapter 5 sketches how these four pursuits, once autonomous discourses, became subsidiaries of a new anthropology. It begins by examining the relationship between literature and the genre of ethnography. Indians filled the pages of American literature in the nineteenth century, most importantly perhaps in the work of James Fenimore Cooper. At the same time, ethnography was developing as another way of describing Indians in texts. By the end of the century, it was ethnography, not literature, that had become the single authoritative way of translating Indian culture into writing.

At the same time, physical anthropology developed as a way of addressing the questions of race and racial distinctions that were also central to the field of inquiry called ethnology. The story of how race was studied "scientifically" is well known to most students of nineteenth-century America, but my purpose in this chapter is to examine how it contributed to the formation of an American anthropology. Finally, this chapter considers the institutional matrix in which anthropology matured. It pays particular attention to the Bureau of American Ethnology, the growth of museums, and the emergence of university departments of anthropology. By the end of the nineteenth century, the study of Native Americans had become almost entirely anthropological. And as anthropology, the study of Native Americans, while interested to some extent in the Native American past, had become largely ahistorical.

The last chapter considers American historical writing proper. Having examined how the historical considerations of these other practices shrank, it looks at how Indians fared in the writing of history. I begin with romantic historians, particularly Francis Parkman, regarded by many as the last, greatest example of that school, and finish with Herbert Baxter Adams and Frederick Jackson Turner. In between, I pause to consider what I have called "the prehistoric revolution," the creation in the mid-nineteenth century of a conceptual space that existed before history. This, I believe, had an enormous effect on how Native American history was conceived. Having been removed from the mainstream narratives of histories being written in the nineteenth century, Indians could be put into this other, prehistoric category, and viewed as a people before and without a history.

The chapters in this book, like intellectual disciplines themselves, represent an artificial order and a categorization imposed on an otherwise messy situation. They are a convenience, and although I think that the choices I have made clarify a set of issues in America's nineteenth-century intellectual life, I should warn at the outset that there is considerable overlap between chapters—of people, of ideas, of events. I have done my best to disentangle them.

Each chapter of this book sketches a long arc, which begins with the founding of the republic, or thereabouts, and ends with the 1890s, approximately. Although Indians certainly drew the attention of writers and scholars before the late eighteenth century, the events of independence and nationhood, along with the shifts in knowledge and learning that took place as part of the American enlightenment, changed the context in which people asked questions about Indians. I end, roughly, in the 1890s, which may strike some readers as an almost perverse choice. After all, our understanding of Native Americans, both present and past, changed dramatically because of the Boasian revolution in anthropology and all that flowed from it in the first half of the twentieth century. I have made this choice because I remain convinced by John Higham's argument made some while ago that the decade of the 1890s witnesses a significant "reorientation" in American culture.[13] But whereas Higham, and others, see the 1890s as prefiguring many of the cultural struggles of the twentieth century, I want to view the decade as a culmination of a century-long process of thinking about history, and how that thinking was stalked by its shadow.

A note on usage: first, my considerations are confined geographically to the space we call the United States. There may well be a companion story here to tell about how the Indian civilizations of Central and South America were viewed, but that is for another time and another scholar. Likewise, it is a gross generalization to lump Canada in with the rest of North America. I refer to the United States, America, and North America almost interchangeably for style's sake, and because this usage reflects the way the terms were used in the nineteenth century. Likewise, I use "Indian," "Amerindian," and "Native American" in the same way. I recognize that for some academics these have become fighting words, but I have chosen not to engage in those fights here.

Studying the Noble Savage

Tocqueville's description of Native Americans is worth lingering over in some detail. He begins his observations by telling readers that, unlike the "vexatious contrast" of European societies where rich and poor confront each other daily, "the Indian, all poor and all ignorant, are also all equal and free." "Indifferent" to the trappings of European civilization now presented to them, "there was in their manners a habitual reserve and a sort of aristocratic courtesy." Tocqueville continues:

> Gentle and hospitable in peace, in war merciless even beyond the known limits of human ferocity, the Indian would face starvation to succor the stranger who knocked in the evening on the door of his hut, but he would tear his prisoner's quivering limbs to pieces with his own hands. No famed republic of antiquity could record firmer courage, prouder spirit, or more obstinate love of freedom than lies concealed in the forests of the New World. The European made but little impression when they landed on the shore of North America; they were neither feared nor envied. What hold could they have on such men? The Indian knew how to live without wants, to suffer without complaint, and to die singing.[14]

The description weaves a marvelous tapestry of contradictory clichés: savagery and aristocracy; kindness and cruelty; peacefulness and war-mongering. And the paragraph resonates with familiarity: it is as succinct, indeed as breathless, a formulation of the idea of the noble savage as one is liable to find. That Tocqueville resorted to this trope, borrowed from his fellow countryman Jean-Jacques Rousseau, should come as no surprise. One suspects, in fact, that this was the description of Native Americans Tocqueville already had in his head when he set sail for the United States.

In recalling the noble savage, however, in his welter of oppositions, Tocqueville implicitly admitted something else. No better or more persuasive understanding of Native Americans had emerged by the time Tocqueville toured the country. Simply stated, Indians largely remained a mystery for white Americans in the first half of the nineteenth century. As Isaac McCoy put it in 1829, almost exactly the moment when Tocqueville arrived for his visit, "it is remarkable that with the opportunities of more than two centuries to become acquainted with the Aborigines of our country, their character and condition should at all times have been so imperfectly understood by us."[15]

Remarkable to be sure, because the very nature of Native Americans had perplexed Europeans beginning in 1492. The misnomer by which they came to be known—Indians—reflects after all a fundamental misunderstanding about who these people were and what their relationship to the rest of the world was. As David Bidney pointed out some years ago, Indians posed both theoretical and practical problems for the colonists who came in growing numbers in the sixteenth, seventeenth, and eighteenth centuries.[16]

For much of this period, theory and practice intersected on the terrain of religion. For believing Christians, as Anthony Pagden has noted, it became crucial that non-Christians be brought into the fold, "indeed, cajoled or forced into entering it." For some Catholic Spaniards and Frenchmen, and for New England Puritans, the missionary encounter with Native Americans lay at the heart of their errand into the wilderness.[17] The missionary encounter, however, forced European colonists to confront a set of intellectual dilemmas. The first of these was language—how to communicate the word of God when Indians and Europeans understood not a word of each other's languages? The next set of problems revolved around figuring out just how Indians fit into the history and teleology of God's plan as revealed in the Bible. This, then, as Pagden points out, amounted to a problem of classification.[18] By the eighteenth century, this focus on classification enabled a shift in the study of Native Americans away from the theological to include the world of natural history. Late in the eighteenth century, Benjamin Smith Barton, one of the most important American naturalists, titled his study of Native Americans, "An Essay towards a Natural History of the North American Indians."[19]

The study of natural history, and the particular way it emerged during the American eighteenth century, laid important foundations for how Native Americans would be studied and understood through much of the nineteenth. It was no accident that Tocqueville put his long description of the noble savage in the very first chapter, entitled "Physical Configuration of North America."

IN 1775, AFTER having "had them years standing before me," and having "lived with them as a friend and brother," James Adair published *The History of the American Indians*. In it, Adair argues that the Indians descended from the Jews, and he spends the vast bulk of the book proving this by examining "their religious rites, civil and marital customs, their marriages, funeral ceremonies, manners, language, traditions, and a variety of particulars." A quick sampling of his evidence: "Argument I, both have tribes. . . . Argument VI, they count time after the manner of the Hebrews. . . . Argument VII, they have prophets and high priests. . . . Argument XI, Mosaic law." And so it goes, through 23 arguments, for 200 pages.[20]

We won't bother to pause in order to figure out just exactly how Adair deduced Mosaic law among the Indians with whom he had spent time. In fact, the theory that the Indians constituted a lost tribe of Israel circulated widely and persuasively in the late eighteenth century, and survived well into the nineteenth. Adair's book is remarkable only in the thoroughness with which he argued the theory, and in the authority with which he spoke, because, as he announced at the outset, he had lived for some years with Indians.

Despite the weightiness of this tome, Adair did not put the question of origins to rest. In his essay, Barton reviews several major theories on the origin of Indians, an "almost endless list of hypotheses." He first considers the idea, put forth by a Mexican mathematician named Siguenra, that Indians descended from Nephtuhim, the grand nephew of Noah, and that they had journeyed to the New World "a short time after the confusion of Babel." Barton points out that some writers "have brought the Carthagenians across the Atlantic" and claimed them as the progenitors of the Indians. Others had attempted "to prove that the greater part of the world was peopled by the inhabitants of Scandinavia." Others still saw Wales or Ireland as the place from which the Indians first came. By the time he reached Adair and the theory of the Jewish origin, Barton quite dismisses what he calls this "strange opinion."

Barton ran through these theories in order to get to one he feels is, finally, right. After looking at the "conjectures" of Edward Brerewood, coupled with the discoveries of Captains Bering and Cook in the North Pacific, Barton was convinced: "I imagine there can no longer be any doubt that America was principally peopled from Asia." He too offered a list of reasons to support the claim, and though it ran only to four items, rather than Adair's twenty-three, it included the fact that "the languages of the Tartars, and of other Asiatic nations, have a very considerable relation to those of the Americans."[21]

From our vantage, Barton's conclusion seems remarkably sharp, even if his claim about language is a more than a bit dubious. Most who have studied the question of how the New World was first populated agree that migration from northeast Asia via the Bering Strait is the most likely answer. In a well-known textbook on the archaeology of North America, Jesse Jennings, in the first line of the chapter on the "origins" of Native Americans, writes with a sense of finality on the subject: "At once the most important and the least dramatic event in American history was the passage of the first human from Asia into the New World 30,000 or more years ago."[22]

In the early republic and antebellum periods, however, Barton's sound reasoning failed to close the case. Caleb Atwater, the first person systematically to explore the intriguing and mysterious mounds that dotted the river valleys of Ohio, published the results of his surveys in 1820 (discussed further in chapter 4). Atwater virtually circled the globe searching for points of comparison. Looking for the "authors of our ancient works," Atwater found similar mounds not only in biblical lands, but in England, Wales, Scotland, Turkey, and across the Russian Empire. "Thus," he concluded, "we learn from the most authentick sources, that these ancient works existing in Europe, Asia, and America, are as similar in their construction, in the materials with which they were raised, and in the articles found in them, as it is possible for them to be."[23]

By 1837, M. M. Noah returned to the Israelites in an energetic book entitled *Discourse on the Evidence of the American Indians being the Descendants of the Lost Tribes of Israel.* He repeated some of what Adair had said over fifty years earlier, particularly about the similarities of language. "The number of Hebrew words in their religious services is incredible," he offered at one point and then elsewhere noted, "the Indians, like the Hebrews, speak in parables." However confidently Noah wrote about the topic, he did have to acknowledge that "it is a singular fact that history is exceedingly confused, or rather I may say dark, respecting the ultimate dispersion of the tribes among the cities of the Medes."[24]

By midcentury, then, the questions of who the Indians were and where they had come from remained open for debate. Evidence that the Welsh had sailed west to populate the New World, or that the Etruscans had done the same, continued to surface in the pages of books and magazines throughout the 1840s and 1850s. Superintendent McKenney summarized the state of the intellectual dilemma thoroughly, if a bit breathlessly, in 1846: "Who are the Indians? Whence they came? When and by What Route was their exodus from the land of their origin. . . .Who were they, if any, that preceded them in the occupancy of this country?" Through no lack of trying, Americans seemed no closer to answering these questions in the middle of the nine-teenth century than they had been at its beginning. In 1849 the author of *Peter Parley's Tales* for children had to confess to his young readers, "The origin of the aborigines of America is involved in mystery."[25]

That the basic question should still be a mystery, given the attention it had already received by 1849 from writers, scholars, and armchair specula-tors, would seem a stunning failure of America's intellectual community. Rather than indict them for that failure, however, or even poke fun at it, we ought to remember that Americans struggled to understand the Indians within the only historical frameworks available to them, those from the classical world, and, most importantly, the Bible. Indeed, Atwater began his exegesis on who built the mounds with reference to biblical history, and in-terspersed it with references like "The land of Ham, seems to have been the place where the arts were first nursed."[26]

Indeed, religious conviction more than anything else may have pre-vented Barton's Asian hypothesis from being more widely accepted. After all, one had to move quite far beyond the human history as revealed in the Bible to accept that theory. Or, as in the case of Caleb Atwater, who did seem to believe that Native Americans descended from the "tartars," one had to engage in extraordinary extrapolations to connect the corner of northeast Asia with "the land of Ham." As Superindendent McKenney put it emphat-ically: "There is, however, but one source whence information can be de-rived on this subject—and that is the Bible."[27] For Christian believers in the antebellum period, the origin of the Indians was an intellectual square peg, and writers worked with great if tortured vigor to jam it into the round hole of biblical and classical history.

The geographic origin of Native Americans was only one way in which the authority of the Bible was strained in the first half of the nineteenth cen-tury. As Benjamin Barton noted in 1797, those who debated the question of origins actually fell into two camps: the first of these speculated about which part of the Old World Indians had come from; the second "embraces those who suppose that the Americans are in strict language the aborigines of the soil, and not emigrants from other parts of the world."[28] Suggesting that Indians were autochthonous, that they had not come from anywhere else on the globe, was an even more radical proposition than arguing that they had arrived in the New World as a result of some set of historical events not described in the Bible. Genesis is quite clear about this: all human groups trace their lineage back to a single pair. As aborigines, "in strict lan-guage," Native Americans would fall outside the biblical genealogy.

Thomas McKenney minced no words as he drew the contours of this debate and hinted at its stakes. "If," he posited, "the garden of Eden is nowhere in America, Adam (the Adam of the Bible, and we have no authentic record of any other), could not have been created here." So far, so good. Then came the obvious conclusion: "The Indians cannot be, therefore, *indigenous* to America, but, being descendants of the original pair, they must have come of some one of the families that settled and peopled some one of the divisions of the globe. In other words, they must be of Asiatic, of African, or of European descent." McKenney sounds almost impatient at having to explain all this. After all, "that the whole human family sprang from an original pair, that pair being the product of the power of God . . . is a truth so universally admitted, as to render any elaborate argument in its support superfluous." Likewise, New York doctor Samuel Forry made the same point, although it took him over fifty pages to elaborate it. In assessing "the natural history of the American aborigines," he argued that "Revelation and Science are both beams of light emitted from the same Sun of Eternal Truth."[29]

But McKenney did have to make this point, despite the universality of its truth, because he wrote in the midst of a great debate over the nature of race, a debate in which the characteristics of the Native American figured prominently. On one side stood McKenney and other "monogenesists," who believed that all human beings had sprung from "an original pair," and thus believed in the essential unity of the human species. On the other side, the "polygenesists" argued that different races had different and separate origins, and thus had different capacities and destinies. Those in the monogenesis camp derived their conviction and authority from the Bible's story of Genesis; polygenesists fancied themselves as empirical researchers, relying on the most current and sophisticated interpretation of scientific data.

In retrospect, this debate strikes us as so weighted with ideological baggage that it hardly seems worthwhile to evaluate it as science. Southerners, like Josiah Nott, bellowed loudly among those proponents of polygenesis, as a way of offering a thinly veiled defense of slavery. But polygenesists also claimed among their number some of the leading northern figures in American nineteenth-century science, most prominently Harvard University naturalist Louis Agassiz, probably the most celebrated scientist in the country during the mid-nineteenth century, and Samuel Morton, the Philadelphia physician who studied race by measuring skulls. Agassiz came to his views in part through his science and in part because of the physical revulsion the Swiss naturalist felt the first time he encountered black people on a trip to Philadelphia to visit Morton. When *De Bow's Review,* a southern magazine, ran a piece supporting polygenesis and denying a common origin of Caucasians and Africans, it quoted liberally from Nott, Morton, and Agassiz.[30]

The debate between the monogenesists and the polygenesists, and the relationship between that debate and the scientific construction of racial categories (not to mention racism) has been well documented.[31] In the racial schema devised by polygenesists, all races were not created equal, but existed in a hierarchy, which these scientists worked hard to define with precision. As chapter 5 documents, in the scientific—ethnological—study of race, especially Morton's work with skulls, can be found the origins of the field we now call physical anthropology. What bears noticing here is just how much scientific energy was devoted to the study of race in the mid-nineteenth century. Once Americans set out looking for evidence of racial distinctions in earnest, they found it everywhere. Charles Pickering ventured forth with one of the United States Exploring Expeditions in the 1840s, convinced that five races inhabited the globe. By the time he returned his list had grown to eleven, "though I am hardly prepared to fix a positive limit to their number."[32]

Rather than review the racial ideologies that undergirded the science of race, I want to examine briefly the theological dimension of this discussion. We should be clear: both monogenesists and polygenesists maintained their belief in the divine creation and in most of the Christian tradition. Indeed, after 1859 Agassiz saw his life's work as defending religion from what he took to be the corrosive assaults of Darwinism. The critical difference between the two camps lay in the particular details of the Book of Genesis and the Hebrew Bible. Monogenesists believed that the story of creation as told in that text needed no revision. Polygenesists, however, weren't so sure. As Josiah Nott put it: "My main object . . . is to cut loose the natural history of mankind from the Bible, and to place each upon its own foundation, where it may remain without collision or molestation."

Nott understood the stakes when he entered the debate. In an essay for the *Southern Quarterly Review*, he offered that the Bible provided no "rational chronology" to explain "this wide spread and diversified population from a single pair." The scientific "facts" being accumulated about races and racial differences "cannot be explained . . . without, in my humble opinion, doing violence to the Mosaic account." A few years later, he was more direct. "The unity of races," he told a lecture audience, "can only be deduced from forced constructions of the Old and New Testaments." Later, he asked his audience, "Where is the evidence of the descent of the black and red races from Adam, so clear as to upset the whole physical history of man?" Rejecting the details of the Old Testament need not mean, Nott assured readers, rejecting the Bible altogether. Indeed, denying the unity of the human race "so far from infringing on the veracity of scripture, will, I am satisfied, become one of the most solid grounds of its defense." The anonymous writer for *De Bow's* agreed: "The interests of sound and heaven-inspired theology are identical with those of physical truth. There is but one Author to the physical and moral universe, and every investigation tending to reconcile the two together of which they must be capable, is a sacred and noble work."[33]

Monogenesists could be just as emphatic, though perhaps not as sanguine about how the debate between science and religion would resolve. M. M. Noah reminded his readers what they all ought to know already: "God that made man in his own image gave to the Indians an origin and parentage like unto the rest of the great family of mankind, the work of his own almighty hand." Dr. Forry undertook his review of the natural history of American Indians to demonstrate the unity of "the great family of the human race." He concluded by telling his readers, "On the one side, he has the conclusions of Dr. Morton . . . and, on the other side, supported by the arguments of this paper, he has *the authoritative declaration of Moses that all human kind have descended from a single pair.*" Despite the proofs offered by Noah, Forry, and many others, James Southall, another monogenesist, understood that an epic battle had been joined. He wrote ominously that "there must be a trial of strength between the Bible and Science."[34]

The politics of this antebellum debate can be easily deduced. Polygenesists used science, first and foremost, as a defense of slavery; in addition, their conclusions about race could be used to justify the treatment of Native Americans in the era of Removal and immediately after. For some monogenesists, the essential unity of the human species implied all sorts of moral and Christian duties toward Native Americans and enslaved Africans. As Herman Humphrey, the president of Amherst College, put it in an impassioned speech denouncing the removal plan, "if the people sit still and look calmly on while the Indian are abandoned to their fate, in violation of the most solemn compacts . . . who in a foreign land will ever hereafter be willing to own that he is an American?"[35]

In the intellectual discourse that surrounded Native Americans during the first half of the nineteenth century, religion functioned in two ways. On the one hand, the intellectual constraints imposed by clinging to biblical frameworks of human history made it difficult to conceive of the history of Indians in other terms. As Noah put it, sounding almost exasperated: "If the Indians of America are not the descendants of the missing tribes [of Israel], again I ask, from whom *are* they descended?"[36] Whom indeed?

If commitment to biblical explanations retarded a more extensive understanding of Indian origins, then in the other direction biblical literalists did get it right on the question of monogenesis, even though evolutionary scientists today put that "original pair" not in a garden roughly five thousand years ago, but on the African savanna some several million years earlier. Resting their case only on the authority of scripture, rather than on the empirical weight of science, monogenesists insisted that the human family was a unity, and in this way they did nothing less than preserve, at least a little bit, the idea that Native Americans had a humanity.[37] For a believer like Indian Affairs Superintendent McKenney, the treatment of Indians at the hands of Euro-Americans caused a twitch in his faith. Looking back at what had happened in the wake of Indian removal, he wondered: "How are we to harmonize these conflicting events with our conceptions of the all wise, and good, and merciful God?" Asking whether all this destruction was a necessity, he concluded, "I think not."[38]

Searching for Indian History

James Adair understood the problem exactly in 1775. "In tracing the origin of a people," he wrote, "where there are no records of any kind either written or engraved, who rely solely on oral tradition for the support of their ancient usages, and have lost a great deal of them . . . the undertaking [is] difficult."[39]

Difficult to be sure. For Americans in the early republic, the question of just how to study the history of Indians proved vexing and complicated. In fact, the late eighteenth and early nineteenth centuries witnessed the rise not only of a new historical consciousness among Americans, but new standards of historical practice and a growing formalization of how history could be studied. Indians and their history wound up at the center of these shifts.

Euro-Americans had known for some time that native groups did have an understanding of their own past, an indigenous set of historical traditions. For the more sympathetic among them, native creation stories corresponded closely enough with biblical ones to admit Indians to the fraternity of Christianity. Henry Schoolcraft, for example, found that "Cherokee tradition preserves an allegoric version of the deluge which is quite peculiar." One implication of this sympathy, as missionary John Heckewelder asserted, was that since "they have no historians among them," they thus had no one to plead their case to "a sympathizing world." Heckewelder took this sympathy to a logical conclusion: "Why, then, should not a white man, a Christian . . . defend them as they would defend themselves."[40]

But as Adair observed, native histories existed entirely as "oral tradition," not as written texts. And as Schoolcraft, a remarkable student of native America, put it in 1830: "all unwritten tradition, extending beyond the era of Columbus, may be considered as entitled to little credit."[41] The distinction was central to this new conception of how history proper would be recovered. It would have several consequences for how Indian history was studied.

First, this definition of history's epistemology threatened to exclude Indian history altogether. As Alexander Bradford recognized in 1843: "The term history, in its usual acceptation, is somewhat restrictive in its scope. If its extent were strictly limited to authentic narratives and records . . . only a small portion of the human race has preserved any very ancient written memorials; and with the exception of the historical facts contained in the Sacred Volume, we should be left in ignorance of the most important occurrences of the early ages of the world." This recognition underscored that Indian history needed to be recovered and understood outside the boundaries of history proper, as it had come to be defined. By the end of the eighteenth century, as Pamela Regis has observed, people without writing could not have a history.[42]

As a consequence, anthropologist Clark Wissler noted some years ago, echoing Benjamin Barton, "almost from the first, it was recognized that the recovery of this lost history must be achieved, if at all, by natural history methods." And as Regis has demonstrated in her study of eighteenth-century American natural history, natural historical representations of America tended to depict the country as existing outside the flow of historical time.[43] Subsumed under this ahistorical mode of representation, and without "any ancient written memorials," Indian history would have to be natural history, not quite human history. Indians became, in the eyes of Euro-Americans, a people with a past, but without a history.

Additionally, the definition of history as a text-based enterprise meant not only that Indians could not have a history, as it was coming to be defined, but it also meant that they could not function as their own historians. William Moore, writing in 1855 as John Frost, put the dilemma succinctly. In attempting to study Indian history, "the Indians can give us no assistance; for of their own history, beyond the traditionary records of two or three generations, they know nothing; and the strange notions which some of them entertain of their origin need not to surprise us." Likewise, in his 1862 study of the Cree, F. V. Hayden echoed the now familiar historical conundrum when he wrote, "Among people where no written records exist, and whose only method of preserving their national histories is oral tradition . . . little can be extracted worthy to be considered of historical value." But he went on to be quite specific: "In regard to the Crees, all appears obscure farther back than 1760. . . . From 1760 down to the present time the history of the Crees can be traced with a fair degree of certainty."[44] If Indians were to have any history at all, they would require as their champions interlocutors like John Heckewelder.

Indians in the nineteenth century told their own history to be sure, though in ways that went largely unrecognized and misunderstood by white Americans. Some, like the Ojibway chief Kah-Ge-Gah Bowh, tried to bridge these cultural divides. Known to the white world as George Copway, he brought out *Copway's American Indian* in 1851 with supporting testimonials from people like Thomas McKenney, Washington Irving, William Gilmore Simms, Henry Schoolcraft, and James Fenimore Cooper. In the prospectus, Copway, who identified himself as a "Christianized Indian," announced that the journal would be "devoted entirely to subjects connected with the past and present history and condition of the people of his own race." Copway acknowledged that the publication was "certainly a novelty in the literary history of the United States, that an Indian should propose to conduct a paper devoted to the cause of the Indian." Copway recognized that "the inquisitiveness of the Anglo-Saxon Races is very large"; his publication endeavored "to answer questions, which have been put to us in every part of the country . . . for the benefit of our 'pale-face' friends." *Copway's American Indian* did not survive beyond its first year, and few Indian voices contributed to the writing of mainstream history in the nineteenth century.[45]

Locating history only in written records meant that those indigenous oral traditions must be something other—less—than history. By and large, that something became "myth." History moved, it evolved, it existed in the flow of time; myth, on the other hand, was understood to be static and to have no relation, therefore, to history. This opposition of history and myth in the first half of the nineteenth century became a central foundation, as Joshua Bellin has argued, upon which ethnology was built.[46] Indeed, "myth" as a term came into common usage only in the early nineteenth century. At the same time, as Lionel Gossman has noted, only by the end of the eighteenth century did history emerge as something distinct and apart from literature.[47] Thus the modern conception of myth and the modern practice of history may well have grown up as mirror images of each other. In the United States, at least, the process of removing Native Americans from the realm of history helped define what was meant by myth. In fact, as this book illustrates, in the early years of the nineteenth century history de-

veloped in relation to several other fields. Many in the early republic attempted to understand history in different ways by relying on different
sources—grammars, vocabularies, artifacts. This book, in part, tells the
story of how boundaries of historical studies hardened across the span of
the nineteenth century to exclude much of this nontextual material.

Chapter 5 explores in more detail how the Indians moved from the
realm of history, to natural history, and finally to ethnology and anthropology—all of which treated Indians largely ahistorically, or outside the
boundaries of any specific chronology. For the moment, it is enough to
keep in mind the observation of Josiah Nott: "*Chronology* [] may be regarded as the touchstone of history." This development tracks another shift
in which the scientific study of race we touched on earlier was deeply impli-
cated. As race emerged as the "scientific" category into which Native Americans were put, they could be more easily removed from the category of nation. As Benedict Anderson has observed, nations have histories, while race
has been conceived of as largely a fixed and unchanging category.[48]

As American intellectuals confronted the questions posed by Native
Americans in the first half of the nineteenth century, they helped shape a
definition of history that simultaneously excluded Indians, and made relying on Indian sources intellectually illegitimate. As Samuel Drake reminded
readers, "their notions . . . can no more be relied upon than the fabled stories of the gods in ancient mythology."[49]

The study of Indians, and the search for Indian history, also helped
drive the shift from speculation to empiricism, from the armchair theorizing of the colonial era to the science of the new republic. This shift, of
course, occurred across the intellectual landscape in the Western world, but
it is worth remembering how much the encounter with the New World, and
with its puzzling inhabitants, drove this shift. As Anthony Padgen has
pointed out in his tracing of these developments in the Spanish new world,
by the eighteenth century texts about Indians written by people with actual
first-hand experience replaced those written from an intellectual and actual
distance. What's more, these writers insisted that only this kind of research
could guarantee the accuracy of the findings.[50]

Over and over again, as later chapters will demonstrate, American
scholars and others who wrote about Native Americans stressed that they
had done the investigations themselves. Artists like Charles Bird King and
George Catlin; linguists like John Heckewelder; archaeologists like Caleb
Atwater and Ephraim Squier—all extolled the virtue of their own empirical
research. In his 1847 synopsis of Indian research, John Russell Bartlett made
the point with satisfied confidence: "Out of confusion, system began to de-

velop . . . what seemed accidents, were found to be characteristics. What was regarded as anomalous, was recognized as a type and feature of a class."[51] For people like these, any remaining confusions would only be resolved by more of the same.

This new empirical, scientific positivism had a complicated side. More research might well help answer questions that had thus far eluded Americans, but there was a risk for those who did this research, who immersed themselves in the lives, languages, and cultures of native peoples. They might develop a sympathy for those they studied, which could lead them to portray Indians as something other than obstacles to white progress. Thomas McKenney, for example, concluded from his experiences that Native Americans possessed "the capacity . . . for the highest attainments in civilization," and even more provocatively he claimed that, "the Indian in his intellectual and moral structures [is] *our equal.*" Even the historian of Indians might run this risk. Army surgeon Edwin James wrote in his own history of Indians that the historian "will find many instances of generous feeling, of dignified and manly conduct . . . and genius; which require only the 'purchased page' of history to make them admired." Lewis Henry Morgan, regarded by many as the father of American anthropology, wrote to William Stone about the need for a vast "repository" of Indian material, not simply for study or preservation: "another of the leading objects should be to . . . encourage a kinder feeling toward the Red Man."[52]

Sentiments like these, needless to say, flew in the face of prevailing prejudices and ideologies. Although few would argue today that scientific inquiry takes place wholly outside the world of values and ideologies, the study of Native Americans was a particularly charged enterprise in the nineteenth century.

Indians and the Cycles of History

In defining their notion of history as a textual study, rooted in chronology, and thus locating Native Americans outside the boundaries of that history, Americans underwent a shift in the nature of their historical consciousness and in their understanding of how history worked. This shift capped a nearly four-hundred-year process of reversal in the way time itself was perceived in the West, what Anthony Kemp has charted as the shift from "an image of syncretic unity and essential sameness" to one of "dynamic change."[53] By the eighteenth century, many perceived history to work in ever-repeating, ever-oscillating cycles of rise and fall. The writings of classical antiquity, of course, had expounded on this theme, but these were rediscovered with a new enthusiasm in eighteenth-century Europe. From there, this notion followed so many other European exports across the Atlantic to become, by the time of the Revolution, what Stow Persons described some years ago as "the distinctive historical conception of the dominant social group in America."

Benjamin Smith Barton, a member of that founding generation, certainly believed "that civilization has been constantly preceded by barbarity and rudeness." History also taught, he cautioned, "a mortifying truth, that nation may relapse into rudeness again; all their proud monuments crumbled to dust . . . it may be our lot to fall into rudeness once more." In 1820, the members of the American Antiquarian Society echoed that view of history when they commented on the origins of their new group: "The decline as well as the rise of nations is in the course of nature—like causes will produce like effects; and, in some distant period, a decline may be the state of our country."[54]

Americans in the early republic manifested their connection to this sense of the classical past in all sorts of ways—from the creation of a national senate to the founding of towns called "Athens" from Georgia, to West Virginia, to Ohio; from filling up those towns with examples of "Greek Revival" architecture to clothing George Washington—our own Cincinnatus—in a Roman toga. Yet even in the midst of this extended homage to the classical past and its ideals, a cyclical notion of history disturbed increasing numbers of Americans. In the early years of the nineteenth century, Americans could certainly tell themselves that they existed in a "youthful" stage of history's great cycle. Even so, a cyclical view of history's motion meant that even this new nation must age and fall eventually and inevitably—the victim of some exogenous force or of its own corruption.

Perhaps, some Americans began to reason, the very act of establishing the nation itself represented a break from the inexorable cycle of history's rise and fall. And in that break, as Dorothy Ross has argued, they began to replace the cyclical view of history with one in which "perpetual life" might be possible.

Linear progress—with all that it implied of improvement, perfection, and distance from an oppressive past—rather than a cycle with its decline and decay. This could be both America's historical fate and the way Americans would come to understand their history. With each passing year of the nineteenth century, scientific discovery and technological innovation only underscored the distance between the present and the quickly receding past. By the mid-nineteenth century, a dominant view had come to prevail that the Greek and Roman past, far from being models to emulate, represented examples to be avoided. By the Gilded Age, as Dorothy Ross believes, Americans were surely and mostly a progressive people.[55]

Still, like any shift in intellectual life, this one was neither complete nor abrupt, and the older view of how history operated lingered even as a new one emerged. As we will see in chapter 5, James Fenimore Cooper grounded his Leatherstocking Tales in a cyclical view of history. This view of history also appears in the work of the landscape painter Thomas Cole, whose painting Cooper admired—"one of the very first geniuses of the age" according to Cooper. Most dramatically perhaps in his ambitious five-painting series *The Course of Empire,* which Cooper thought of as "a great epic poem," Cole used landscape painting as a way to comment both on history and on the state of American society.[56]

Cole received the commission that became *The Course of Empire* from New York businessman Luman Reed, and completed the cycle in 1836. At first glance, the five paintings trace a straightforward rise and fall, not of a particular empire, but of some generic one, in some indeterminate past. All five are set in the same, equally indeterminate place: a natural harbor with a dramatic rock outcropping towering over it in the background. Across the series, nature remains constant amidst the comings and goings of human activity.

The first painting, *The Savage State,* shows swirling clouds at daybreak. The scene is thick with trees and vegetation, and dark with shadow. In this rough, untamed wilderness a few equally wild hunters, clad in skins, chase a deer. These men inhabit the circle of teepees on the far right of the painting, occupying the only human-made clearing in the scene.

In the second painting, *The Pastoral or Arcadian State,* the light has brightened and softened. Nature here, its trees and clouds and rock features, is decidedly gentle, pleasant, and without threat. The figures seem more or less Greek—especially the bearded old man seated in the left foreground. But these Greeks have built something that looks remarkably like Stonehenge in the center of the canvas. Religion, in one form or another, has arrived.

By the time we arrive at *The Consummation of Empire,* the third and largest in the series, nature has disappeared entirely, save for that one outcrop. It has been buried under a Greco-Roman architectural fantasy of columns, pediments, and sculpture. These buildings serve as the set for a bewildering number of figures and a dizzying activity. Boats arrive in the harbor; a hero marches triumphantly across a bridge, all under the glare of a midday sun.

Thomas Cole, *The Course of Empire: The Savage State*, ca. 1836. In a five-part series, Cole presented a "gloomy" view of history's progress. © Collection of the New-York Historical Society.

Thomas Cole, *The Course of Empire: The Arcadian State*, ca. 1836. © Collection of the New-York Historical Society.

Thomas Cole, *The Course of Empire: The Consummation of Empire*, ca. 1836. © Collection of the New-York Historical Society.

Thomas Cole, *The Course of Empire: Destruction*, ca. 1836. © Collection of the New-York Historical Society.

Thomas Cole, *The Course of Empire: Desolation,* ca. 1836. © Collection of the New-York Historical Society.

The architecture of *Empire* might be indiscriminately classical, but the decadence and corruption implied in *The Consummation of Empire* were surely Roman. By painting four, *Destruction,* it has all gone bad. Back are the swirling, ominous clouds, giving an atmospheric echo to the scene of catastrophe playing out in the harbor city. Flames leap into the air, engulfing boat and building; helpless people tumble from a collapsing bridge into the water; the survivors risk death at the hands of invaders.

As the sun goes down on *Desolation,* nature has returned, creeping literally over the ruins of Empire. Gone are the human beings, replaced by new trees, vines, and a family of birds nesting on top of a Corinthian column in the foreground. The series ends, therefore, just before its beginning, as the scene reverts to its original nature, awaiting the next cycle of human ascension. So goes the course of empire.

The setting for this series is generic both in time and place because Cole wanted it to serve as a historical allegory. So goes the course of all empires. In this sense, the series presents what art historian Alan Wallach has called Cole's essentially "pessimistic philosophy of history." Cole was also convinced that viewers would miss the point of the series when it went on display in fall of 1836. In a letter to his patron Luman Reed, he complained: "very few will understand the scheme of [the paintings]—the philosophy that may be in them." To some extent he was right. The critic for the New

York *Mirror* saw in the paintings "*that* which *has been* in all past times," not what was presaged in the United States where "the perfection which man is hereafter to attain, will be based upon a more stable foundation: political equality; the rights of man; the democratick principle; the *sovereignty of the people*."[57] Two views of history collided with the exhibition of *The Course of Empire*. By 1836, Cole's was already on the wane.

There is much of contemporary politics too in *The Course of Empire*, of the debates between Whig federalists and Jacksonian democrats.[58] Cole's pessimism wasn't simply about the past and the course of history, but about the present and future of American society as well. How could it have been otherwise, given his essential historical sensibility? But like his view of history, Cole's political allegiances were to principles and ideals that were disappearing fast.

It comes as no surprise that a progressive view of history should find a congenial reception in Jackson's America. In an age of greater democracy and more fluid class lines, the ideal of progress must have resonated with Americans who wanted to believe in their own abilities to rise in society. Indeed, Persons suggests that for most of the founders, "the notion of progress was repugnant," because at some level it rejected both social hierarchies and Enlightenment thinking. Cole, for his part, had no use for Jacksonianism either.

But to root this change in historical consciousness entirely in the politics of Jacksonian America, or to see a progressive view of history as incipient in eighteenth-century republican ideology as it grew in the nineteenth-century United States, right though I think those explanations are, misses another force behind this change of historical attitude. The first painting in Cole's series, with its teepees and reference to savages, returns us to the question of Native Americans, even if the figures in the painting look approximately European and not native.

By the 1830s when they were so brutally "removed," the perceived fate of Native Americans, I suspect, was shaping American ideas about history. Whatever the debate over their past, American scholars who studied Indians in the antebellum period found themselves in virtually unanimous agreement about the future. That fate seemed self-evident to Americans: extinction. This consensus of opinion itself reflects the way in which Indians were increasingly viewed as part of natural, rather than human, history. The notion that species could disappear from the earth as a result of natural processes and quite apart from any biblical flood was one of the remarkable developments of late eighteenth and early nineteenth-century natural science, straining the relationship between science and religion. So novel and difficult was the idea of natural extinction that no less a scientist than Thomas Jefferson believed that there might still be herds of mastodons roaming the continent somewhere. Indians were not simply animals in the view of most Americans in the nineteenth century, but they were surely headed down the same road as the iguanadon and the giant sloth.

Indeed, the only real disagreement took place over whether individual Indians might assimilate into Euro-American society or whether, unwilling or unable to do this, they were indeed headed for extinction in a biological sense. Either way, "Indianness" was doomed. Even Ojibway chief George Copway believed that the Indians' days were numbered. Plaintively, poignantly he wrote about the purpose of his journal: "That race is fast vanishing away; a few years more and its existence will be found only in the history of the past: may not an Indian, then, hope for countenance and support in a modest and unambitious effort to preserve . . . the still lingering memorials of his own people, once numerous and strong?"[59]

This was not necessarily the consensus of the founding generation, who, as Bernard Sheehan has noted, believed that Indians would see the obvious desirability of civilization, and thus that they would give up their own savagery happily and voluntarily.[60] That hope had largely faded by the early national period. Indeed, extinction became such a constant and familiar refrain in the literature of the nineteenth century that it is almost not worth quoting. It was a conviction, rather than a prediction, and it was such a ubiquitous belief that it did not exist so much in the realm of empirical observation as in the world of unquestioned assumption. A quick sampling can stand for a whole literature: for L. Bliss, the task of recording the history of this "ill-fated" race would be "of mournful interest," and amounted to "something almost holy"; an anonymous writer for the *Southern Literary Messenger* managed to kill off the noble savage when he wrote, "this wild, but noble and unhappy race, is rapidly becoming extinct," and as a consequence, the historian faced a "melancholy task." He might well find himself "weeping over the final extinction of the aboriginal natives of America." William Pidgeon hoped that Americans would "value researches which have been made with a view to perpetuate the memory of nations that have preceded those that are now falling into ruin."[61]

Pidgeon's use of the word "ruin" gives us a striking, if altogether inadvertent, connection to Cole. Cole had described his concept for *The Course of Empire* to Reed by saying that he would illustrate "how nations have risen" and how they all "become extinct."[62] In Cole's view of history, of course, ruin is what empires fall into. Ruins remain to dot the landscape, serving as "melancholy" if evocative reminders of that process. But by the mid-nineteenth century, Indians were so clearly falling into ruin that Euro-Americans need not worry that they themselves might suffer the same fate. White Americans were fruitful and multiplying; Indians were all on the verge of extinction.

American scholars did not generally give Native Americans credit for having risen much on the scale of civilization, but they certainly agreed about their fall. Euro-Americans thus shifted the inevitability of decline, with all its attendant anxiety and gloominess, onto the people progress was displacing. In this way, they created the imaginative space to conceive of their own history as the unfolding of linear progress.[63] As an American historical consciousness took shape in the antebellum period, its definition located Indians outside of the progressive, chronologically marked time whose ticking clock measured the history of Euro-Americans alone.

Several scholars have examined the relationship between conceptions of Indians and the formation of American identity: Elise Marienstras, for example, sees popular images of the vanquished Indian as helping Americans conceive of themselves "as a collective entity." Philip Deloria, in fact, observing the ritual and practice of "playing Indian," believes that it has been impossible to conceive of an American identity without Indians.[64] Equally important, however, it is impossible to create a national identity without first creating historical narratives around which a collective sense can draw legitimacy and sustenance. In the new United States, that historical understanding was shaped by the ways scholars and intellectuals defined the history of Native America.

This may also explain a secondary debate among those who studied Native America in the first half of the nineteenth century. Did those tribes and groups who currently inhabited the continent represent the denegerate, degraded descendants of earlier more civilized Indians—Aztecs perhaps? Or was the continent first populated by a more enigmatic people called Mound Builders, whom we will meet in chapter 3, who were quite distinct from contemporary Indians and who had already disappeared entirely?

Most who considered the issue ultimately came down on the side of the latter. As John Bartlett put it in 1847, it "has been developed to show that a people, radically different from the existing race of Indians, once occupied the valley of the Mississippi . . . they were to a certain extent advanced in the arts of civilization."[65] To admit Indians into a great cycle of history meant that, while they were currently in decline, they might rise again. For expansion-minded and increasingly progress-minded Americans, this thought proved too uncomfortable. Writing in 1872, J. D. Baldwin made the point quite clearly. Although it might be true that "the history of the world shows that civilized communities may lose their enlightenment, and sink to a condition of barbarism," the Indians of North America demonstrated no such thing. Theirs "was original barbarism. There was nothing to indicate that . . . the Indians inhabiting our part of the continent . . . had ever been civilized even to the extent of becoming capable of settled life and organized industry."[66] Thus, such American scholars moved Indians out of progressive history and into cyclical history incompletely. Indians could experience decline, without ever having experienced a reciprocal rise.

From our vantage, the consequences of this seem nothing short of vicious and destructive. As anthropologist Johannes Fabian has pointed out in his examination of the relationship between anthropology and colonialism, "expansive, aggressive, and oppressive" societies require both space in which to expand, and "Time to accommodate the schemes of a one-way history: progress . . . in short, *geopolitics* had its ideological foundations in *chronopolitics.*"[67]

The widespread (again, almost ubiquitous) belief that savage Indians and civilized whites simply could not coexist may have been a consequence of this "chronopolitics." Beyond the now-obvious inability to coexist in the same physical space, they could not inhabit the same historical space and likewise could not share the same present. As a reviewer wrote in the *North American Review* in 1830, "year after year, the cultivated border advanced bearing before it the primitive people, who would not mingle with their invaders, and who could not stop their progress." What else to conclude but that "a barbarous people . . . cannot live in contact with a civilized community."[68]

It is surely right that, in this sense, American intellectuals in the first half of the nineteenth century participated in a colonial enterprise. And yet, just as we need to take more seriously the strained, almost desperate attempts to fit Indian history into a biblical framework, we ought to acknowledge just how difficult and daunting it must have been in the first half of the nineteenth century to conceive of a history for Native Americans. At a moment when the power of writing as a preserver of history—Greek, Roman, Egyptian—was growing more and more potent, how could scholars study people who had no writing and had left no texts? In an age when the differences between past and present grew not only more pronounced with each passing year, but could even be measured along that chronology, how could historians understand people who did not fit onto that timeline?

Earlier in this chapter we turned to Alexander Bradford, who in 1843 recognized that the emerging practice of history would necessarily exclude "most important occurrences of the early ages of the world." Undaunted, he went on to suggest just how Native American history could be studied: "Thus of necessity are mankind impelled . . . to examine other channels by which the events of remote antiquity may have been transmitted, and to study and compare the languages, customs, traditions, science, religion and monuments of nations."[69]

The rest of this book will examine just how American scholars, across several different intellectual pursuits, tried to answer Bradford's challenge, and how American intellectual life and an American sense of history during the nineteenth century was shaped in the process.

2

IMAGES OF HISTORY: INDIANS IN AMERICAN ART

It seems to us that the Indian has not received justice in American art.

THE CRAYON, 1856

Up and down the Indian country roamed . . . artists.

CLARK WISSLER, 1938

Indians were everywhere when the American nation was born, present at some of the critical moments of revolution and founding. When angry New Yorkers pulled down the equestrian statue of George III in a symbolic act of regicide, Indians stood by as onlookers. Some were milling around in front of the Old State House—Independence Hall—on July 4, 1776, including "the Indian who bore the Declaration to the camp of Washington." At the end of the Revolutionary War, when General Washington arrived by boat in New York harbor, Indians rowed a canoe next to him. And when Washington made his triumphal entry into the city, Indians were thick in the crowd.

Or so they were depicted in popular images of these events made during the first half of the nineteenth century—I have just given the briefest description of four such images. Given the space that Native Americans occupied in American intellectual life, and in the cultural imagination, it should come as no surprise that American visual culture was populated with Indians as well. After all, images of Indians constitute the very earliest representations of the New World brought back by explorers and conquerors in the fifteenth and sixteenth centuries. Just as Indians remained a common sight on the streets of the nation's cities in the early Republic, so too they were recorded visually as part of the historical action from that period.

No surprise either that the volume of visual representations of Native Americans reached a crescendo during the nineteenth century before dissipating somewhat during the twentieth. Indians turned up in the works of "serious" painters like Benjamin West and Albert Bierstadt, and in those of more middle-brow artists like Frederick Remington. Early photographers focused their new apparatus on them, and Indians were reproduced in popular illustrations, lithographs, posters, and knickknacks too numerous to count. It exaggerates only a little to say that Indians filled the visual field of nineteenth-century Americans.

It is not my purpose here, however, to give a thorough or complete treatment of the ways Indians were represented visually across the nineteenth century—a task so enormous that it deserves a separate volume. Rather this chapter examines a few artists and a few kinds of images to explore the relationship between art and history, the place of Indians in both, and how that place changed over the course of the century. The chapter thus constitutes a particular, perhaps idiosyncratic history of nineteenth-century American art, looking at some familiar figures like Benjamin West, George Catlin, Albert Bierstadt, and Edward Curtis, as well as some more obscure figures, like Charles Bird King and Elbert Ayer Burbank.

These names by no means exhaust the list of nineteenth-century artists who treated Native Americans. Rather, I have chosen them because their careers, and the ways they used Native Americans in their work, loosely chart the trajectory of Indians in American intellectual life, which will be explored in more detail in subsequent chapters. In this way, their work prefigures the issues central to this study. In the images these men produced we can watch Native Americans move from the realm of history, to natural history and ethnography, and finally to extinction and elegy. In this sense, these images also track a reciprocal change in how Americans understood history and in how iconographic material disappeared from that understanding as the nineteenth century wore on. Viewing images like these, and countless others besides, nineteenth-century Americans could almost literally watch Native Americans disappear from the realm of history and enter the more inchoate world of the past.

American History in the Grand Manner: Benjamin West

In 1834, Stephen DuPonceau apologized to an audience at the Historical Society of Pennsylvania for his own shortcomings as a historian, and in so doing underscored the connection between art and the presentation and interpretation of history. He regretted "that we cannot make a more splendid display on this occasion," and went on, "we leave that to the painter and the poet."[1]

DuPonceau's self-deprecation reminds us that in the late eighteenth and early nineteenth centuries history had not yet become the domain solely of historians. We saw in the last chapter that the practice of history, as it evolved from the late eighteenth century, developed almost entirely as a textual business. Relying more and more on texts, usually excavated from archival sources, as the evidentiary base for their narratives, many historians grew almost phobic of what Drew Faust has called "iconographic" evidence.[2]

Yet it bears remembering that as a modern historical consciousness began to take shape in the eighteenth century—an outgrowth of the European Enlightenment—historical narratives were often presented visually, sometimes with tremendous currency and power. These visual narratives took the form of the so-called grand manner history painting—canvases often big and bombastic, filled with swirling drama, or violence, or touching pathos. In turn, history painting rose to the place of highest esteem in the world of art. Students drilling with Charles Peirce's 1811 primer on manners and morals were asked this question: "What are the most esteemed paintings?" and were to give this answer, "Those representing historical events."[3] This children's quiz summarizes as aptly and succinctly as anything the consensus that had arisen in both Europe and the United States about the hierarchy of painting's genres. At the moment when history's boundaries were still fluid, history could be both a textual and a visual affair.

History painting, as it matured in the eighteenth century, was not merely the practice of transcribing historical events in paint. It was a genre that followed its own set of rules, codified most importantly in the Anglo-American world by British painter Sir Joshua Reynolds. Grand manner history painting in the eighteenth century attempted to weave together the heroism of individuals with universal moral messages embodied by those individuals at particular moments—specific scenes illustrating eternal truths. Reynolds himself recognized that a painter "must sometimes deviate from vulgar and strict historical truth, in pursuing the grandeur of his design." In his thirteenth discourse on art, Reynolds drew a prematurely postmodern distinction: "It is allowed on all hands," he told his listeners, "that facts, and events, however they may bind the Historian, have no dominion over the Poet or the Painter. With us History is made to bend and conform to the great idea of Art."

The traffic went in both directions. Samuel Goodrich, in his modestly titled *History of All Nations,* introduced his readers to the topic of history by asking them, "What is the philosophy that history should teach?" and answering, "Virtue, the moral improvement of man." Like Sir Joshua, Goodrich realized that this "philosophical" purpose transcended the merely factual: "The love of truth is the first duty of the historian, but it is not his whole duty. In laying before us the occurrences of past times, he must animate and excite our feelings." Likewise, C. S. Rafinesque in 1836 asserted that "history does not merely consist in accumulating facts . . . it seeks results, teaches lessons of wisdom, brands with infamy the foes of mankind, and inspires veneration . . . it presents examples worthy to be followed, and records the crimes to be avoided."[4] Compositionally, many painters underscored their lessons by making reference to earlier works from the Christian and classical traditions—lamentation scenes, crucifixions, pietas, for example. In the grand manner, the past was infused with didactic intent and moral truth.[5]

This is precisely what grand manner history painters hoped to achieve, and in this sense the best of them may have been more successful historians than the historians themselves. As David Levin has written, that first generation of nineteenth-century American historians routinely compared history to painting. The romantic historian, according to Levin, "considered himself a painter."[6]

Sitting at the apex of painterly achievement as the nation was founded, grand manner history painting posed an immediate, almost insistent problem for American painters who would take it up. Where could Americans find historical scenes worthy of painting in the first place? In the Bible to be sure—but scenes from classical antiquity, so popular with European painters and viewers, did not seem to belong properly to the American province. Still, American painters did aspire to the grand manner, and Benjamin West was the most important to do so.

West was born in 1738 in the hinterland of Philadelphia. From this humble, almost frontier beginning, he made his way to Europe, rose to succeed Sir Joshua as president of the Royal Academy, and became the king's favorite painter—a remarkable accomplishment for a colonial. Though he, like his compatriot painter John Singleton Copley, never returned to America, West became the touchstone for American history painters in the early republic.

That West considered his most significant work to be his grand manner history paintings is well documented. His enthusiastic biographer John Galt organized the events in West's life so that they pointed toward history painting. In his 1820 edition of *The Life and Works of Benjamin West,* Galt reports that no less a person than the Archbishop of York "endeavored, by all the means in his power, to procure encouragement for Mr. West to devote himself exclusively to historical composition," rather than waste his time and talents on mere portraiture. Likewise, in an 1832 biography, Galt reports that "a gentleman of the name of Cox" came to have a portrait done of his daughter, but was so impressed by another image, because "it appeared to him to evince such a taste for historical painting," that he immediately "gave an order for an historical picture." In the end, "he made choice of the trial of Susannah."[7]

These were not simply the flatteries or exaggerations of a biographer trying to elevate the reputation of his subject. In a letter to West from Philadelphia, Charles Willson Peale reported on the great success West's history paintings were enjoying in his native city. "I was anxious to know," Peale began to his fellow painter, "in what degree people of this city might be interested with an exhibition of large, historical works . . . considering that little has been published to excite curiosity." Much to Peale's delight, "the number of visitors to the Academy has given upwards of 8100 per month since we hung up your pictures."[8] West's history paintings were indeed well esteemed.

The grand manner history paintings of West's early career, predictably enough, included both biblical scenes and scenes from classical antiquity, like *Agrippina Landing at Brundisium with the Ashes of Germanicus* (1767). These established his reputation as a master of the genre. In 1770, however, he astonished the art world, and reoriented the nature of history painting besides, with his *Death of General Wolfe.*

The painting commemorates the death of a British general in battle against the French outside Quebec. The general swoons at the point of death in the sort of "S" curve familiar to Christian pieta scenes. With Wolfe's eyes rolling toward heaven, it is also a scene filled with pathos of the sort common to grand manner painting. To depict an event of recent historical vintage—Wolfe had died only eleven years earlier—was not unprecedented. But in portraying this scene West chose to put all the figures in contemporary costume, rather than dressing them up as actors in a classical drama. This raised eyebrows both in the studio and at the Royal Academy, where it was exhibited in 1771.

West, so the story goes, had been told while he worked on the canvas by none other than Sir Joshua to "adopt the classic costume of antiquity" in depicting the soldiers. West resolutely refused. According to a biographer, West told Reynolds "the event took place on the 13th of September in a region of the world unknown to the Greeks and Romans, and at a time when no such nations, nor heroes in their costume, any longer existed." He went on: "It is a topic that history will proudly record and the same truth that guides the pen of the historian, should govern the pencil of the artist."[9]

Whether he meant to do so deliberately or not, in making this statement West challenged Reynolds over just exactly how to define the nature of artistic truth and accuracy, an issue that would recur repeatedly in the nineteenth century.

The result was a triumph, and it has become one of the stock stories in the history of art. Upon seeing the finished work Reynolds announced: "Mr. West has conquered. He has treated his subject as it ought to be treated. I retract my objections against the introduction of any other circumstances into historical pictures than those which are requisite and appropriate." Further, Reynolds predicted that *The Death of General Wolfe* would bring about "a revolution in art."[10]

To some extent, it did, at least in American art. *The Death of General Wolfe* seemed to promise that the moral and ethical imperatives of grand manner history painting could be preserved, even while a new standard of historical reportage was defined. More than that, the critical success of the painting made it legitimate to paint contemporary events without hiding their recentness behind togas. This had important implications for Americans who continued to be haunted by the sense that their national identity existed in a kind of historical vacuum. After all, as West had pointed out, neither the Greeks nor the Romans—the source of both history and its moral lessons—ever made it across the Atlantic.

Finally, in painting *The Death of General Wolfe*, West effectively shrank the distance between the present and what was considered historical. In addition to the moral messages of history painting, lessons about heroism, nationalism, and sacrifice, *The Death of General Wolfe* implicitly told its viewers that they too lived in historical time, that the processes of history were not confined to the classical past, and that therefore they too might be part of history.

There is a Native American figure in *The Death of General Wolfe*. Kneeling in the left foreground, with his head resting on his hand, this warrior stares impassively at the dying general. If the story of West's *General Wolfe* is familiar, at least in art historical circles, then perhaps less well remembered is that immediately on the heels of his success with *General Wolfe*, West embarked on a history painting of quite a different kind, one in which Indians figure centrally, rather than peripherally.

West's *Penn's Treaty with the Indians* (1771) remains, perhaps, the painter's best-known, most often reproduced work. It stands certainly as the most famous attempt to include Indians as part of the narrative and didactic structure of grand manner history painting. More than that, by putting Indians at the center of a history painting, West made an attempt to include

Benjamin West, *Penn's Treaty with the Indians*, 1771. Painted at a time when Penn's peaceable kingdom had fallen apart, West's painting reminded viewers that Indians were central to one of the most important moments in colonial history. Courtesy of the Pennsylvania Academy of the Fine Arts, Philadelphia. Gift of Mrs. Sarah Harrison (The Joseph Harrison Jr. Collection).

them as part of American history itself, at a time when a prevailing narrative of American history had not yet been defined.[11]

Even today, the image comes easily to mind. A rotund William Penn stands slightly to the left of center, hands outstretched in a welcoming gesture, amidst a crowd of Europeans and Indians. Bows and arrows have been conspicuously laid down in the foreground of the painting, while the Delaware River and the construction of Penn's new city occupy the background, framed by blue skies and leafy trees.

The history here being commemorated is also still the stuff of junior high school history classes. Having chosen the site of his new city he called Philadelphia along the banks of the Delaware River, Penn wanted to negotiate peace with the local Indians. The treaty he struck with them constituted the first test of his utopian vision for "brotherly love." No conquest or bloodshed, no chicanery or duplicity, but openness, honesty, and love instead—the only treaty ever concluded between Euro-Americans and Indians not to be broken. So the story goes.

West included Indians in other of his paintings, and he famously remarked, gazing upon a Roman statue, that the figure struck him as looking like an Indian warrior. Even more than this, Indians figured prominently in West's self-creation as a painter. His biographer John Galt recounts that West had a childhood encounter with some local Indians who "taught him to prepare the red and yellow colours with which they painted their ornaments." His mother helped him grind up some indigo, and voilà, "he was thus in possession of the three primary colours." In case the reader missed just how redolent this scene was with Rousseauian symbolism, Galt concluded that: "the mythologies of antiquity furnish no allegory more beautiful . . . than the real incident of the Indians instructing West to prepare the prismatic colours."[12]

Perhaps the story, in part or in whole, is true. Perhaps it isn't. Either way, it seems clear that part of West's success as both a painter and as an artistic figure moving to London from the colonial hinterland rested on his presumed connection with noble savages, and on how that connection informed his art. These same Indians, Galt goes on, also taught the boy West how to shoot with a bow and arrow. Indians were a part of West's own history or at least his mythos, and this may well have added an authority and authenticity to his inclusion of them in his paintings. West had claimed the New World as the province of history in *The Death of General Wolfe*, but in truth he had never been to the plains of Quebec. He had, on the other hand, grown up almost literally in the shadow of the famous "treaty elm" in Philadelphia. The founding of his home town was history with which West himself could feel a personal connection.

Penn's Treaty came about as a commission from Penn's grandson Thomas, who by 1771 was running the colony as proprietor from the great distance of his country estate in England. Thomas Penn was an embattled ruler—none other than Benjamin Franklin tried to have the crown replace him—and, as Ann Uhry Abrams has noted, when Thomas Penn asked West to paint the scene, he wanted to draw upon the already mythic power of his grandfather's "peaceable kingdom." West, of course, had grown up around Quakers and doubtless heard the story of Penn's treaty any number of times. It constituted, as Abrams puts it, part of the "mental baggage" West took with him when he left Pennsylvania in 1760.[13]

Compositionally, *Penn's Treaty* is thoroughly conventional. The painting is arranged in an easily read triptych. To stress the "peacefulness" of the scene, West has employed diffuse, even light, rather than dramatic contrasts of light and shadow, a balanced rectangular grid, a horizontal arrangement of almost all the elements in the scene, and figures who are standing or sitting.[14] West has studied and drawn upon Renaissance composition for this work.

Yet Penn makes an unlikely hero. Usually, the central figure of a grand manner history painting is caught in the act of suffering, dying, or making some heroic sacrifice. Here, Penn is doing very little, and he looks like a well-fed, contented burgher. The historical importance of the scene, then, is embodied not so much in the central actor but in the meaning of the treaty itself. After all, "Treaty," and not "Penn," is the very subject of the title. In this sense, it is the possibility of peaceful relationships between Euro-Americans and Native Americans, rather than Penn himself, that is being memorialized.

Strictly speaking, the painting is not accurate in its details. Plenty of viewers, then and now, have observed that the contemporary dress in which West put his figures was contemporary to the eighteenth century, not the late seventeenth. Likewise, those buildings under construction in the back of the painting simply would not have been there in the 1680s. Philadelphia naturalist Benjamin Smith Barton, for one, took offense. Writing in a shipboard journal in 1789, he complained: "Mr. West's Picture of the Treaty of the Indians [is] in a great measure . . . fabulous, or rather imaginary. . . .This is not a license which, I think, Historical Painting warrants."[15]

Jigsaw puzzle, *William Penn's Treaty with the Indians*. By the mid-nineteenth century, reproductions of *Penn's Treaty* were hard to avoid, even for children who just wanted to do a puzzle. (Note that this image reversed the original because it was probably made from a lithograph or other reproduction.) Courtesy of the Library Company of Philadelphia.

West, for his part, admitted as much without compunction. To his brother William he wrote in 1775 that "I have taken the liberty to introduce the likeness of our Father—and Brother of Reading into the picture in the group of Friends that accompany Wm. Penn."[16] Thirty years later, he made an even fuller explanation to H. Darton: "The leading characters which make that composition are the Friends and Indians—the characteristics of both have been known to me from my early life—but to give that identity which was necessary in such a novel subject, I had recourse to many persons then living for that identity."

West had introduced a new level of historical accuracy in grand manner history painting with *The Death of General Wolfe*, but he still drew a distinction between mere historical accuracy and artistic truth. As he explained to Darton: "The great object I had in forming that composition was to express savages brought into harmony and peace by justice and benevolence . . . as well as a wish to give by that art a conquest made over native people without sword or dagger." He went on to call the likeness of his father and brother in the painting "the materials to give it truth."[17] This pursuit of a higher moral and artistic truth makes *Penn's Treaty* a history painting in the grand manner. In those terms, only a few cared that William Penn's hat was anachronistically out of place.

From Grand Manner to Kitsch: The Strange Career of *Penn's Treaty*

In fact, by 1771 Penn's peaceable kingdom, his city of brotherly love, had dissolved into bickering, recrimination, and conflict. The governing of the colony was in turmoil, and the city itself roiled with the radicalism that would shortly put it at the center of the break from England. In this sense, Abrams is surely right that West conceived *Penn's Treaty* as an allegory of Pennsylvania politics, a comment, by contrast, on the nasty turn of events in Penn's peaceable kingdom. Likewise, whatever harmony the founder might have achieved in his relationship with the Indians had fallen apart into tensions punctuated with violence.[18] At one level, then, the painting yearns for a sweeter, more innocent past as much as it records a historical event.

West's ability to capture a sense of what might have been, rather than what simply was, lies, I think, at the heart of what makes *Penn's Treaty* such an enduring image even today. The painting, or more to the point reproductions of it, became a succinct visual encapsulation of the William Penn myth, which grew during the nineteenth century, both as proof that whites and Indians could live together peacefully and as a scolding reminder of how little Penn's example had been followed. The myth was powerful enough to cross the Atlantic. It was Voltaire, after all, who made the remark that Penn's treaty stood as the only one whites had never broken.

That myth became something of a commonplace. Here is N. Hale in an essay in the *North American Review*: "William Penn and his followers treated [the Indians] with great kindness and friendship and this kindness was reciprocated by the Lenape. But the other English settlers treated them with great injustice." Stephen DuPonceau, in a public speech, acknowledged that we might not really know all the details about what transpired under that elm, but the essential conclusion did not change: "The true merit of William Penn, that in which he surpasses all the founders of empires whose names are recorded in ancient and modern history, is . . . in the honesty, the integrity, the strict sense of justice with which he constantly treated the Aborigines of the land."[19] It hardly mattered whether West's *Penn's Treaty* depicted the event in any way Penn would have recognized. Accuracy need not stand in the way of truth.

In his 1838 *The American Speaker,* John Frost included "The Character of William Penn" as one of the pieces students could memorize to practice their public speaking. It is worth quoting at some length because the essay gives us a good sense of how the treaty story had been reduced like a sauce to an essential lesson, premised on "seeing" the scene that West had made iconic:

> But see William Penn, with weaponless hand, sitting down peaceably with his followers in the midst of savage nations, whose only occupation was shedding the blood of their fellow men. . . . See them bury their tomahawks in his presence. . . . Here was a spectacle for the potentates of the earth to look upon, an example for them to imitate. But the potentates of the earth did not see or if they saw they turned away their eyes from the sight: they did not hear, or if they heard, they shut their ears against the voice, which called out to them from the wilderness. The character of William Penn alone sheds a never-fading luster on our history.[20]

And chances are that anyone preparing this recitation had seen some version of West's image.

While the painting itself remained in England until the middle of the nineteenth century, reproductions of it proliferated almost immediately across the United States. According to Ellen Starr Brinton, at least thirty-one engravers and fifteen lithographers in England, France, Germany, Italy, Mexico, and the United States produced reproductions—Currier and Ives did three separate versions.[21] Thomas Clarkson, who wrote a study of

Quakers and Quakerism in 1806, reported that although most of these plain people eschewed filling their houses with new furniture and decorative items, nearly every family had a framed print of *Penn's Treaty*—and some households had multiple copies. By midcentury, one could admire a framed print hanging in a parlor, while eating from a plate with the scene, that was served from a tray with a hand-painted version of it. If the dinner conversation grew dull, one could stare through windows curtained with the scene. Later, one could put oneself to bed with a shot from a *Penn's Treaty* whiskey glass and stay warm underneath William Penn and the Indians figured on a quilt.[22]

Putting aside the tricky question of whether a scene done as a grand manner history painting can retain its moral authority underneath steaming vegetables on a dish made by the Staffordshire China works—the only reproduction of an American scene they ever put on their ceramics—it seems clear that West's *Penn's Treaty* achieved a kind of ubiquity, at least in the domestic world of the middle and upper classes. That ubiquity preserved in the historical memory of nineteenth-century Americans the sense that once, at least, settlers and Indians had gotten along. Subscribers to the *Philadelphia Ledger* received an engraving of *Penn's Treaty* as a New Year's thank you in 1857, complete with this Hallmarkian doggerel:

How beautiful the scene portrayed above
A treaty, framed in Justice, Truth and Love,
Our City's Founder and the peaceful "Friends"
Stoop to no subterfuge, to gain their ends;

While with unswerving confidence around
Their Indian brethren occupy the ground,
This incident, a maxim may afford,
And prove *our* PENN was "mightier than the sword."

Little else, I suspect, needs to be said about the translation of West's painting and the story of William Penn into the middle-brow imagination.

Although *Penn's Treaty* had an extraordinary life across the first half of the nineteenth century, the painting itself remained in England until 1851 when it was purchased by Philadelphian Joseph Harrison. The Harrisons, with their painting in tow, came back to Philadelphia some time later, and it appeared in public on several occasions before it was presented to the Pennsylvania Academy of the Fine Arts in 1878, a gift from the widow Harrison. By that time, of course, grand manner history painting as a genre of

P. Haas, "Penn's Treaty/Boon and the Indians," ca. 1840. The story of Penn's treaty became a touchstone for everything that had degenerated in relations between Indians and whites in the antebellum period. Courtesy of the Library Company of Philadelphia.

high art had largely died on both sides of the Atlantic—the victim of changing tastes, vanishing patrons, and hide-bound academies, which had trained painters in the style and methods used to produce these works, but had not changed with the times. In the United States as well, the Civil War caused a crisis of representation to which the conventions of the grand manner simply could not respond.[23] Emmanuel Leutze's *Washington Crossing the Delaware* may well be the most famous grand manner history painting depicting an American scene. It may well be the last to become in any sense "iconic." Ironically, he painted it in 1851, the same year Joseph Harrison bought *Penn's Treaty* with the intention of bringing it and its important message back to the United States.

An anonymous critic for *The Crayon* wondered in 1856 why Indians were not the subject of more history paintings, and he offered several possible vignettes for any painter who happened to be reading. "Here is an original action," the critic opined after suggesting a hunting scene, "picturesque, composing agreeably, wholly American, full of lively incident, and telling its story perfectly."[24]

Despite helpful advice like that offered by *The Crayon*, however, never again would a major American artist use grand manner history painting, or indeed any other genre, to convey the moral lesson that the nature of relations between Indians and Euro-Americans could be anything other than violent—its result anything other than conquest. West's lesson carried the pathos of what might have been. This surely contributed to its sentimental appeal. As mid-nineteenth-century Americans were covering themselves with *Penn's Treaty* bed linens, the possibility had vanished that Indians and whites might live harmoniously as William Penn did with the Lenape. It had become yet one more loss to mourn. The trajectory of Benjamin West's *Penn's Treaty with the Indians* tracks the shift from the moral use of history to the nostalgic use of the past.

THE TREATY ELM is long gone, and so too are the Lenape. At least legally. Three centuries after Penn shook hands with his Native brethren, two centuries after West memorialized the event on canvas, neither the federal government nor the commonwealth of Pennsylvania officially recognize the existence of the Lenape tribe. Indeed, Pennsylvania—Penn's holy experiment and his peaceable kingdom—is, as of this writing, one of only thirteen states without any officially recognized tribes at all. No small irony to be sure—especially for the thousand or so Pennsylvanians who identify themselves as Lenape and who call Robert Red Hawk Ruth, a businessman from suburban Philadelphia, their tribal chief. Given the number of times members of the Lenape have been invited to the state capital in Harrisburg for plaque dedications or other such ceremonies, one might think the commonwealth could at least offer the Lenape formal recognition.

The issue, of course, is gambling, and the fear of conservative state legislators that recognition will lead inevitably to Indian casinos in Pennsylvania. Repeated assurances from the Lenape that they won't pursue casino development, and the fact that any tribe needs Federal certification before it could even consider casinos, have not persuaded the Republican gatekeepers in Harrisburg to budge. (The Lenape did file for federal certification in 2000, but that process can drag on for years.)

For the Lenape, according to Ruth, the issue is purely one of dignity and identity—simple recognition that the Lenape were the first people to inhabit Pennsylvania. The push being made now at the state and federal level for that recognition has a familiar-sounding, if also ironic urgency. Having survived for over three centuries since the arrival of Europeans, the Lenape seem now about to disappear, at least according to Ruth. "Unless we get some help soon," he said, "so much of the knowledge, the history, the culture of our people is passing away."[25]

Portraiture as History: Charles Bird King

Benjamin West hoped to use commissions for history paintings as a way of escaping the remunerative but dreary work of portrait painting. His student, Charles Bird King (1785–1862), however, made his living almost entirely by painting likenesses. And he achieved his fame by painting portraits of Indians.

West was already in London by the time King was born in Newport, Rhode Island. An inheritance received when his father died—killed by Indians in the Ohio territory, as it happens—enabled King to study in London, where he went in 1806. He stayed on at the Royal Academy until 1812, returned to the United States, and tried to set up shop in Philadelphia, but relocated to Washington, D.C. by 1816. There he distinguished himself by painting competent portraits of local luminaries and politicians, including John C. Calhoun, Henry Clay, and Mrs. John Quincy Adams.

In 1821, however, he wound up with an extraordinary commission from the Department of War to paint the portraits of Indians coming through Washington as part of official diplomatic delegations. Over the course of twenty years, King painted 143 such pictures, the vast bulk of them in the 1820s.[26]

William Dunlap, among the earliest chroniclers of the nation's art history, described King, while he was still alive, as hard-working, rather than talented: "It appears that all he has acquired has been by very hard study; and Mr. King is an example of a man of very moderate genius who has acquired much in his profession"—this from a man who acknowledges King as a friend. King reversed the cliché of the artist's fate: successful during his own lifetime, he has faded into obscurity since. Still, as Dunlap observed in 1834, King "commanded that employment which has made him independent in his circumstances, and an object of attention in society."[27]

He enjoyed much of that attention because of his Indian portraits. They were a popular attraction, drawing a generous remark even from the usually acerbic English traveler Mrs. Trollope. To see these portraits one went to visit the "Indian Gallery" on the second floor of the War Department in the office of Thomas McKenney. McKenney began his official connection with Indians as the superintendent of Indian Trade, a position he held from 1816–1822. After that, he was appointed the first head of the newly created Bureau of Indian Affairs, an office, fittingly enough, of the War Department. King's commission to paint Indian portraits had come not so much from the War Department, but from McKenney himself. The portraits, along with some Indian artifacts McKenney had accumulated, constituted the first public, or quasi-public, museum in the nation's capital, which McKenney called "The Archives of the American Indian."[28]

The portraits also constituted an early example of public funding for the arts, and as such became part of the fuel for a political fire that drove McKenney from his post in 1830. The portraits seem to have remained on the walls of the War Department until 1858, when they were removed to the Smithsonian's newly completed "Castle." There, they joined another large collection of Indian portraits by John Mix Stanley to create a remarkable gallery of Indian likenesses. The gallery did not last long. Virtually all the paintings—over three hundred by the best estimate—were destroyed by the famous fire that tore through the Castle in January, 1865.

Frances Trollope wrote after seeing King's portraits on display in 1830, "it cannot be doubted [they] are excellent likenesses."[29] One wonders how she could know, not having seen any of the sitters herself. We have no way of evaluating these images purely for their verisimilitude. The difficulties we have in assessing just what King accomplished in these paintings, however, are further compounded by the fact that almost none of the originals survive. But unlike Stanley's work, which was erased by the fire almost without a trace, King's painting did live on in the form of a lavish three-volume set put out by Thomas McKenney and James Hall between 1837 and 1844.

These volumes stand as a monument in the history of American publishing, the first "large-scale lithographic project attempted in this country and the first large-folio illustrated work entirely produced here," according to Patricia Murray, and "one of the largest and most splendid works which the literature and arts of this country have ever produced," according to Philadelphia's *Saturday Courier.*[30] The project was done in Philadelphia, where painter Henry Inman made oil copies of King's originals, which had been shipped up a few at a time from Washington. These copies in turn provided the basis for the lithographs that illustrated the volumes. Thus, any assessment of King's work comes through two sets of lenses.

With that said, it seems clear that some of King's portraits, like *Ma-Has-Kah, Chief of the Ioways,* were quite remarkable presentations of their subjects, while others, like *Keokuk,* were somewhat flat and stylized. Most are three-quarter length busts depicting the sitter in particular dress. Some are presented in their own costume; others, like the Choctaw Push-Ma-Ta-

Charles Bird King, *Portrait of Shaumonekusse (L'Ietan)*. King tried to present his subjects as distinct individuals, and he was lauded for his "accuracy" by people who had never seen the sitters. Courtesy of the Joslyn Art Museum, Omaha, Nebraska. Gift of M. Knoedler & Co., New York.

Ha, had adopted western clothes and are shown wearing them. We know that these were studio portraits, yet King has set some of his subjects in generic nature—with trees or mountains in the background. Others sit in no particular place at all against blank backgrounds. In all, I think it is fair to say, he makes an honest attempt to depict these subjects as individuals, not as types or representatives. That each was labeled by the name of the sitter underscores King's attempt to make sure each portrait, and thus each Indian, had a unique identity.

That sense of individuality and particularity is surely what Mrs. Trollope meant when she commented on the faithfulness of these paintings. Secretary of War James Barbour, who wrote an introduction to the three-volume set, also lauded King for achieving a "faithful resemblance" of his subjects and for triumphing in his task "with fidelity and success, by producing the most *exact* resemblances." The same was said about Stanley's work as well. In pleading for a public appropriation to pay poor Stanley for his paintings (he never did get any money for them before they burned), the 1857 *Journal of the Regents* recommended the paintings for their attention to all the "particulars" and for their "fidelity of the individual details." As Julie Schimmel has noted, the question of accuracy dominated the discussion of all images of Indians in the nineteenth century, more so than judgments about artistic merit.[31]

Significantly, McKenney and Hall titled their project *History of the Indian Tribes of North America.* The history came in two parts: the first two volumes consist almost entirely of lithographs of individual Indians accompanied by two- or three-page biographical sketches. This underscored the connection between history and the visual. As an 1830 guidebook to Washington, D.C., put it, describing the Indians presented in King's portraits: "He must be seen to know him."[32] The third volume, however, is taken up with a lengthy essay on the history of the Indians written by James Hall. Largely a compendium of the ideas circulating about Indians in the 1830s, Hall wrote his history hoping to bring about a change in Indian policy. He also recognized that understanding Indians past and present required changing one's point of view. "It is necessary," he wrote, "to go back beyond our own times, and to examine events in which *we* are not immediately concerned as a people."[33] When these three volumes are taken together, the history of Native Americans is conceived of as both textual and visual. In this sense, these volumes, beginning with their very title, help us chart the way the relationship between painting and history, and the place of Native Americans in both, shifted in the middle part of the nineteenth century.

Portraiture has always served the purpose of preserving for posterity the image of an individual, and in this sense King's portraits are no different. Given that he painted members of high-level Indian diplomatic delegations, it was easy for viewers to recognize that these were significant individuals—"some of the most distinguished among this most extraordinary race of people," in Secretary Barbour's words. The portraits acknowledged for viewers at the time both that the Indians were "extraordinary" and that there were "distinguished" individuals among them.

Distinguished individuals, of course, were seen as the central actors in history, and we can see these portraits as the visual analogies to biography. Just as biographies write the stories of important individuals, using their lives as exemplary for the rest of us, so too these portraits make an attempt at Indian biography, especially as assembled with the text in these volumes, preserving the likeness of significant, individual representatives of the "race." C. S. Rafinesque went on in the description of history quoted earlier to list several "departments" of history, the first of which he gave as "biography."

At one level then, King tried, like his teacher Benjamin West, to make Native Americans a part of American history, through a different representational strategy, however. West drew upon an event from the past to comment on the current state of Euro-Native relations. King tried to capture what was distinguished about these individuals as a way of asserting the respect to which they were entitled. As historian Karen Halttunen has argued, Americans in the antebellum years were obsessed with the notion of "character," and especially with how to recognize it in others, an obsession she has called "a crisis of social confidence." Believing that the exterior person could be "read" to reveal the true nature of the inner person, antebellum Americans developed a set of measures by which to make such evaluations.[34] Placed in this context, King's portraits are nothing less than a demonstration that these Indians did indeed have character.

Yet by linking the individual and the "race" in his evaluation of these portraits, Secretary Barbour pointed to a slightly different way in which they were seen. While these images might represent specific, worthy individuals, their significance, at least for many, lay in their creating a visual record of a people on their way to inevitable extinction. Secretary Barbour, after commenting on the importance of the individuals King painted, reminded readers that he believed "that this race is about to become extinct." The paintings, thus, "would be full of interest in after times." In recommending a visit to McKenney's "Indian Gallery," an 1830 guidebook described its importance in these terms: "But for [this] gallery, our posterity would ask in vain: 'What sort of a being was the red man on this country?' In vain would inquirers be told to read descriptions of him. . . . Here then is a gift to posterity."[35] So too for John Mix Stanley's portraits—"Centuries hence," the Smithsonian's Regents believed, "most of the tribes here represented shall have disappeared." These paintings, then, should be viewed as the visual contributions to the larger discussion of Indian extinction taking place in print.

Moving, as these portraits prompted viewers to do, from the mortality of specific individuals to the extinction of an entire race, they help move Indians out of the realm of human history, as understood through individual lives and careers, toward natural history. The lithographic reproductions of King's oils emphasized this. Although King included generic settings for some of his paintings, the lithographs removed setting and background altogether. In so doing, the lithographs turned figures into something akin to specimens. No accident that an 1838 review celebrating these volumes described their importance as "second only to Audubon."[36]

The substitution of natural history for history underlies the emphasis on the "faithfulness" and "exactness" of these images quoted above. These images, so writers would have it, displayed an almost scientific accuracy and drew their authority from that. That same 1838 review complained that "poets and novelists have given reign to their imagination in describing the poetical life and picturesque eloquence, of the Indians. The representations they have given are utterly false"[37]—unlike King's portraits presented by McKenney and Hall. King's portraits, and the use made of them in *History of the North American Indians*, stand as markers both for the way Indians were represented in art and for the purposes to which history should be put. West had not included a single "faithful" likeness of an Indian in *Penn's Treaty*, but he had included them in the flow of historical events, and they were central to a great moral lesson. The new conception of history demanded accuracy above moralizing, and as a consequence the portrayal of Indians in painting moved from the didactic to the documentary.

Historian of the Present: George Catlin

In 1836, James Hall, still in Philadelphia working to bring the publications of *History of the Indian Tribes of North America* to fruition, wrote to George Catlin, whom he had recently met. After describing his publication project, Hall then proposed that Catlin join himself and McKenney: "Your collection contains many portraits which it would be very desirable to unite with ours, as they are those of Indians of the more remote tribes."[38] Catlin, as events played out, turned the offer down. But the invitation is a nice reminder that by 1836 Catlin had already achieved a measure of celebrity for his renderings of Native Americans. If King's portraits, translated into lithographic reproductions by McKenney and Hall, put painting more in the service of natural history, then Catlin's work—indeed, his whole career—also moved Indians away from history and into the realm of ethnography even more emphatically.

Catlin's biography is fairly well known, in part because Catlin himself promoted the story at almost every chance he got.[39] Born in 1796, he grew up in the wilds of Pennsylvania. By 1820, he had made his way to Philadelphia and had taken up painting—he exhibited at the Pennsylvania Academy of the Fine Arts annual show in 1821. He spent that decade trying to make a career of portraiture, but having seen a delegation of Indians pass through Philadelphia on their way to Washington in 1824, he had already decided to go west to pursue his life's great work. Or so he claimed.[40] Whatever prompted him, he had made his way to St. Louis by 1831 and spent the better part of the next six years traversing the Great Plains, painting at a furious rate. By 1837, he had returned east, and had begun exhibiting his "Indian Gallery" in major cities. In 1839, he took his show across the Atlantic to London where he became a huge, if brief, sensation. After the mid-1840s, he spent most of the rest of his life in a failed attempt to reclaim that success. Catlin spent much of the 1840s and 1850s pleading with officials in Washington to buy his paintings. Congress was not swayed. He turned out a few more books about his western adventures, including one for children titled *Life among the Indians*, but the productive period in his artistic life was over.

Drowning in debt, Catlin made a deal with Philadelphia industrialist Joseph Harrison, the purchaser of *Penn's Treaty*, whereby he gave Harrison his paintings and in exchange Harrison took care of Catlin's bills. Harrison had the paintings shipped back to Philadelphia from London in 1852–1853, West sharing space with Catlin. There they languished in storage until Harrison's widow was persuaded to donate them to the National Museum in 1879. In Washington, Catlin's paintings replaced the King-Stanley paintings that had burned in 1865, and the public could once again see Indian portraits on display. Impoverished by the time he died in 1872, his paintings had not been seen in public for almost twenty years.

His obscurity has not lasted. Catlin's paintings have had an active exhibition life ever since they made their way back to the United States, including a major retrospective which inaugurated the Smithsonian's newly renovated Museum of American Art in the fall of 2002. They stand as a remarkable, prephotographic record—of individual Indians, of details of costume and custom, of a way of life that was changing even as Catlin painted it.

At the height of his fame, Catlin filled the London catalogue of his paintings with encomiums from the press. In fact, he had received a mixed critical reception. William Dunlap considered Catlin "utterly incompetent" as a painter, and considered his chosen subject matter beneath the dignity of serious art. Sardonically, Dunlap did concede that Catlin "has no competitor among the Black Hawks and the White Eagles," because he had "nothing to ruffle his mind in the shape of criticism."[41] That view, softened at the edges perhaps, remains persistent. Recently, William Truettner has called Catlin's production "uneven," and that seems right. A few of the portraits are genuinely striking; many seem flat and uninspired. To be fair, Catlin did rough out these paintings at tremendous speed. In his *Letters and Notes*, he claimed to have done 310 portraits, and 200 other scenes, between

1832 and 1839—sometimes he did six in a single day. Further, as he made his way through the Missouri basin he traveled with only a dozen or so colors. These circumstances go some way toward explaining why there is a certain sameness to many of his paintings.

The uneven response viewers have had to Catlin's paintings, then and now, may simply reflect the quality of the work itself. It may also stem, however, from the fact that people have not been quite sure how to look at these paintings, or into what category they ought to be put. Without stepping into the treacherous waters that swirl around what constitutes the canon of fine art, we can say that Catlin's paintings were, and are, admired primarily for their documentary, rather than their artistic, achievement.

In an age that prized seeing as a way of understanding, the power of these visual representations of Indians and Indian life cannot be overstated, especially because they came from a region still quite remote to most white Americans. Henry Schoolcraft underscored the importance of Catlin's paintings in a *North American Review* essay. "Others have described the physiognomy and dress of the Indians," Schoolcraft wrote, "Mr. Catlin has painted them."[42] If, as the guidebook entry for King's paintings insisted, the Indian must be seen to be known, then Catlin provided the richest source of that knowledge. "It may be in truth be esteemed," the *United States Magazine* declared in 1842, "the most valuable work on the inhabitants of the vast untrodden west which has been as yet produced."[43]

In this sense, Catlin's work, almost as soon as it appeared, was viewed as an ethnographic project. Catlin himself described his goal in what we might recognize as "ethnological" terms. In the introduction to his 1844 collection of folio-size lithographs, he told subscribers that he had hoped to record "faithful portraits of their principal personages, both men and women, from each tribe; views of the villages, games, sports, &c; and full notes on their character and history. I designed also to procure their costumes, and a complete collection of their manufactures of all kinds, including their implements of war and the chase."[44] He also insisted on his own detachment and observational objectivity in language that surely echoed that of other natural scientists. He told his readers and viewers that "I am traveling in this country not to advance or to prove theories, but to see all that I am able to see."[45]

The relationship between observation and knowledge was a central component in nineteenth-century science, and statements like these make Catlin appealing as a scientific painter. As with King's portraits, the accuracy of Catlin's renderings was both prized and unquestioned, although, as with King's paintings, few of his viewers had any real way of judging. "Of the

George Catlin, *Bird's-Eye View of the Mandan Village, 1800 Miles above St. Louis,* ca. 1837–39.
Working quickly and with a limited palette, Catlin executed dozens of paintings of Native
Americans and Native American life in the trans-Mississippi West. Courtesy of the Smithsonian
American Art Museum. Gift of Mrs. Joseph Harrison Jr.

truthfulness of his representations," one critic wrote, "there can be little or
no doubt." Thomas Donaldson, who compiled a massive catalogue of
Catlin's oeuvre shortly after it had been bequeathed to the National Museum, concluded: "The value of Mr. Catlin's pictures does not depend
merely upon their artistic merit, but upon the question as to whether they
are correct portraits of persons and dress and of scenes and events." Indeed,
Donaldson seems to have regarded these paintings as accurate in large part
because they made no other claim. Drawing this distinction between the
artistic and the accurate, Donaldson's assessment of Catlin in 1887 helps us
measure how the debate over the relationship between fact and truth, the
same debate that Reynolds and West had carried on, had changed.

It was not only the product but the process of Catlin's efforts that
proffered him membership in the scientific club. King had sat in Washington waiting for his subjects to arrive, as they did periodically and unpre-

dictably. Catlin, on the other hand, had gone out west, had pursued his quarry in native habitat, never mind the personal risks. Central to the autobiography Catlin repeated in all his publications—and a large part of what made him such a celebrity for a time, no doubt—was the image of a painter as intrepid adventurer. At the beginning of his 1844 London book of folios, he described his project to readers in this way: "I started my arduous and perilous undertaking with the determination of reaching, ultimately, if my life should be spared, every tribe of Indians in North America."[46] He was a field-worker, in the way that other natural scientists were, not an armchair dilettante. "*Every painting has been made from nature,* BY MY OWN HAND," he told visitors in his London catalogue to underscore this and to assure them of the authenticity of what they were about to see. For reasons like these, William Truettner concludes his study of Catlin by saying that, whatever his shortcomings as a painter, after Catlin, "no self-respecting artist could paint Indian life without venturing forth from his eastern studio."[47] Statements like these made it easy enough to see Catlin as an incipient ethnographer, by method as well as by his concerns.

Both Donaldson and Truettner much later stress that Catlin must certainly have breathed deeply in the scientific atmosphere of Philadelphia in the 1820s. Donaldson told readers, "Mr. Catlin's mind was on the subject of an ethnological and natural history museum and collection early in 1824," while Truettner believes Catlin to have been influenced by visits to Peale's Museum, still open in Philadelphia when Catlin sojourned there.[48] Indeed, Truettner has put him in the tradition of other "artist-naturalists" of the antebellum period. By 1896, when William Youmans included Catlin as one of his "Pioneers of Science in America," a consensus of sorts had been reached about Catlin's work and its significance: "George Catlin's work was undertaken not from a scientific, but rather an artistic impulse. It became, nevertheless, truly scientific in spirit."[49] In the end, Catlin came to be seen as a scientist because his method of producing paintings was more ethnographic than artistic, and the results seemed to belong less in a gallery than in an encyclopedia. Even as I write, several of Catlin's paintings still hang in the halls of the North American Indian at the Field Museum in Chicago.

One wonders what Catlin would have thought about this assessment. In his 1844 book, Catlin certainly sounds like a natural scientist using his art as the basis for an encyclopedia of Indian tribes. Should his life be spared, he hoped to record "every tribe of Indians in North America." As Truettner has interpreted his purpose: "What he meant to do, in effect, was to classify the principal tribes: to describe the chiefs, warriors, medicine men, and other noteworthy members of each; to examine and compare habits, amuse-

ments, and religious beliefs, and to collect a representative group of costumes, weapons, and domestic articles." And in his 1867 book *Last Rambles*
Catlin does spend some time evaluating "ethnological" theories, largely so
that he can contrast himself and his experiences with those who never saw
Indians firsthand.[50]

Nevertheless, Catlin started his career with loftier artistic aspirations.
Indeed, his decision to travel through the Great Plains seems to have come
largely as way for Catlin to jump-start an artistic career that was otherwise
sputtering. As a conventional portrait painter, he wrote to General Peter
Porter in 1829, "My feelings are becoming too enthusiastic for the limited
and slavish branch of the arts which I am now pursuing, and in which I am
wasting my life and substance for a bare living." Life is short, said the thirty-
year-old Catlin to the general, and "I find that I have already traveled over
half of it without stepping out of the beaten path in the unshackled pursuit
of that Fame for which alone, the Art, to *me* is valuable."[51]

Once he arrived in the Great West, it comes as no surprise that he found
what he was looking for. In an 1832 letter, he gushed that he was now surrounded by "almost unlimited models, both in landscape and the human
figure, exactly suited to my feelings." Finally, "I am now in the full possession and enjoyment of those conditions on which alone I was induced to
pursue the art as a profession, and in the anticipation of which alone my admiration for the art could ever have been kindled into a pure flame."

The language that Catlin uses in this letter comes straight from the
noble savage tradition as it translated into art in the late eighteenth and
early nineteenth centuries. Away from the corrupting influence of civilized
circles, "entirely divested of those dangerous steps and allurements which
beset an artist in fashionable life," Catlin finds "beautiful models" all around
him—"hundreds of graceful youths . . . arrayed in all their gorgeous colors." That Catlin's enthusiasm for "the noble races of red men" sounds entirely conventional, almost hackneyed, is not the point. Rather, it is a reminder that Catlin went west looking for artistic inspiration, rather than
scientific researches. Confirmed in his opinion "that the wilderness of our
country afforded models equal to those from which the Grecian sculptors
transferred to the marble such inimitable grace and beauty," Catlin found in
the Indians of the Great Plains a muse, not a set of specimens.

What is more, the muse he came looking for was Clio. At the outset of
his career, the ambitious Catlin aspired to the most respected of painting's
genres: history. One of his earliest attempts to paint Indians, a portrait of
the chief Red Jacket (1826–1828), started out as a history painting, and
Catlin asked his father and Timothy Pickering for their memories of meet-

ing the Seneca leader. Although the painting ultimately turned into a full-length portrait with Niagara Falls in the background, Catlin had by this time decided that he would be the history painter of Indians. Just as he began work on Red Jacket, he visited painter George Harvey at his Wall Street studio and "disclosed the ambition of his life to become the historian and limner of the aborigines of the vast continent of North America." Later in his letter to General Porter, he suggested an appointment to "some little agency among the savage Indians [where I] could have the benefit of the finest school for an Historical painter now to be found in the world, where, among the naked savage [I] could select and study from the finest models in Nature, unmasked and moving in all their grace and beauty."[52]

Catlin went west thinking of himself as a history painter. He returned east and went to Europe believing that he had accomplished a historical task. He continued to describe his paintings as "a full *pictorial history*" and as documenting "the history and customs" of the Indians. With his characteristic drama, Catlin continued to believe that "nothing short of the loss of my life shall prevent me from visiting their country and becoming their historian." The *American Daily Advertiser* saw the paintings this way and said of them: "The collection embraces a wonderful extent and variety of national history." No wonder Catlin included this clip as part of an 1848 catalogue of the paintings. Even when he complained to Congress, as he did in an 1852 letter to Daniel Webster, the appeal came from a historian. "So much I am doing for the history of our Country," Catlin wrote, "and I do think the government, from which I never yet had a shilling, should call my Collection home and pay me for my labours."[53]

It is easy to see how this would-be historian in paint became transformed posthumously into an ethnographer. Thomas Donaldson, whose book stands as the first, most thorough consideration of Catlin's career to appear after the painter's death, ignores Catlin's description of himself as a historian. Instead, Donaldson stresses the way in which Catlin recorded the ordinary and mundane: "One great merit of Mr. Catlin's 'North American Indians,'" Donaldson tells us, "is that he writes of the Indians in their everyday and domestic life." Catlin's eye caught "their eating, sleeping, hunting, fishing, birth, death; details as to dress, religious belief and the other things which make up the economies of the Indian." These constitute the kind of data that the ethnographic scientist requires: "Their domestic and everyday customs, habits, and manners are the essentials to the proper study of their origin and descent, and herein lies the chief value of his books and pictures." Just as importantly, Catlin did not clutter either his paintings or his books with the kind of material unnecessary for ethnographic understanding. "He does not constantly prate about [the Indians'] heroic acts," Donaldson writes because, "the heroic side of their life is but an incident."[54]

Whether he meant to or not, Donaldson has offered a nice description of the distinction between ethnography and history as the two had evolved by the last quarter of the nineteenth century, and which we explore further in chapter 5. "Heroic acts" are by their nature singular, extraordinary; they happen at fixed, identifiable moments in the flow of chronological time. They represent the ways in which individuals intervene and shape the processes of history. This "heroic side" of life is the stuff of history—the kind of thing featured in biography, that important "department" of history—Donaldson has implicitly suggested, and as such is incidental to understanding Indians. By contrast, the questions that concern us about the Indian past borrow their language from biology, "origin and descent." That these two words form the subjects in the titles of Darwin's two books was probably coincidental, but significantly so nonetheless. To understand this natural history, scientists need all those trivialities of "everyday and domestic life," and that is what Catlin has given us.

It would remain for a later generation of social historians to reclaim "everyday and domestic life" as part of Euro-American history at least. Still, it is worth examining a bit further why Catlin kept calling himself a historian and why he believed his paintings to be historical.

None of the paintings Catlin did during the 1830s could be considered in any way a grand manner history painting. This much seems unarguable, and in this sense Catlin's history paintings spring from a different impulse than those of Benjamin West and his contemporaries. There are no classical or biblical allusions here, no didactic work being done, no lessons taught or timeless truths conveyed. Furthermore, Catlin emphasized repeatedly that he painted scenes and people he himself had witnessed or met. West might have shrunk the distance between past and present with *The Death of General Wolfe*, but Catlin eliminated that distinction entirely.

Catlin's productive years corresponded with the period of Indian removal, and it remains a curious irony that he does not seem to have commented explicitly on this brutal event in any of his paintings. Yet just as he participated in the rhetorical conventions of the noble savage, so too like so many others he believed without qualification that extinction loomed as the only future for Native Americans. Even as he rhapsodized in 1832 about the artistic possibilities afforded him by these "thousands and tens of thousands of knights of the wilderness," he saw them "melting away" and about to be "lost to the world." In his 1840 London catalogue, he wrote that he painted "these interesting but dying people" because for some years he had "become fully convinced of the rapid decline and certain extinction of the numerous tribes of the North American Indians." He reiterated all this again in 1861 when he wrote that "the vanishing races of native man in America" were disappearing "before the approach of civilization."[55]

Catlin, then, would save all this. Not the Indians themselves, of course, or their way of life, but a record of it and them on canvas. In the midst of certain doom—"for they are 'doomed' and must perish"—Catlin believed "I have flown to their rescue . . . phoenix-like they may rise forth from the 'stain on a painter's palette,' and live again upon canvas."[56]

Here was Catlin's historical project—not to resurrect the "heroic" events of the past, even the very recent past, so that they might usefully instruct the present, as West and the other grand manner painters of an earlier generation had done. Nor to recover and reconstruct forgotten parts of the past so that they might be restored to the human memory, as other historians would do. Rather, Catlin the historian was saving a disappearing present for the benefit of the future. Here was what drove his desire to be comprehensive, both to record everything about the Indian's way of life and to "visit every tribe of Indians on the continent." He offered his Indian Gallery in this spirit, "for the use and instruction of future ages," believing in "the vast importance and value which a full *pictorial history* . . . might be to future ages."[57] As a historical painter, Catlin did not simply look to the past for inspiration. He waded directly in the flow of history—a process he saw as inevitable and inexorable—to catch and preserve a glimpse of the Indians *before* they became consigned to the lost past.

That his work became seen, at least for some time, as primarily of ethnographic rather than historic value measures two reciprocal developments. First, this categorical shift from history and art to ethnography and science mirrors the larger process by which Indians ceased to be central to the historical inquiries of nineteenth-century Americans. At the same time, this shift underscored that history itself would be a textual not a visual enterprise. Painting might have illustrative or even scientific use, but by the time Catlin died, it was no longer part of historical consideration.

THERE WAS ONE final way in which Catlin appeared to be more an ethnographer than the historian he wanted to be. To many it seemed, both at the time and after Catlin's death, that Catlin had succumbed to the easiest and most dangerous temptation facing any Euro-American who spent too much time among the Indians. He went native, or practically so.

Catlin's sojourn among the Indians of the Great Plains did prompt him to speak out, at least generally and generically, against the treatment they suffered at the hands of encroaching America, and he attempted to dispel some of the erroneous conceptions about their savagery. Certainly one of his London viewers came away convinced. After seeing Catlin's display, Arthur James Johnes told his readers that "it is impossible to peruse Mr. Catlin's living picture of the manners and social habits of the North American Indians without being deeply impressed with the conviction that these Tribes, both intellectually and morally, are as highly gifted by nature as those nations who have inherited the blessings of a refined civilization."[58]

As the *United States Magazine and Democratic Review* complained, however, "this over enthusiasm for savage life forms almost the only fault we have to find with Mr. Catlin," blaming this on the fact that he had become "at least *semi-indianized.*" The *Southern Literary Messenger* spoke even more angrily, charging that Catlin had chosen the Indians over the settlers and government "in that interminable warfare between the races." "He prefers savage to civilized life," the *Messenger* sneered.[59]

In truth, Catlin's experiences with Indians did lead him to lament the treatment they received both by settlers and government, despite his belief that Indians were, inevitably, doomed. Sometime around 1870, for example, Catlin responded to an inquiry from one Professor Harper with a long, impassioned denunciation of American Indian policy. Fittingly, he called upon Clio to make his condemnation: "Historians of the old world, who are watching these disgraceful scenes . . . are putting down in indelible ink, these blots in the pages of our Countries [*sic*] history."[60]

With Catlin dead, Thomas Donaldson could afford to be a bit more generous in his assessment of Catlin's Indian enthusiasm. He too believed that "the Indian, of necessity, had to give way to the progress of the age," and certainly acknowledged that "Mr. Catlin took the sentimental side of the Indian question in the matter of state policy." No doubt, Donaldson told readers, "Mr. Catlin permitted his sympathy for the Indian to warp his judgment."

The reasons for this, Donaldson suggests, are innocent enough. He chalks them up to Catlin's own historical circumstances and to his temperament. Catlin knew the Indians for only a few years in the 1830s, and thus "Mr. Catlin saw but little of the American Indian after 1839. Since that date we have had the most serious and dreadful Indian massacres." Catlin was a painter, not a military man or government official. Consequently, "Mr. Catlin saw but the man. He queried not at policies. His plea was humanity." Yet, while history moved on, Catlin's "creed never changed. The facts of 1830–1839, on which it was based, did change, however, but he was unalterable."[61] There is condescension here, especially because Catlin certainly did pay attention to developments in Native America after 1839 and still found American Indian policy appalling. But, Donaldson intimates, Catlin's view of Native Americans belonged to an earlier age, when Euro-Americans might still entertain the idea of noble savages. From Donaldson's vantage, that age had disappeared.

Like the Indians he attempted to save from the historical dustbin, history had passed George Catlin by.

Landscape into History: Albert Bierstadt

The grand manner tradition in history painting might well have been dying by the middle of the nineteenth century, but questions of history remained on the minds of many American painters. Rather than translate those concerns onto canvas, using the conventions of the grand manner, some turned instead to landscape painting. The American landscape, and the vastness of the western landscape in particular, became the stage upon which these painters sketched historical narratives.

With the eruption of Civil War in 1861, several painters used landscape as a way of symbolically depicting the struggle. Some, like Frederic Church's *Our Banner in the Sky*, strike us now as a bit overblown. Here, in a painting Church created in response to the firing on Fort Sumter in 1861, the Stars and Stripes have been felicitously formed by the swirling of clouds in the midst of a lurid sunset, anchored visually to a dead tree serving as a "flagpole." Others, like Albert Bierstadt's 1863 *Mountain Brook*, are more subtle. In this forest scene, Bierstadt has depicted the moment after a storm has just passed, sometime in late summer, as the transition to fall has just begun. The Belted Kingfisher—a bird named by Audubon "the United States Kingfisher" because it was common in both the North and the South—suggests a note of national unity. In both these paintings, and many others as well, painters used landscape to explore political debates and historical meanings.[62]

At the same time, landscape painting served as a way to document American natural history. More specifically, as Rebecca Bedell has so astutely analyzed, some landscape painters shared with many Americans a fascination with the science of geology and with the way it provided a visual record of the continent's history. By painting the American landscape, especially its spectacular natural features, these painters saw themselves as participating in the scientific project of the geologists who described, documented, and explained the natural world. Landscapes could thus capture history, both human and natural.

While this tradition of depicting the natural history of the landscape began in the East, it flourished most dramatically in the West. After the Civil War, many American artists did indeed follow in Catlin's footsteps, heading west to observe and paint firsthand the landscape and the people in it. Albert Bierstadt memorialized these intrepid painters in his 1884 *The Little Yosemite Falls.* Although the painting is mostly a landscape, Bierstadt has included a small group of men under a rock shelter in the foreground. Upon closer inspection, those men turn out not to be explorers or trappers, but painters.

In the second half of the nineteenth century, Native Americans were portrayed as part of the natural history of the western landscape. Just as the study of Indians became shaped by the intellectual apparatus of natural history in the nineteenth century, a process we will examine in greater detail in subsequent chapters, so too painting felt the influence of midcentury natural science. Through the landscape tradition that developed in the midcentury, especially the depiction of the west, Indians became part of the scenery eastern viewers expected to see, along with towering mountains, yawning canyons, or primeval forests.

In fact, Albert Bierstadt's first great popular success came with just such a painting. Like Catlin, Bierstadt had gone out west—the first time in 1859 and again in 1863 and 1871. Painted in 1863, the same year he commented on the Civil War in *Mountain Brook, The Rocky Mountains* brought Bierstadt national and international attention when it was displayed at New York's Metropolitan Fair in 1864, just down the corridor from Leutze's *Washington Crossing the Delaware.* Size alone must surely have impressed viewers. At a whopping six feet by ten feet, *The Rocky Mountains* seems to reach almost for a life-sized verisimilitude. In 1864, it must have overwhelmed those who came to see it. At the conclusion of the fair, *The Rocky Mountains* reportedly sold for $25,000, the largest sum ever paid for an American painting at the time.

The arrangement of *The Rocky Mountains* is quite conventional. Three broad horizontal planes move the viewer from the open meadow of the foreground to the brilliantly lit waterfall and pool of the middle ground before coming to the immense peaks, a bit hazy through diffused light, in the background. It is a magnificent painting of a magnificent scene. "Mr. Bierstadt's picture," one critic wrote, "deserves to take rank among the highest existing productions of American landscape art." The critic James Jackson Jarves recognized Bierstadt's connection with the science of natural history. "The botanist and geologist," he wrote in 1864, "can find work in his rocks and vegetation. He seizes upon natural phenomena with naturalistic eyes . . . with truthful effect."[63]

Albert Bierstadt, *The Rocky Mountains, Lander's Peak*, 1863. Native Americans as a part of the natural history of the landscape. Courtesy of the Metropolitan Museum of Art, Rogers Fund, 1907 (07.123).

That foreground, however, interests us most. There, a band of Native Americans have made an encampment. Teepees are already up, horses mill about, and people engage in a variety of domestic activities. Their activity is all subdued and in no way distracts from the contemplation of the overall scene. Their lives, lived in the shadow of the great mountains, are dwarfed by the great peaks. In this way, Indians are an integral part of this natural landscape, as seamlessly incorporated into the scenery as the "rocks and vegetation." Jarves, who pointed out the interest *The Rocky Mountains* might have for botanists and geologists, also noted that "Bierstadt uses the landscape . . . to illustrate Indian life. His figures are picturesquely grouped, prosaically true to actual life, giving additional interest to most observers." Those figures added a "human warmth" to the scene, according to a writer for the *New York Times*.[64]

Bierstadt had tried this arrangement not too many years before, in *Sunset Light, Wind River Range of the Rocky Mountains* of 1861. In this canvas, however, the viewer has been placed lower to the ground, almost literally in the Indian camp, which connects us more directly with the scene. Rocks and mountains loom up in the middle and background, but the Indian figures themselves here are larger, more specifically rendered, and presented with more immediacy. In addition, the group of Indians on horseback, located between two teepees on the right-hand side, are lit most directly, making them the visual focus of the painting. More than that, this foregrounding creates the impression that the mountains serve as backdrop for Indian life, that the natural scenery is the stage set upon which these figures act out their dramas.

Sunset Light, Wind River Range of the Rocky Mountains did not create the same critical splash that *The Rocky Mountains, Lander's Peak* would two years later. Although there well might be many reasons for this, I think it is fair to speculate that part of the reason may lie in the different way the two paintings handle the relationship between the Native Americans and the larger setting and between the Native American figures and the viewer.

Between the 1861 work and his 1863 composition, Bierstadt moved the viewer to a more indeterminate place. Without too much stretching, one might call it a more omniscient location. In this place, the viewer can take in the whole of the scene with a grander sweep, without being, as in the case with *Sunset Light,* stuck too much on a particular spot on the ground. This helps create an effect of greater distance between the viewer and the scene, and certainly between the viewer and the Indians arrayed across the foreground. In creating a more seamless presentation of this western scene as natural history, complete with rocks, vegetation and Indians, Bierstadt has also accomplished a more complete separation between that natural history and his viewers. Native Americans inhabit that natural history. Euro-Americans, at least the ones who saw Bierstadt's work, came as tourists.

Bierstadt's success as the premier painter of American landscapes did not last long. His biographer Gordon Hendricks dates the beginning of his declining critical reputation to 1873. The slide would continue, according to Hendricks, more or less until his death in 1902. One measure of Bierstadt's fading fortunes came in 1889 when the committee charged with selecting American paintings for the 1889 Paris Exposition passed on Bierstadt's only entry to the competition. He put up a brave show to a reporter, calling the rejection "a matter of indifference" to him, but Bierstadt felt the blow. Later in the same interview he went on: "Why my picture was rejected I, of course, do not know. . . . I consider my picture one of my very best."[65]

The rejected painting had been done a year earlier and titled *The Last of the Buffalo.* The reasons the painting did not make the trip to Paris are probably many, including the fact that it might have been too big—*The Last of the Buffalo* matches the enormity of *Rocky Mountains* almost to the inch. For our purposes, however, we can look at *The Last of the Buffalo* as a late attempt by Bierstadt to incorporate Native Americans into the landscape of the Great West.

In this painting, now among his most famous works, Bierstadt depicted an Indian buffalo hunt, picking up a theme first explored by Catlin. The action is dramatic, and the viewer is put front and center in the midst of it. An Indian on a rearing white horse is poised to thrust a spear into a charging buffalo, while the rest of the herd is scattered around the canvas. A half dozen or so Indians come charging in from the right-hand side. The bones of dead buffalo are scattered at our feet in the foreground, amidst dead and dying animals. The flat plain on which this action takes place recedes for a great distance into the background, though it fades into an increasingly diffuse and indeterminate horizon. We are left fixed on the drama between hunter and hunted.

Dramatic though it is, the painting seems confused on two levels. First, by his own admission, Bierstadt was primarily interested in the buffalo, not in the Indian hunters. "I have endeavored," he told that reporter from the *New York World*, "to show the buffalo in all his aspects and depict the cruel slaughter of a noble animal now almost extinct. The buffalo is an ugly brute to paint."[66] Yet, while Bierstadt called the painting *The Last of the Buffalo*, there are lots of them in this scene. Dozens, probably, painted individually, giving the impression of even more—a vast herd stretching out toward that hazy horizon. Painting at the moment when Americans had begun to recognize the imminent extinction of the bison, Bierstadt has chosen in this canvas to create a scene of natural abundance. It is not clear, therefore, how this painting functions metaphorically or what message is to be read from it.

More than this, however, at another level the painting implies something almost insidious. By calling a painting that depicts an Indian buffalo hunt *The Last of the Buffalo*, Bierstadt seems to suggest that Indian hunting bore some responsibility for the ecological disaster that Americans now acknowledged. In this sense, Bierstadt has neatly sidestepped one of the most obvious results of Euro-American expansion into the otherwise undisturbed, pristine natural landscape he painted so reverentially in other pictures. White Americans, crudely put, ruined the landscapes that Bierstadt sought to present, yet he can't quite bring himself to say so in paint, at least not in this painting. When Bierstadt portrayed these Indians in domestic tranquillity, they became of a piece with the natural surroundings. When he portrayed them in *The Last of the Buffalo* participating in aggressive, masculine action, as having some recognizable agency, they are responsible for ruining the landscape's natural history.

But perhaps Bierstadt's painting proved a success after all. It prompted a survey of the nation's remaining bison, a count that came to 551. That, in turn, prompted a national effort to save them, at just the moment when the

Albert Bierstadt, *The Last of the Buffalo*, 1888. Who exactly was responsible for the near-extinction of the American bison?

Indian wars came to their conclusion. Some began to imagine a time when the West might be repopulated with bison, but not necessarily with buffalo hunters.

GEORGE DE FOREST BRUSH also followed Catlin out west looking for artistic inspiration. Indeed, Brush even claimed to have witnessed the Indian ritual that Catlin had painted whereby leather thongs were inserted into the slit flesh of young Indian men. Brush trained academically in Paris. He returned to the United States in 1880, cast about a bit trying to figure out his artistic future, and then headed out west. He stayed long enough to turn out a few Indian pictures before returning to the East Coast and a modestly successful career painting sentimentalized portraits with titles like *Idle Moments* and *The Young Violinist*, which looked increasingly out of place in the art world, as the nineteenth century turned into the twentieth.[67]

We won't linger here over those paintings of Native Americans, portraits with titles like *In the Dark Forest*, save to say that by the time Brush made his journey out west, as we have previously mentioned, Bierstadt's reputation was already in decline. That decline mirrored a larger dissolution of the relationship between landscape painting and the study of natural history. Brush's sojourn in the West then provides a useful window onto the changing use of landscape painting and the changing role of Indians in those landscapes.

Although his experience was brief, Brush did manage to illustrate several magazine articles with western scenes and to write one of his own. Calling himself "An Artist among the Indians," Brush begins by both summoning and dismissing his artistic forebear George Catlin: "In reading Catlin, one is oppressed with a certain partiality, a constant tendency to throw into relief all their good and subordinate the bad." The complaint here is familiar, yet even in making it Brush acknowledges American art's debt to Catlin.

Like Catlin, Brush came looking for artistic beauty, but unlike Catlin, he will not be bogged down by any other agenda. "It is not necessary," he wrote, continuing to poke at those who took up the Indian "cause," "that an Indian learn to spell . . . before we see that his long locks are beautiful as he rides against the prairie winds." And most decidedly not like Catlin, Brush has no ambitions to be the historian of the Indians: "in choosing Indians as subjects for art, I do not paint from the historian's or the antiquary's point of view." Stressing the point, he went on, "I hesitate to attempt to add any interest to my pictures by supplying historical facts. If I were required to resort to this in order to bring out the poetry, I would drop the subject at once."

If, in this art-for-art's-sake rationale, Indians hold no historical, political, or scientific interest, then where do they fit into the larger scheme of things? As part and parcel of the landscape, Brush told readers of the *Century.* "It is when we detach them from all thoughts of what we would have them be, and enjoy them as part of the landscape, that they fill us with lovely emotions," he wrote at a moment when the last of the Indian wars were still bringing news of fresh casualties and when "subdued" Indians were being herded onto reservations. And with this all brushed aside, Brush concluded, "So the Indian is a part of nature."[68] Catlin had hoped to capture Indian history in paint and believed he was making a record of people trapped within an inevitable historical process. Bierstadt, among others, figured them into the record of the landscape's natural history. By the end of the nineteenth century, Brush evinced no interest even in this. Instead, Indians merely decorated the landscape of the West, or at least the imaginings of the West, no more than an aestheticized "part of nature."

Archives of Extinction: Elbridge Ayer Burbank and Edward Curtis

Bierstadt's fall from artistic grace coincided with a shift in the way American painters constructed the image of the West. As Alex Nemerov has argued, after 1880 or so, the West became a canvas on which people could respond to the dislocations and anxieties of an increasingly industrialized,

urbanized America whose very processes of progressive history were eroding the landscape, and its restorative, near religious power along with it.[69]

In this new context, Indians simply became part of what was disappearing in the West. But as we have already discussed, the belief that Indians
verged on extinction had been potent for some time. Catlin had responded
to this in the 1830s. By the end of the nineteenth century, the impulse to document and to archive became even more powerful.

Of all Catlin's painterly descendants who took up the business of depicting Indians, Elbridge Ayer Burbank stands perhaps as the most direct.
Burbank came from Illinois and had easy access to the world of turn-of-the-
century natural science. His uncle, Edward Ayer, was founding president of
Chicago's Field Museum of Natural History. Ayer, in fact, helped push Burbank out west in the first place.

A connection like that proved important in a host of ways over the
course of Burbank's career. For our purposes, it may have helped him occupy the space that Catlin had inadvertently defined where ethnographic
and historical concerns overlapped. That Burbank's portraits had ethnographic significance there can be no doubt. He either exhibited them or sold
them to the Peabody Museum at Harvard, the University of Pennsylvania
Museum, and the Field Museum (being his uncle's nephew surely did not
hurt here). And Burbank insisted, like Catlin had before him, that he always
worked from life, never from photographs or in a studio setting. His work
was a pure product of "out west where," as Burbank put it, "I belong."

At the same time, his portraits were also recognized and appreciated,
like Catlin's, for the disappearing history they recorded. In the foreword to
Burbank's episodic story of his adventures in Indian country, Charles Lummis insists that "no one at all rivaled Burbank as an historical painter of Indians." In fact, Lummis was prepared to go one better: "His work has historic truth and value for which we seek in vain, from Catlin down to date."
Lummis, describing Burbank, sounded in 1944 much like Thomas Donaldson in 1885 when he described Catlin: "his portraits are done with rigorous
exactness. . . . He neither idealizes nor blinks." With a clear, scientific eye,
Burbank gives us Indian faces, wrinkles and all, because "scientifically this
insistence upon the lines in which life indexes character, is very important."
And just as importantly, "Mr. Burbank preserves not only the facial type
with extraordinary fidelity and sympathy; his portraits are as well a graphic
and accurate record of the characteristic costumes, tribal and ceremonial."
A remarkable achievement and a legacy "not only to the future but to the
present."[70] This was a thoroughly familiar characterization of the Indian

painter as preservationist, including the familiar insistence on the accuracy of the work by people in no position to judge.

Burbank was most active as an Indian portraitist in the early years of the twentieth century, in the years immediately following the closing of the frontier, when the Indian problem had been resolved as far as most Americans were concerned. No wonder then that Burbank's project seemed even more vital and urgent than Catlin's had in his time. And yet, since we know a bit about how Burbank worked, we know that these portraits do deceive, their "extraordinary fidelity" notwithstanding. In fact, by the time Burbank got to them, many of his sitters no longer dressed in "characteristic costumes," and rather than acknowledge this he often had his subjects "dress up" instead.

Not surprising perhaps, but significant all the same. As it turned out, Burbank was too late. The Indian life he had come to rescue and preserve for the future had already passed away, already consigned to history. If Catlin had worked in a genuine "ethnographic present," then Burbank wanted to do so as well, and when he found himself in the wrong "present," he invented the one he had come looking for in the first place. Out west, where he belonged, Burbank turned the past into the present in order to save it for the future.

Burbank might have used "genuine" Native trappings to underscore the Indianness of his subjects, but he simultaneously acknowledged this sense that it was all slipping away before his eyes by his choice to paint so many old Indians. As Barbara Gallati has noted, unlike Charles Bird King's portraits of the 1820s, which portrayed Indians who "were physically powerful, able to maintain a semblance of authority because of their masculine vigor," Burbank's "paintings of famous chiefs . . . often featured aged men."[71] Indeed, the colored frontispiece to *Burbank among the Indians* is a reproduction of Burbank's 1898 portrait of a shrunken, shriveled Geronimo.

Catlin went west and found his calling recording scenes from a way of life he felt was destined to disappear. He arrived on the scene just in the nick of time, and in this way, history blurred with ethnography. Burbank started his work with similar impulses, understanding the way these two intersected, and yet he was haunted perhaps by the sense that he had arrived too late. As a result, his paintings quickly moved from ethnography to elegy.

THE PAINTERS WHO depicted Indians after the Civil War might well have been motivated by sensibilities different from Catlin's, because by that time, the work of pure "historical" documentation had been taken over much more efficiently by the camera. Photography had several advantages over painting, not the least of which were speed and easy replication, although, as Brian Dippie has pointed out, photography largely followed the two traditions of Indian portraiture already pioneered by painters: the studio portrait and the depiction of Indians in their "natural" setting. Much in common with the painters we have already discussed, most photographers of Indians in the late nineteenth century recorded, in Dippie's words, "a picturesque yesterday" or "a hopeful, if less colourful, present, serving as propagandists for assimilation."[72]

It is well known that the camera followed closely behind the advance of federal troops and the wagon wheels of settlers into the trans-Mississippi West. It is also well known that of the photographers who went west into Indian country, none was more prolific, well-financed, or better at self-promotion than Edward Curtis. Curtis spent nearly thirty years taking pictures of Indians and published over two thousand of them. Simply put, Edward Curtis probably did more to shape the way we imagine Native Americans visually than any other single individual.[73]

Curtis's work belongs largely to the first few decades of the twentieth century, and thus falls outside the chronological boundaries I have drawn around this book. Nonetheless, he stands as the best-known producer of the best-known images of Native Americans, and it is thus worth ending this chapter with a brief consideration of his work.

Curtis first came to national attention as the official photographer to the Harriman Alaska Expedition of 1899, a privately funded scientific exploration of the Alaska coastline. His photographs, especially of indigenous Alaskans, drew great acclaim and won Curtis prizes. On the strength of this success, Curtis spent several years trying to secure funding or patronage to finance his big idea: a comprehensive photographic survey of all the North American Indians.

His break came when he met J. P. Morgan early in 1906. Morgan, apparently very impressed with the photographs Curtis brought with him, agreed initially to fund the fieldwork at $15,000 a year for five years. Curtis would then have to publish the results on his own and sell them by subscription. The next year, 1907, the first two volumes of the magisterial *The North American Indian* appeared. The twentieth and final volume of the project came out in 1930. At the end of volume 20, Curtis concluded with an almost exhausted hubris enviable to any scholar: "Great is the satisfaction the writer enjoys when he can at last say to all those whose faith has been unbounded, 'It is finished.' "[74]

It is worth asking, however, just exactly what had been finished. The twenty volumes of *The North American Indian* are not solely or simply books of photographs, though they are surely all that most people, if they have heard of Curtis at all, remember from the project. In addition to the images, Curtis included lengthy written descriptions of Indians, tribe by tribe, "a complete and systematic text," as he put it, sketching, "every phase of Indian life . . . taking up the type, male and female, child and adult, their home structure, their environment, their handicraft, games, ceremonies, etc." A complete ethnography, "so seriously handled that the most critical scientific worker cannot take exception."[75]

The results were well received. Reviewing the first two volumes in the *American Anthropologist*, the anthropologist George Byron Gordon praised the accuracy of Curtis's work: "the illustrations present vividly to the eye such facts of Indian life as can be accurately recorded by means of the camera." Even those pictures of the "homely phases of aboriginal life," which have been made visually appealing, suffer not "the slightest loss of scientific accuracy."[76] In lauding the accuracy of these images Gordon gave Curtis the highest critical accolade, like Catlin and King before him, except now the power of the photograph made the accuracy a sure guarantee.

Likewise, in the language of system and completeness and accuracy we hear the familiar echoes of nineteenth-century natural history as it was applied, through ethnography and anthropology, to the American Indians—a record, both visual and written, of everything about every tribe. We hear as well the echo of Catlin, whose ambitions were no less grand, if much less realized. Curtis, in a sense, picked up where Catlin left off, and no painter, even one as quick as Catlin, could keep up with the pace of a camera. And despite the doubts of people like Edward Ayer—who did not believe the task could be accomplished, and said as much to the managers of the North American Indian Fund: "it would take ten to fifteen of the best anthropologists in America twenty years to write the history of the North American Indians as it should be done," not one photographer with a small staff[77]—Curtis was also pushing the whole business of anthropology to its logical limit. Rooted, as we will see, in the systematics of nineteenth-century natural science, the anthropological study of Indians late in that century still aspired to a kind of encyclopedic completeness and finality. Curtis believed that his volumes of *The North American Indian* represented the culmination of the encyclopedic project that Catlin had first imagined. Further, since this was a photographic project, *The North American Indian* represented the final triumph of accuracy, the yardstick against which all painters of Indians had been measured, and the goal of an increasingly scientific study of Native peoples. Perhaps Curtis thought he spoke not just for himself, but for a larger anthropological endeavor, when he wrote triumphantly: "It is finished."

As the apotheosis of the systematic and encyclopedic ethnographic impulse, the Indians in Curtis's *North American Indians* do not exist much as individuals. Although Catlin and King had gone to great lengths to preserve the likenesses of particular Native Americans, Curtis was more concerned with presenting group types—"the Apache" and "the Navajo." Many portraits of individuals do not record their names in the titles. Biography, that important "department" of history, has largely disappeared.

This is the same language Gordon, for one, used in his review, underscoring just how in tune Curtis was with the currents then running in anthropology. This reduction to ethnographic type, however, also served to keep ethnography and history at a distance from one another. As Gordon pointed out to his fellow anthropologists, Curtis's "labors are almost purely ethnological," and as such, "we must not expect to find . . . in these pages much matter dealing with the relations between the Indians and the white man. Mr. Curtis does not feel called upon to deal with these aspects of American history."[78] All of history, at least as it had become defined and understood by the turn of the twentieth century, had disappeared.

It is worth pausing over the significance of that observation. As several critics have pointed out, including William Cronon and Mick Gidley, Curtis deliberately erased any sense that Indians and whites had been interacting for decades, at least by the time Curtis "found" them out there.[79] In this sense, Curtis was little different from many anthropologists who through their studies positioned themselves as the silent, undisruptive observers of uncorrupted cultures. Curtis imagined a precontact, Edenic world, and then snapped its picture. Indeed, he even titled one of his most famous images "Before the White Man Came." The photograph was taken in 1924.

At one level, it would seem to take an almost comical suspension of disbelief to look at a photograph taken in 1924 titled "Before the White Man Came"—who, exactly, was taking the photo after all?—but at another level, Curtis is playing with a complicated dilemma inherent in his photographic project. Part of the power of photography, as Alan Trachtenberg reminds us, lies in what he has termed a "disruptive event." Every photograph, whatever it depicts, records the very act of taking the image itself, of the camera having been at that place at some very specific, datable moment in time.[80] At the same time, we need to notice that the Native world Curtis constructed through his photographs attempted to remove Indians from the events and flow of history altogether. Charles Bird King had acknowledged that the Indian world and the Euro-American world intersected when he painted his sitters in European dress or with medals and trinkets given to them by whites, but Curtis did not. And, as Gidley has argued, Curtis glossed over or ignored completely the political divisions within Indian groups, or the fact that in some cases he simply couldn't find the information and subjects he came looking for.[81] In this way, Curtis's Indians have no sense of politics, of an internal set of historical forces driving them. They are wholly and entirely part of nature and respond only to their natural environment. These images are precisely timeless because they do not represent Indians as Curtis found them early in the twentieth century—Curtis acknowledged this implicitly when he referred repeatedly to his "old time" Indians—nor can we ever know whether they represent Indians at any particular point in the past.

Curtis's photographs, of course, are not entirely what they seem. Since the 1970s, Curtis has had something of a revival, at least to measure by the exhibitions and re-publications of his work, and through this rediscovery we know now that he dressed his subjects up, posed them, and moved them around. They represent artifice as much as artifact. Yet these careful stagings were motivated by exactly the same impulse that drove other artists in depicting Indians: the impending disappearance of the Indians and the need to document them before that tragically but inevitably happened. Gidley has called Curtis's work "salvage ethnology."

If there is a narrative through-line in this fact-laden, detached work of ethnographic science, it is surely captured in the image Curtis chose as the very first illustration in the very first volume: *The Vanishing Race* (1904). This photo is classic Curtis, heavy on the chiaroscuro, and presents us with Navajos on horseback, riding away from the camera. These Indians are vanishing from our view, and so too they stand for their "race." At some level, it is possible to read almost all of Curtis's images through this lens of "vanishing." Given the careful crafting Curtis applied to his photographs, the scenes he depicted had indeed vanished. Certainly no one who went chasing after them was likely to find them. They were so valuable to us because they represented the fleeting moments of an imagined and thus ephemeral past.

Without weighing in on the ethical and moral debates that surround Curtis's use or misuse of his subjects, however, one thing, I think, remains unarguable: the photographs are beautiful. They penetrate, they captivate, they haunt. They speak to us, powerfully, across nearly one hundred years. This, surely, explains why in the last quarter of the twentieth century even as his position within the world of anthropology had become problematic, Curtis found a new home in museums and galleries of art. His skill as a photographer, his handling of light and shadow and composition, his way of

Edward Curtis, *The Vanishing Race*, 1904. Curtis used this image in the first volume of his encyclopedic photographic endeavor, *The North American Indian*, and with it set the tone and the rationale for the entire project. Courtesy of the Library of Congress.

putting figures into the landscape, made his elevation to the realm of fine art easy. Observers at the time recognized as much, although Curtis himself considered his a labor more of science than of art, and was doubtless pleased when George Gordon noted in his review that Curtis did not let the art in these photographs interfere with their scientific purpose.

Curtis, then, completed the process through which Indians moved from history, through ethnography, and finally to aesthetics. In that movement, we have perhaps and ironically come full circle.

More completely than Burbank, Curtis used the trappings of history— settings and costumes—to aestheticize, rather than historicize his Indian subjects. Yet there were historical consequences nonetheless. None other than Theodore Roosevelt wrote the foreword to volume one of *The North American Indian*. Roosevelt had seen some of Curtis's work, had heard of his ambitious plans, and had lent him his enthusiastic support for the project. In the equally enthusiastic foreword, Roosevelt echoed familiar refrains in underscoring the importance of Curtis's work. The Indians themselves are "on the point of passing away," and he recalls Catlin when he reminded readers that Curtis "is an artist who works out of doors and not in the closet. . . . He lived on intimate terms with many different tribes" and was "both an artist and a trained observer." The result, Roosevelt said, was that his "work has far more than mere accuracy, because it is truthful."

Accuracy and truth. We have come back to Benjamin West and Joshua Reynolds, only Roosevelt suggests Curtis has done them one better because he did not have to sacrifice accuracy to achieve artistic truth, the way Sir Joshua said was sometimes necessary. Photographs, after all, never lie. The truth Curtis achieved was not simply to have documented the fact of the Indians vanishing, but to have caught—or constructed—the pathos, the nostalgia, the elegiac quality of that fact. Given all that surrounded this vanishing—a history of warfare, disease and dispossession—for Euro-Americans in the early years of the twentieth century truth was probably less unsettling to look at than fact.

3

FADE TO SILENCE: INDIANS AND THE
STUDY OF LANGUAGE

The history of American philology is a subject far too extensive to be entered
upon in the present work.

JAMES COWLES PRICHARD, 1845

He was a powerful fixture of my childhood imagination. Long-haired and
dressed in buckskins, he stared at me—trash at his feet—and with a single
tear lamented all that had been destroyed in the American environment.

Of course, he stared at me from a television screen, this nameless Indian, and he was the centerpiece of an antilittering public service campaign.[1] Even for a child, growing up in the mid-1970s, the message was not
hard to decipher. Part of the growing environmental awareness of that era
had it that Euro-Americans had trashed the land while the Native Americans had lived in harmony and balance with nature, until we came along
and trashed them too.

There he stood, generically representing all Indians, and there went a
car and its litter-tossing occupants standing for all the pollution that modern, industrialized, white society had generated. Simple symbolism, but
effective.

Nameless, and voiceless too. Even while other antilittering campaigns
of the era gave a cartoon owl the chance to say: "Give a hoot. Don't pollute,"
this Indian remained stone silent. He didn't speak, and he didn't need to
speak. That single tear rolling down his cheek said all that needed saying.
And in his silence too he stood generically for all Indians, who in the Euro-
American perception didn't speak, or hardly ever spoke. Men—almost always men—of few words, inscrutable and opaque, whose utterances were
not so much conversational as oracular or who conversely grunted in
monosyllables. Indeed, the silent Indian has become such a stock figure that
it has entered the world of Native American humor. The narrator in Sher-

79

"Various Indian Hieroglyphicks," ca. 1780, from Pierre Eugène Du Simitière, *Original Journals & Extracts*. Native Americans were thought to have had no writing and therefore no history of their own that could be relied upon. But perhaps as these "hieroglyphicks" hint, the situation was a bit more complicated than that. Courtesy of the Library Company of Philadelphia.

man Alexie's story "What You Pawn I Will Redeem," describes himself as "living proof of the horrible damage that colonialism has done to us Skins," quite in contrast to his friend who is so "good-looking . . . like he just stepped out of some 'Don't Litter the Earth' public-service advertisement." But the narrator isn't going to let on about his fears and anxieties: "I'm a strong man, and I know that silence is the best method of dealing with white folks."[2]

It hardly needs saying that Euro-Americans invented the silent Indian and that they have continued to prefer silent Indians. Silent Indians, after all, are far less likely to demand or debate, complain or contradict. Silently, they can be the recipients of our consternation, concern, sympathy—pity even—without challenging any of our assumptions about them in the first place.

It does need remembering, however, that Indians, even in the Euro-American perception, have not always been so laconic and taciturn. Indeed, when the nation was founded and into the early nineteenth century Indians were often seen as loquacious and eloquent. In the years before the Civil War, people pursued the study of their languages with enthusiasm. The scholars who did so believed that understanding Indian languages would unlock the answers to a host of questions about their origins, interrelationships, the degree of social advancement they had attained, and their history. Furthermore, some of these students of language at the turn of the nineteenth century believed that the study of Indian languages would form the foundation upon which a new and distinctly American science of language would be built.

It did not turn out precisely that way. By the end of the nineteenth century, the study of Indian languages, rather than being a field unto itself, had become one of the four legs upon which the "chair" of anthropology sat. Instead of being the center of philology and linguistics, or even an independent field of inquiry itself, the study of Indian languages was largely neglected by European and American language scholars except by those in the new disciplinary field of anthropology.[3] One consequence of these intellectual and disciplinary shifts was that vocal Indians became silent ones.

Speaking in Eloquent Tongues: The Power of Indian Oratory

In 1849, the Ojibwa chief Kah-ge-ga-goh-bouh, or someone writing under that name, mused on the state of American Indians for readers of the *American Whig Review*. During the uneasy calm in white-Indian relations, between the calamity of Indian removal in the 1830s and the "age of Indian wars" that would commence after the Civil War, Kah-ge-ga-goh-bouh believed that some of the Indians' problems were rooted in language. Advocating a plan to create one big reservation for Native Americans, he recognized that differences in language would make it difficult for different tribes to live together. "I have tried to convince the different missionaries," he complained, "that it is better to teach the Indians in English rather than in their own language." He went on, "A great amount of time and money have been expended in the translation of the Bible into various languages . . . when [Indians] might have been taught English."[4]

At the beginning of the twenty-first century, when English appears to have triumphed, for better or worse, as the global *lingua franca,* Kah-ge-ga-goh-bouh's complaint rings remarkably modern and prescient. A shared language, both between the various tribes and between Indians and whites, might have proven the base upon which a solution to the "Indian problem" could arise.

But the second part of Kah-ge-ga-goh-bouh's complaint must have carried an inadvertent sting. The translation of the English bible into different Indian languages had been the first goal of seventeenth-century Puritan missionaries, and it remained perhaps the most significant, enduring accomplishment of their often ill-fated and unsuccessful evangelizing. Indeed, the first translation of the Bible into an Indian language remains one of the landmark events in the history of American intellectual life, and it is probably not an exaggeration to say that throughout the seventeenth and eighteenth centuries the serious study of Indian languages was inextricably bound up with the missionary impulse. The faithful of many stripes, Jesuits and Calvinists first, Protestants of other denominations later, learned Indian languages in order to harvest souls more effectively in the fields of Indian heathen.

Kah-ge-ga-goh-bouh's remark would have come as a surprise to Puritan divine and Bible translator John Eliot, who believed that differences in language were not a serious impediment to conversion.[5] Though Kah-ge-ga-goh-bouh may well have meant the comment to be offhanded, his impatience with Bible translating records a shift in attitudes about the utility of studying Indian languages. The missionary zeal of seventeenth-century New England generated considerable interest in Indian languages. According to Raoul Smith, of the twenty-seven books about language published in British North America during that century, twenty-three of them were about Indian languages.[6] That interest faded in the eighteenth century along with the errand into the wilderness, but it revived again for different reasons with the founding of the republic. What had been seen primarily as a religious tool in the colonial period became viewed increasingly as a way to answer comparative questions about the state of Indian social development, genealogical questions about the relationships between different Indian groups, and most especially historical questions about who these people were, where they had come from, and how they were related to other peoples in other parts of the world.

The eighteenth century drew to a close with the study of Indian languages largely dismissed in the trans-Atlantic intellectual discourse. With the important exception of the work done by Wilhelm von Humboldt, theories of languages generated in the European Enlightenment largely ignored Native American languages, despite the fact that some of those languages had been known and discussed in Europe for well over a century. Diderot, for example, included Huron as the only specific example of an Indian language in his encyclopedia. Of those languages in general he was derisive: "The language of these savages is guttural and very impoverished because they have knowledge of only a very few number of things."[7]

Students of Native American languages, therefore, had to swim against the tide of scholarly dismissal, by arguing that their studies ought to be taken seriously in the first place. Jonathan Edwards, a link between the older religious impulse and the newer study of language, offered his book *Observations on the Language of the Muhhekanaew Indians* as a corrective to erroneous notions circulating in the middle of the eighteenth century. "It has been said," he told readers, "that savages have no parts of speech besides the substantive and the verb. This is not true concerning the Mohegans, nor concerning any other tribe of Indians, of whose language I have any knowledge." He went on, "It has been said also, that savages never abstract, and have no abstract terms, which with regard to the Mohegans is another mistake."[8]

Thomas Jefferson perhaps most significantly of all took up the charge of defending the complex and therefore fascinating nature of Native languages against detractors, both at home and in Europe. His responses to the queries of French diplomat François Marbois, published famously as *Notes on the State of Virginia*, address the issue at several points. Among other things, he told Marbois that despite the paucity of "our knowledge of the tongues spoken in America, it suffices to discover the following remarkable fact. Arranging them under the radical ones to which they may be palpably traced, and doing the same by those of the red men of Asia, there will found probably twenty in America for one in Asia."[9] One can almost hear Jefferson's voice swelling with a defensive pride.

Jefferson implicitly argued that Indian languages were worthy of study because of their richness and diversity. He underscored that argument by introducing his readers to the idea that Indians were eloquent. Exhibit A in Jefferson's case was the speech given by Chief Logan to Lord Dunmore in 1774. In a dramatic rhetorical flourish, Jefferson prefaced the text of the speech by saying: "I may challenge the whole orations of Demosthenes and Cicero, and of any more eminent orator, if Europe has furnished more eminent, to produce a single passage, superior to the speech of Logan."[10]

That Jefferson invoked Cicero when describing Logan's eloquence, startling though it must have been, is generally well remembered. Three other things about Jefferson's discussion of Logan should be reiterated, however. First, the claims he made for Logan's oratorical prowess caused something of a controversy. Not everyone was persuaded. The otherwise unidentified B. T. C. found "that the speech, as published by Mr. Jefferson is not worthy of those high encomiums which he bestows upon it."[11] Worse than that, the speech itself was dismissed as a forgery, and some accused Jefferson of being the author. In response, Jefferson felt compelled to add an appendix to subsequent additions of the book defending the veracity of the Logan story, including what amounted to signed affidavits that the massacre of Logan's family had indeed taken place.

Second, the discussion of Logan takes place not in the chapter dealing with "Aborigines," but in the one titled "Productions Mineral, Vegetable and Animal." Jefferson used the story of Logan's eloquence as the culmination of his description of Indians as objects of natural historical interest, a discussion that includes, among other things, a meditation on body hair. Working, as it were, from the corpus inward, Jefferson moves to a consideration of the Indian's mental capacities. With the accumulation of more information, Jefferson concludes, "We shall probably find that they are formed in mind as well as in body, on the same module with the 'Homo sapiens Europaeus.'" As proof of this bold assertion, Jefferson then offers Logan. And at the end of the text of the speech, Jefferson adds, "Before we condemn the Indians of this continent as wanting genius, we must consider that letters have not yet been introduced among them."[12] Here, then, was the crucial equation: to demonstrate that Indians possessed complex languages, and could use them to eloquent and affective ends, bestowed a measure of humanity, perhaps even equality, on the speakers.

Finally, Jefferson, of course, was not the first Euro-American to remark on the eloquence of Indians. As Matthew Lauzon has pointed out, "the notion of the 'savage poet' was common in 18th-century Britain, and those found in North America were a part of the construction of British identity during the colonial period." In 1775, just a year before the Declaration of Independence, James Adair wrote that "their language is copious and very expressive . . . and full of rhetorical tropes and figures, like orientalists."[13] But in *Notes* Jefferson has wrestled eloquent Indians away from the British and made them a province of the new United States.

Chief Logan's speech was probably the best known among several examples of Indian eloquence that turned up often in the printed discourse of the early republic and antebellum periods, although William Stone, author of an 1866 biography of Red Jacket, assumed that in addition, "The name of Red Jacket, as the great orator of the Six Nations, is among those most familiar to the American ear." He went on to credit the Six Nations "above all others of the American aboriginals" as "lovers of eloquence, and cultivators of the art." Historian Carolyn Eastman believes that in the early republic alone "hundreds of representations of Indian voices" turned up in a variety of publications. School children learned their elocution and public speaking by memorizing, among other things, examples of Indian speeches, Samuel Drake filled his 1836 volume with "noble specimens of Indian eloquence," and John Frost included Red Jacket's story in his *Book of Good Examples*. Indeed, Stone organized his entire biography of Red Jacket around the texts of his speeches, and underscored the ubiquity of both his subject and the idea of eloquent Indians at the very outset of the book: When Red Jacket makes his first appearance to readers of Stone's biography, he announces: "I am an orator!—I was born an orator."

John Irving went so far as to suggest that anyone who could not appreciate Indian oratory was the victim of bad translation. Translators, he complained, were "with few exceptions ignorant and illiterate." As a consequence, "the poetical thought, which runs through Indian eloquence, is entirely lost. There was not a savage who addressed us, who did not at times, clothe his ideas in beautiful attire, and make use of wild and striking similes."[14] His two-volume *Indian Sketches* is otherwise a vicious account of Indians in the midst of a crushing social crisis. The book came out in the midst of Indian removal, after all, and participated in creating public justification for that policy. Yet even Irving could find an exceptional place in his narrative for eloquent Indians.

For some, the Jeffersonian equation continued to matter. Herman Humphrey, president of Amherst College, delivered a fiery speech in 1829 calling for more just treatment of the Indians. In it, he quoted Logan and another Indian chief as examples of what this "noble race" might be capable of and as evidence that they deserved more humane consideration. Likewise, Indian Affairs Commissioner Thomas McKenney, writing in 1846, believed that Indian eloquence proved that Indians were "worthy of the Christian teaching and labors, and of the government's protection."[15] As American policy toward Indian nations cast all relations with them in terms of hostility, Humphrey saw an appreciation of language as one way, perhaps, to mitigate increasingly savage policies.

Others saw language as having the power to transform individual Indians—otherwise savage and bloodthirsty, or slothful and dissolute—into something more approaching a masculine ideal. As a writer for the *Southern Literary Messenger* reported a speech by Tecumseh: "His frame swelled with emotion. Every posture and every gesture had its eloquent meaning. And then, language, indeed—the irrepressible out breaking of nature—

flowed from the passionate fountains of the soul." Caleb Atwater, an archaeologist of considerable importance, whom we shall meet in chapter 4, believed that "enthusiasm is the secret spirit which hovers over the eloquence
of the Indian," and when that enthusiasm was aroused—when for example
the subject of selling ancestral lands would come up for negotiation—"his
eyes flash fire . . . every muscle is strained . . . and his voice becomes clear,
distinct and commanding. He now becomes, to use his own expressive
phrase, A MAN."[16] Driven by emotion and "enthusiasm," the Indian body itself becomes eloquent. The achievement of Indian eloquence might or
might not raise the estimation of all Indians, but it had the force to make individual Indian speakers into real men.

By the mid-nineteenth century, the case for Indian eloquence had been
made often enough that some European authors were persuaded. Reviewing a book on American Indians by Frenchman l'Abbé Demenech, an
anonymous English writer told readers of the *Westminster Review* that
"The Indian vocabulary is poor, but the genius of the language seems ex-
tremely poetical. . . . The Indians have a natural talent for oratory."[17] No
quantity of Indian oratory, of course, and no quantity of admiration for it
spared Indians the brunt of brutal federal actions. But Jefferson, at least in
some quarters, appeared to have won the battle he began in *Notes* by elevat-
ing Indian oratory, as a distinctly American production, to a place of international admiration and respectability.

Language, American Nationalisms, and the End of Eloquence

Jefferson himself was an avid student of Indian languages, collecting and
compiling vocabularies of different tribes. By the 1780s, he had outlined a
plan for the systematic collection and study of vocabularies and grammars.
In 1817, he deposited what remained of this work—much of the manuscript
material was unceremoniously dumped overboard in 1809 by thieves rifling
through his trunks as he moved from Washington back to Virginia—in
Philadelphia at his old haunt, the American Philosophical Society.

And fittingly enough. The revival of interest in Native languages in the
early republic took an important institutional step in 1815. In March of that
year the American Philosophical Society in Philadelphia created a new Historical and Literary Committee. With Stephen DuPonceau as its corresponding secretary, the committee became the hub of language study
throughout the 1810s and 1820s and of a new, largely secular approach to the
problem. As DuPonceau wrote to Jefferson in 1817, "You will be pleased to
hear, that our Committee have particularly turned their attention to the
languages of our Indian nations."[18]

DuPonceau remains one of those extraordinary intellectual figures about whom we don't know enough.[19] Born Pierre Etienne in France in 1760, he wound up in America in 1777 as a youthful revolutionary sympathizer. A year later, he was a captain in the Continental Army and, through the intercession of Benjamin Franklin, a member of General Washington's staff. Settling into the intellectual life of Philadelphia after the war, his interests ranged from history, to constitutional theory, to silk production. In the midst of all this, he developed an insatiable appetite for languages. DuPonceau stands, with Albert Gallatin and John Pickering, as the most energetic and influential student of Indian languages in the antebellum period.

DuPonceau understood, and helped foster, the shifts in the study of language that took place as the United States emerged from the colonial period and grew in the nineteenth century. He recognized the role that religious missionaries had played in establishing what was known about these tongues, and he was respectful of it. After all, he had to rely on the vocabularies that were still being gathered by ministers in the field. To the Reverend Daniel Butrick, he wrote: "To Religion we are indebted for what little has been done on the subject. The Indian languages have been studied as a means of converting the Savages to the Christian faith." And in case the good Reverend remained skeptical about DuPonceau's avowedly more scientific interests, the latter assured him that science and religion worked hand in glove to illuminate the plan of the creator. To Jefferson, however, he complained that "the study of languages has been too long confined to mere 'word hunting' "[20] That is what missionaries had done, as they compiled utilitarian vocabulary lists of the particular tribes among whom they proselytized. To a committee of the American Philosophical Society, he sounded a more positivistic note: "It is only since the beginning of the present century, that barbarous languages, as they are called . . . have been seriously attended to. . . . Before that time, missionaries and travelers alone paid attention to the languages of savage nations." Triumphantly he told the Society, "Philosophy, at last, took hold of the subject and thus began a new science called 'the comparative science of languages.' "

Scientist though he thought himself to be, DuPonceau was also enamored of Indian eloquence, because he considered it the logical product of the languages with which he was so fascinated. In corresponding with John Heckewelder, perhaps the most talented, thorough, and engaged linguist among the missionaries of the late eighteenth and early nineteenth century, DuPonceau wrote enthusiastically, "You speak to a convert when you observe upon the richness of the American language." Indeed, DuPonceau believed that American languages surpassed all others in their eloquence and poetry. "To me," he wrote somewhat self-effacingly, "it appears, from the very slight book knowledge that I possess, that the Indian languages are the richest in the world in Grammatical forms." And in a gesture worthy of Jefferson, he concluded "one would rather think those languages formed by Philosophers than by Savages."[21] His scientific studies would provide the intellectual framework for better understanding that beauty and philosophy.

Like Jefferson, DuPonceau was motivated by a booster's sense of national pride and by the defensiveness that sprang from a national cultural and intellectual inferiority complex. In an exchange with Heckewelder about a German book on American Indians, DuPonceau reported himself "very much disappointed and mortified by the bad opinion [the author] seems to entertain of the Indian Languages."[22] Corresponding with Jefferson about several new books published in Europe about Indians, he found himself of two minds: "While you will be pleased with me Sir, to see our country so often and so respectfully noticed by the learned in the most distant parts of Europe, you will regret I am sure, that their notions of it should be so imperfect." Admitting that he was both "mortified as well as astonished that so much knowledge respecting the languages of the aborigines of our country should be possessed at the furthermost end of Europe [St. Petersburg and Germany], while we know so little," he promised Jefferson that the Historical and Literary Committee "are sensible of this difference and I hope will be able to convince the world that the true, full and correct knowledge of America and all that belongs to it can only be obtained in & from America." And in a near-crescendo he concluded with the former president: "I beg you will excuse this effusion of patriotic zeal. It is the spirit which has dictated this letter."[23]

DuPonceau was not the only student of languages moved by "patriotic zeal." Henry Schoolcraft similarly complained about the "vague and erroneous notions of the character and structure of our Indian languages . . . on both sides of the Atlantic," which derived from "preconceived opinions." How could it be otherwise: "It is hardly to be expected that a people, whom we were so often called upon to measure swords with, should at the same time inspire the literary zeal, necessary to enable men of letters to analyze their words, and unravel their syntax." Likewise, when he wrote an essay on "Indian Languages" for the *Encyclopedia Americana,* James Pickering echoed that sense of nationalistic pride: "It is also a fact that the American languages are rich in words . . . [this has] attracted the attention of the learned in Europe as well as in this country." He went on to hint at the slightly unsettling conclusions that might be logically drawn once scholars recognized the sophistication of Indian languages: "The pride of civilization is reluctant to admit facts like these."[24] DuPonceau's work demonstrated that the more one learned about Indian languages, the less tenable became the "prejudices" that scholars had held against those who spoke them.

According to Edward Gray, DuPonceau sought in the study of American languages the basis for an "indigenous aesthetic experience," one that would be noticed favorably in Europe and bring cultural laurels to the new nation. There is a bitter irony that DuPonceau should share this project so enthusiastically with Jefferson, whose own policies while president only facilitated the destruction of Indian cultures, and, as Anthony Wallace argues, paved the way for the calamity of Jacksonian removal.[25] Still, this exchange reveals a strange dialectic. Military, diplomatic, and economic policies all posited opposition and conflict between the Indian nations and the United States. For purposes of writing the nation's cultural declaration of independence, however, Indian languages could be embraced, or appropriated, as part of "our country."

If patriotic zeal motivated DuPonceau's linguistic project, his method was comparative. Using his post at the American Philosopical Society as a kind of central command, DuPonceau solicited from his correspondents in the American hinterlands all the information he could about as many different languages as possible. This distinguished his activities from "mere 'word hunting.'" Rather than simply assembling vast lists of vocabularies, DuPonceau was a pioneer in the study of comparative grammar. As he explained to Jefferson: "Perhaps a comparison of the grammatical forms of the different nations may produce more successful results."[26] The comparative method would be the heart of a new science of language, bringing rationality and system to Babel. This new scientist, as John Pickering envisioned it, "under the guidance of his Newton and Linneaus," would be able "to class and systematize . . . the perplexity and confusion" until "order reigns through the chaos, and each object settles into its place."[27]

At the heart of this scientific conception of language study lay the accumulation of data. Data—vocabularies and grammars—and the conclusions drawn from their comparison would replace armchair speculations. As Pickering put it: "the world has been long enough amused with theories of man . . . it is time now . . . to study men and things as they are." English philologist Arthur James Johnes was even more explicit in his invocation of empirical, experimental science as the guiding principle for studying languages: "the leading doctrine laid down by Lord Bacon as applicable to the investigations of Physical science applies equally in this instance to the researches of the Philologist. . . . Experience is the only legitimate guide to *Truth*."[28] This explains in part why DuPonceau and others believed the United States would prove to be the intellectual center of this new science: where else in the Western world could the scientist find such rich resources so close to hand? And in this sense, the study of Native American languages constitutes the first methodical attempt to gather information systematically about these people.

For linguists today, DuPonceau is probably best known for coining the term "polysynthetic" to describe multiple ideas expressed in a single word, a trait he found remarkable and unique in Native American languages—"it has been observed, that no nation elsewhere can combine so many ideas together in one word," although he would confess later under the weight of further evidence that not *all* Indian languages operated this way.[29] But DuPonceau saw the comparison of Indian languages as the heart of his scientific pursuits. The greater "success" DuPonceau hoped to achieve was in using languages to answer fundamental historical questions about Indians, questions that could not be answered by studying languages in isolation. Languages, DuPonceau argued, held the key to understanding who these people were, how they were related to one another, and where they had come from originally.

In this sense, DuPonceau helped bring to the United States ideas about language that had begun circulating in Europe since the latter part of the eighteenth century. For people without written records of themselves, and without tangible monuments with which to mark the passage of time, words themselves might be used as artifacts. In this strain of natural-historical thinking, language depended for its existence "not on knowledge but on habit," and thus language itself provided a glimpse into the past of people whose history was otherwise completely obscure. As Edward Gray has demonstrated, that "language was historical and that its history corresponded to the progressive history of mind, was accepted by philosophers as an almost unwavering article of faith." In its grandest, most encyclopedic conception, a worldwide comparison of nonwestern languages would yield a single genealogical linguistic map and demonstrate the historical connections between the speakers of those languages.[30] As distilled by Henry Schoolcraft on this side of the Atlantic: "Language is itself so irrefragable a testimony of the mental affinity of nations . . . that it offers one of the most important means for studying the history of the people." "Nothing is more characteristic of the intellectual existence of man," he wrote again, "than language."[31]

IN 1836 AN anonymous writer for the *Knickerbocker* contributed an essay on the subject of "Indian Eloquence." The piece was as familiar as it was lugubrious. "A few suns more, and the Indian will live only in history," it begins, and along the way Red Jacket, White-Eyes, Shenanadoah and several others are remembered for their oratory. In addition to reminding readers both that "Indian eloquence is a key to the character," and that it stands as "a noble monument of their literature," the author also makes the romantic equation between oratory and Indian physical performance: "What can be imagined more impressive, than a warrior rising in the council-room to address those who bore the same scarred marks of their title to fame and to chieftainship? The dignified stature—the easy repose of limbs—the graceful gesture, the dark speaking eyes, excite equal admiration and expectation."

The article is as succinct a summation of the enthusiasm some Americans felt for Indian eloquence as any, including its concluding plea that, whatever might become of Indians in the future, examples of their oratory ought to be preserved: "shortly the question '*Who is there to mourn for Logan*,' may be made of the whole race, and find not a sympathetic reply. Their actions *may* outlive, but their oratory we think *must* survive their fate."[32]

The whole notion of eloquent Indians has a larger than mellifluous significance. Eloquence and oratorical skill were central parts of the American political and cultural discourse in the late eighteenth and early nineteenth centuries. The equation Jefferson made between Logan and Cicero was neither casual nor arbitrary. Just as Americans looked to Greece and Rome for forms of governance, so too they looked to the politicians of the ancient world for models of political speech. The ability to persuade and inspire was seen as intimately connected with the ability to govern and command. In John Quincy Adams' famous equation before a crowd at Harvard in 1805: "In the flourishing periods of Athens and Rome, eloquence was power."[33]

Further, as several scholars have demonstrated, language itself helped to create nations and nationalism during the Enlightenment. Language, and specifically the erosion of a single "truth" language, as Benedict Anderson puts it, stands as one of the three things necessary for "the very possibility of imagining the nation" in the first place. The power of language in creating nationalism for Anderson resides in "its capacity for generating imagined communities building in effect particular solidarities."[34]

Thus, admiring Indian eloquence, acknowledging their oratorical skill, came provocatively close to investing individual Indians with power and with giving Indian groups the ability to imagine themselves as nations. It was no coincidence then that most of the Indians identified as eloquent came from tribes usually identified as "nations"—in a letter to Gallatin, DuPonceau greeted him: "I will now tell you news from the Indian Republic of Letters."[35] In the late eighteenth century, when American nationhood apart from Great Britain was still tenuous and not fully "imagined," and when Euro-American conquest of the entire continent was not yet a foregone conclusion, it may well have been possible for some to figure Indians into the equation that linked eloquence, power, and nationhood.

As the nineteenth century wore on, however, the oratorical power of Indians grew to seem less impressive, and increasingly remote. Caleb Atwater, who saw a more perfect Indian masculinity in the act of speaking, was also clear that appreciation for Indian eloquence could go only so far: "Among savage nations orators do not stand as high as they do among civilized ones." And taking the preeminent exemplar of Indian eloquence head-on, he reminded readers that although Logan's speech was "simplicity itself," the chief "had lived all his days among the whites." He went on to qualify even further the estimation that some still had for Indian oratory: "Such a speech as his was never delivered by an Indian, unacquainted with the whites. There are in that speech a clearness, a simplicity, a pointedness, which belong to a civilized man's speech."[36]

Likewise, DuPonceau and others referred regularly to Indian languages as "American languages." But in 1828 that plural phrase was made singular, and its meaning changed dramatically when Noah Webster published the first edition of his *American Dictionary*. Looking eastward across the Atlantic, the *Dictionary* helped define the English language as Americans used it, and thus it underscored the relationship between language and nationalism we have discussed previously. Americans and Britons might speak a similar language, but Webster, by calling it "American," announced that there could not be a "particular solidarity" with the former colonial ruler. Looking westward, across the vast expanse of as yet untamed Indian country, Webster's *Dictionary* claimed English as the American language, denying that connection to the hundreds of Indian languages spoken by Native Americans. That "particular solidarity" of American nationhood came to be symbolically defined by Webster as those who spoke American English only. What remained of Indian language in the American lexicon were Indian place names—simply underscoring that Indians belonged properly to the natural world.

Of course, even the most avid admirers of Indian eloquence rarely translated their admiration into a sense of social or political equality. The equation between eloquence, power, and nationalism that was central to the construction of American identity in the early nineteenth century did not, in the end, apply to Native Americans. Indeed, as Carolyn Eastman has astutely observed, more often than not the examples of Indian speech most cited by Euro-Americans as worthy focused on episodes of defeat, told in elegiac terms. These allusions to the "dark side of expansion" in the early years of the new republic linked Indian eloquence—Logan most exemplary of all—with the earlier tradition of the American jeremiad, those Puritan sermons that narrated a fall from grace along a trajectory of decline.

In this way, Americans could pay homage to eloquent Indians while simultaneously moving them—rhetorically if you will—"from a position of power to a place in American memory."[37] Americans thus executed a nifty shift in the first half of the nineteenth century: by displacing the historical narrative of the jeremiad, with its sense of declension and repeating cycles of history, onto Native Americans—by making it "their" narrative rather than "ours"—Americans cleared a discursive space to be occupied with the much sunnier, linear narrative of progress that would dominate mainstream historical thinking throughout the nineteenth century. The very notion of American progress was thus dependent on Indian decline.

As that progressive narrative took shape, it should come as no surprise that writers seemed intent on knocking the Indian off whatever rhetorical pedestal Jefferson and others had placed him. An anonymous reviewer was decidedly left-handed in his 1860 assessment of Indian eloquence: "They also aspire to oratory, and, while they are guiltless of the rhetorical atrocities often put into their lips by historians and novelists, their short, popular harangues are not without a certain rude eloquence."[38] Washington Irving's nephew John found some of the Indians he encountered on his adventures west to be predictably monosyllabic. Crossing paths with one Pawnee, Irving reported, "He saluted us with the usual guttural salutation of 'ugh!' "[39]

If examples of Indian eloquence could be used in the antebellum period to consign Native America to the realm of American memory, then after the war, Indian eloquence itself became seen as a thing of the past. Examples might still be trotted out, as in William Stone's 1866 biography of Red Jacket and in a book for children of 1861, which included for their edification several examples of Indian oratory. After the last of these the author pauses: "Let us turn back for a moment to this wonderful speech . . . and read it over again . . . this humble eloquent address . . . that no language, that no diction, and no study could improve. . . . What a beautiful illustration have we here . . . that nature has endowed man, even in his most ignorant wilderness state, with a knowledge of his Creator."[40] The author was George Catlin, whose career belonged entirely to the antebellum period, who was aged and on the verge of death, and who, in any event, had committed the unpardonable sin of going native. Besides, by 1861 few but children had much use for eloquent Indians.

More typically, William Tracy, writing in 1871, critiqued several recent speeches, including one by Red Cloud, and found them wanting: "They are hardly such as would be called eloquent," he complained, "they are very far removed in style and imagery from the fragments of Indian eloquence which have been preserved and became historical." He went on in the same vein, "Few of the race which left us such specimens of eloquence still survive . . . soon it may be that all that shall be left of Indian eloquence will be its history." John Esten Cooke managed racist slurs in two directions in an 1874 essay: "While the African gibbers, jabbers, and grimaces, the Indian is silent, grave, and even austere in his demeanor."[41]

A coup de grace of sorts came in 1851 when Brantz Mayer delivered a speech to the Maryland Historical Society entitled "Tah-Gah-Jute or, Logan and Captain Michael Cresap." Although what constitutes "eloquence" might reside in the ear of the listener, Mayer chose instead to investigate historically the very episode out of which Logan's speech came in the first place. His purpose was to redeem the reputation of Captain Cresap, whom Logan blamed for murdering his family. After an exhaustive recounting, Mayer intoned to his audience, "Thus the famous 'speech of Logan' which has been so long celebrated as the finest specimen of Indian eloquence, dwindles into a reported conversation with, or message from, a cruel and blood-stained savage."[42] No one left to mourn for Logan, and Mayer would make sure that there was no one left to admire his eloquence either.

By midcentury, then, the notion of Indian eloquence had served its purpose. Having successfully shifted any tragic sense of American history out of the mainstream Euro-American historical narrative and placed it centrally as the Indian narrative, Americans no longer had any need for eloquent Indians. Indeed, to acknowledge them at all might be construed as misplaced sympathy for a people doomed by the inexorable processes of history, which were now conceived as linear and progressive. At the same time, the project to study Indian languages as a way of resolving historical problems about the origins of Indians had stalled. These twin developments contributed mightily to the silencing of a once garrulous, eloquent people. Coincidentally but symbolically, in the very same year—1871—that William Tracy belittled Indian eloquence, Congress declared that the United States would sign no new treaties with Indian tribes. Treaties, after all, are negotiated between sovereign nations, and Indian tribes were no longer to be regarded as separate and autonomous nations.

The Key to Indian History

For his part, DuPonceau's comparative study convinced him that there was a shared grammatical structure underlying all Indian languages, or at least all he had had a chance to examine. Much of his correspondence with Jefferson between 1817 and 1820 revolves around what language might reveal about which tribes were descended from which. So, for example, he told Jefferson in 1820 that, based on language comparisons, "It appears to me that the Algonkins or Delawares occupied all the country between Canada & Carolina."[43] This might not be an absolute or exact genealogy and chronology, but it was a start.

These were the highest intellectual stakes for those who championed the study of Indian languages—to use language as a way of answering the most basic historical questions. Indeed, Anthony Wallace believes that Jefferson's "obsession" with the origins of Native Americans drove his interest in Indian languages in the first place. Pickering told readers of the *North American Review* that an understanding of the structures of Indian languages "will have a most important bearing upon the great and long contested question, whether America was peopled from the Eastern continent or not."[44] DuPonceau explained the new science of philology to a committee of the American Philosophical Society in this way: "The object of this Science is from the variety of languages which exist on the surface of the Earth, to trace, as far as possible, the history of mankind." Pickering, too, defined philology, "a science, comparatively of recent date," as purely a historical endeavor, the purpose of which is "ascertaining the relationship and history of nations—even those which are not yet known to have ever had *written* languages."[45] This definition was trans-Atlantic. The Englishman Edward Freeman agreed that "the science of the philologer . . . is strictly historical." Schoolcraft put it as emphatically as anyone in the pages of the *North American Review:* "The early history of the aborigines is taking a deeper hold on literary attention in America," he began. Physical remains— "mounds and ditches"—might demonstrate the work of "ancient labor" but "oral language is the chief object which can in any degree supply literary data from a people wholly destitute of books." And driving the point home: "*Language is the key of history.*"[46]

Pause over the equation being drawn by Schoolcraft. History is a literary pursuit—a commonplace in the eighteenth and nineteenth centuries—and its record lies in books. Language too is a literary matter because it is the foundation of writing, literacy and so forth. People without writing were therefore without books, and thus without a discernible history—in

Schoolcraft's terms "a people who live without letters, must expect their history to perish with them."[47] Language itself, however, if studied deeply and comparatively, could provide that history in the absence of written sources. Indeed, these languages, when preserved for posterity, could themselves become historical artifacts. Edwin James, Assistant Surgeon of the United States Army, wrote his own study of Indian languages with this same motivation: "The languages even of rude tribes could they be preserved by writing and transmitted to future times, would be like coins and monuments . . . by which to confirm or correct the statements of history."[48] Here were the intellectual underpinnings of how language could be used to supply history to those who otherwise had none. Here was the rationale that placed the study of Indian languages at the center of the study of Indians themselves in the antebellum period.

If DuPonceau's linguistic labors pointed toward a magnum opus, a great comparative compendium of Indian languages, he never completed one. Elected president of the American Philosophical Society in 1828, his energies now had to be spent in a variety of other directions. Writing in 1835, he confessed that "after a long intermission, I have returned to the Indian languages."[49] But by 1838 his eyesight and hearing were failing, and he died in 1844. His fellow language student and frequent correspondent Albert Gallatin did, however, make such an attempt. Published as Volume II of the American Antiquarian Society's *Archaeologia Americana* in 1836—the same year that the anonymous author discussed "Indian Eloquence" in the pages of the *Knickerbocker*—Gallatin's "A Synopsis of the Indian Tribes of North America" attempted to use language as a way of classifying all the Indian tribes, at least those east of the Rockies, and sorting out their interrelationships.

Gallatin made his studies of Indian languages in the midst of a long and significant career in public life. Not surprisingly, his "Synopsis" is peppered with observations that have the ring of policy analysis and the prescience of a sage political observer. Gallatin did not see any hope for Indians in Christian conversion. Missionaries "may succeed in converting to Christianity the present generation," he wrote, "but this alone will not prevent the speedy annihilation of the Indian race . . . unless . . . the Indians shall become an industrious people." Writing not long after the disaster of Jacksonian removal, he astutely recognized a fundamental change in the relationship between the United States and Indian nations. As genuine and immediate military threats, the Indians were "objects of execration." But circumstances had changed, and "the natives have ceased to be an object of terror, and they are entirely at our mercy." Given all this, Gallatin saw the future of Native America as bleak: "Let not the Indians entertain the illusory hope that they can persist in their habits, and remain in perpetuity quiet possessors of the extensive territory west of the Mississippi, lately given to them in exchange for their ancient seats."[50] Although the language here is antiseptically euphemistic, the prediction proved dead on.

These commentaries on current conditions were not the heart of Gallatin's study. A separate preface to the volume sketched for readers two parts to "the comparative science of languages": "The first step towards this investigation must be a correct knowledge of individual dialects; the second, a comparison of the various dialects with one another." The preface also highlighted the significance of Gallatin's work in this direction. While other writers had carried out work on the first part of this comparative scheme, "it remained for Mr. Gallatin to bring together in a comparative view, the languages and dialects of all the nations." Gallatin prefaced his study by telling readers that the comparative study of Indian languages revealed that they were all related to each other: "the unity of structure and of grammatical forms proves a common origin."[51] In this, he largely agreed with DuPonceau.

That conclusion held more than merely linguistic significance. While neither DuPonceau or Gallatin could use language as a way of recreating a Native history filled with specific events and populated with real people, the two scholars studied languages against the backdrop of biblical chronology. The common origin of Indian languages, Gallatin told his readers, "may be easily accounted for consistently with the opinion that the first inhabitants came from Asia, and with the Mosaic chronology."[52] To demonstrate a common origin for all Indian languages was, by extension, to demonstrate a common origin for all the speakers of those languages. It was not necessary to sort out that origin with real chronological precision, but only to demonstrate that such an origin,—remote and indeterminate—still fell within the parameters of history as outlined in the Bible. For Gallatin, then, language was the way to answer those most basic historical questions: who were these people, where did they come from, and when?

As we have discussed earlier, assimilating the existence of Native Americans into a biblical framework had preoccupied Euro-Americans almost from the beginning of contact. Studying languages, then, might finally yield a definitive answer to these questions. This belief underscores a slightly ironic shift in the reasons that motivated people to study Indian languages. In the seventeenth and eighteenth centuries, those missionary "word hunters" had learned languages in order to better convert the heathen. By the early nineteenth century, historical rather than missionary zeal drove the enterprise, but the goal remained rooted in theological concerns. Learning Indian languages had not really done much to save Indian souls, but the comparative study of those languages might well help save the historical legitimacy of the Bible.

Gallatin was confident that the data on American Indian languages could be explained within a biblical chronology. His English counterpart Arthur James Johnes was even more sweeping in his *Philological Proofs of the Original Unity and Recent Origin of the Human Race*. He believed the linguistic evidence clearly demonstrated a common origin for the whole of the human race. Relying largely on DuPonceau's work when fitting American Indians into his global theory, Johnes turgidly concluded: "Of the general proposition, that the American Tribes and Nations of the Old World are descended from the same Parent Stock, I conceive the evidence adduced in the previous pages will be deemed conclusive."[53]

More importantly, however, Johnes believed the scientific study of languages only undergirded biblical history. "These propositions," he began in his preface, "of which the Philological evidence is developed in this volume, are supported not only by the testimony of History, Sacred and Profane, but also by the highest Scientific authorities."[54] The "Unity" in the title of his book had an unintended double meaning—a unity of human origin, and a unity of human understanding. Even more specifically, to demonstrate a unity of human origin proved the Adamic descent of all human beings. "This essential and primeval unity of language," concluded an author in the *North American Review*, "points unequivocally to a genealogical unity of man." In the antebellum period, the study of languages could both reinforce theological conservatism by proving the Bible right, and point toward social liberalism by insisting on an essential human unity within a multiracial society. Aware of these implications, the *North American Review* writer trumpeted: "Language itself . . . is the noblest and most characteristic, the most direct and perfect manifestation of the human mind! Hence the study of language has a humanizing tendency." In the years before the Civil War, when political and "scientific" debates over race were becoming increasingly charged, this was no small assertion.[55]

In the years before the Civil War, the work of Gallatin and DuPonceau constituted a high water mark of sorts in the study of Indian languages in the nineteenth century. Neither man would live beyond 1850, and neither left any immediate successors to carry on his research. By the 1860s, the lively interest that Indian languages once generated across a broad spectrum of America's intellectual discourse had largely ebbed. To take one measure of this, Indian languages, by Julie Andresen's tally, had by that

Robert Cornelius, daguerreotype portrait of Stephen DuPonceau, ca. March 1840. Near the end of his life, Stephen DuPonceau, who was a friend of Thomas Jefferson's, sat for one of the first portraits ever taken with a camera. Courtesy of the American Philosophical Society.

decade disappeared from the pages of the *North American Review* as a topic.[56] After the Civil War, the study of Indian languages certainly did continue, but now as a subset of anthropological research, confined largely therefore to that scholarly world and those who worked in it.

To be sure, the work of Gallatin and DuPonceau continues to be regarded as important—in some ways foundational—and according to Lyle Campbell, DuPonceau did succeed in getting noticed by Europeans, particularly by von Humboldt. Humboldt, one of the European pioneers of philology, became through DuPonceau "thoroughly fascinated by Native American languages."[57] Still, the new discipline of philology, which DuPonceau heralded with such nationalistic and scientific enthusiasm, did not, in the antebellum period, achieve the kind of intellectual centrality he thought it would. Despite all the "raw material" ready to hand, European philologists did not flock to these shores to pursue their researches.

The Survival of the Fittest Languages: Darwin and Linguistics

After 1859, philologists and linguists proved no different from other scholars who wondered what implications Darwin had for their researches.
Though it has been said countless times, it bears repeating that the publication of *The Origin of Species* was quickly recognized as the single most significant intellectual event of the nineteenth century. Students of language,
like biologists, historians, sociologists, and philosophers, rushed to figure
out what Darwin might contribute to their work, and conversely, how their
work might prove or deny Darwinian theory.

John Dewey, however, either overstated or misunderstood Darwin's
impact when he wrote that it simply dissolved the old questions that had
been asked and replaced them with new ones. History seldom experiences
such definitive ruptures, intellectual history even less so. In fact, many who
wrestled with Darwin, at least in the latter half of the nineteenth century, attempted to fit his ideas to the received wisdoms of their own, no matter how
square his peg and how round their holes. And in this, those who studied
languages were no different.

Darwin and Darwinism helped pull the study of languages, like so
many things in this era, in the direction of the natural sciences, though in
fact, it had been headed there already. According to an 1851 author, "the science of language is, as it were, the geology of the latest period, the Age of
Man. . . . The remains of ancient speech are like strata deposited in bygone
ages, telling of the forms of life then existing."[58] Given the authority that
natural science enjoyed at midcentury it is no wonder that scholars tried to
apply its schema, methods, and metaphors to the study of language.

In 1874, the *North American Review* carried an essay discussing two new
books on the subject of "Darwinism and Language." Both written by Germans, one book embraced the conclusion that languages offered proof of
Darwinian ideas, while the other argued strenuously against that point of
view. The reviewer, however, chose a more cautious path: "So far, linguistic
science has not been shown to have any bearing on Darwinism, either in the
way of support or of refutation." The whole business of Darwinian theory,
the reviewer judiciously advised, "belongs in the hands of the biologists."[59]

Given the ways in which research in evolutionary theory has moved,
that assessment seems prescient in retrospect. It strikes us today as a stretch
indeed to ask of linguistic research what bearing it has on the mutability of
species or vice versa. Yet, while linguistics probably does not contribute to
our understanding of the mechanisms of natural selection, Darwin did
prove to have a profound impact on the way the relationships between lan-

guages were imagined. This in turn had major implications for the understanding of Amerindian languages.

Reviewing one of those same two books—the one by the Darwin enthusiast, Professor August Schleicher—F. W. Farrar made an astute observation in the journal *Nature*. Before Schleicher had ever read Darwin, Farrar told his English readers, he had "called attention to the struggle for existence among words, the disappearance of primitive forms, and the immense development and differentiation which may be produced by ordinary causes in a single family of speech." For his most recent work, however, Darwin had provided Schleicher with an irresistible image. In the middle of *Origin*, "Mr. Darwin has constructed an ingenious diagram to illustrate the immense scope which must be allowed for gradual divergence of characteristics in animal and vegetable species from an original genus." Likewise, Farrar went on, "Schleicher has made an exactly similar table to serve as a genealogical tree for the Aryan Families of language."[60]

This proved to be a powerful and enduring visual analogy. While others might argue with Farrar's conviction that "Mr. Darwin uses language which may be literally applied without even verbal modification to the phenomena of language," Schleicher's chart provided a way to conceive of languages that easily demonstrated their relationship to each other, their growth over time, and the ways in which new ones grew out of the extinction of old ones. This, in turn, as Stephen Alter has pointed out, refined the historical vision at the root of comparative philology, a vision that organized genealogical relationships around branches stemming from a common trunk.[61] The branching tree of species worked wonderfully well to illustrate the history of the natural world, and it could map out the history of language as well.

Or at least the history of some languages. The branching tree of languages grew out of developments in European language study that traced the origins and relationships of European and Asian languages. These developments were built upon the fantastic discovery—if that is the right word—of "Indo-European," that ur-language which served as the base of the language trunk. As it turned out, there proved to be no room on that tree for Amerindian languages.

As more research accumulated, it grew increasingly apparent that Indian languages were not related to any of the familiar Old World tongues—not to Hebrew or Welsh or Latin, as some had argued in the antebellum period. Consequently, there was no way for linguists to fit Amerindian languages onto any of those branches that now governed the way they conceived of their study. Even worse, it seemed impossible even to construct an

entirely separate tree for these languages, as philosopher John Fiske noted
in 1869: "We cannot point to a single individualized mother-tongue from
which the twelve hundred and sixty four American dialects . . . might have
started." For Fiske the inability of linguistic science to understand Indian
languages was proof not of the limitations of linguistics, but of the failing of
Indians. He explained the absence of a "mother-tongue" as evidence that
"there has been no great political concentration, resulting in wide-spread
organization of linguistic traditions. . . . Their hundreds of dialects have
gone on from the beginning, unstable and fluctuating, never attaining such
an organic shape as the mother-Aryan or mother-Semitic."[62] A remarkable
logic to be sure.

In fact, however, Fiske's assessment of Amerindian languages within
the field of linguistic study described a situation that remained largely un-
changed into the twentieth century. Writing in 1931, Holger Pedersen mar-
veled that "it is still uncertain into what large groups the American world of
languages should be divided . . . we have not got beyond a picture of dizzying complexity." And forty years after that Charlton Laird noted that when
"students of Amerindian languages endeavored to apply the conventional
linguistic patter and terminology to the confusion of New World tongues,
they found both inadequate."[63] It does not exaggerate things too much to
say that Indian languages proved too complicated to fit into this elegant
new conception of languages and that rather than try to solve the problems
these languages posed, mainstream linguistics, especially as it developed in
Europe, simply ignored them.

The author of the 1874 *North American Review* essay comparing Schleicher and Müller was none other than William Dwight Whitney, the leading
linguistic authority in the country in the post–Civil War era and a Yale professor of Sanskrit. Two years after the war, he published *Language and the
Study of Language*, and in 1875, the year after he considered the relationship
between Darwinism and language, he published a magisterial synthesis of
linguistic knowledge, *The Life and Growth of Language*. This book, important and influential as it was, provides a good measure of how language
study in the United States shifted across the divide of the Civil War, and how
as a result of that shift, Amerindian languages ceased to be of central concern for a new generation of linguists and philologists.

Toward the end of *Life and Growth* Whitney did stop to consider Indian
languages. He too noticed just how complex and complicated their relationships seemed to be: "There are a very considerable number of groups,
between whose significant signs exist no more apparent correspondences
than between those of English, Hungarian, and Malay." Remarking on the

structure of Indian languages, he echoed Fiske in finding continental babel, which had not been quieted and harmonized by some more linguistically civilized group. "Of course," he acknowledged, "there are infinite possibilities of expressiveness . . . it would only need that some native-American Greek race should arise, to fill it full of thought and fancy, and put it to uses of a noble literature." And in a swipe, intentional or otherwise, at DuPonceau, Whitney finished his thought: "As it is . . . it is cumbrous and time-wasting in its immense polysyllabism." Where the earlier philologist had found beauty and complexity, Whitney found wasted time.

Whitney came to his chair in Sanskrit after earlier training as a naturalist and collector, which may explain why he worked so well within the new classificatory schemes inspired by Darwin and why he was drawn to the study of the more easily classified European languages. He too had concluded that Amerindian languages bore no connection to the Old World languages with which he was more concerned. "There appears," he wrote soberly, "to be no tolerable prospect that, even supposing the American languages derived from the Old World, they can ever be proved so, or traced to their parentage." As a consequence, he continued, "an exhaustive classification of the American languages is at present impossible."[64] So pronounced the most authoritative linguistic voice in the United States, and with that pronouncement he underscored that the science of linguistics would move forward in directions that did not include Indian languages. Dead languages from the old world, rather than the living languages of the new, were what interested scholars now, European or American. Sanskrit, not Siouan, would prove to be where the linguistic action was.

All that remained, in the years following the Civil War, was to rewrite the history of language study in the United States so that it pointed back to the Old World, rather than west to the prairies and plains filled with Indians. Philosopher Fiske took a stab in his 1869 essay. Looking past and beyond the work of American philologists in the antebellum period, he pointed to the German Bopp as the founder of modern linguistics: ". . . Bopp, in 1816, had shown that inductive philology, like other sciences, can be successfully dealt with only by adhering to fixed methods." Likewise, the anonymous reviewer who greeted Whitney's *Language and the Study of Language* with tremendous enthusiasm in the pages of *The Nation* saw 1816 as the epochal moment: "Previous to the publication of Bopp's masterly 'Conjugation system,' in 1816, no scientific comparison and analysis of verbal forms . . . had been accomplished." Nor did Whitney, in his quick sketch of the history of linguistics at the end of *Life and Growth of Language*, make any mention of studies of Indian languages.[65] Indian languages were growing silent, and in this new history of the field so too were those Euro-Americans who had tried to make sense of them.

Ironically, however, while Indian languages may not have been central to the ways in which linguistics developed in the late nineteenth century, and although scholars who had studied them earlier in the century had been written out of the discipline's history, the old nationalistic anxieties remained. Whitney's reviewer in *The Nation* ended his essay on a patriotic note that would have made DuPonceau and Jefferson smile: "We cannot . . . lay down our pen without giving expression to our pride in the thought that such a book has been written by an American scholar and issued from an American press."[66] Europeans, as it turned out, did not come flocking to America to study language, but with Whitney at least, America had produced a linguist on par with the best in Germany and England.

Ethnographic Languages

In the same year, 1875, that Whitney's *Life and Growth of Language* appeared, John Wesley Powell published his own classic, *Exploration of the Colorado River*. Powell had already achieved fame for his three-month raft journey down the roiling waters of the Colorado and through the Grand Canyon in 1869. His book was the long-awaited account of this unparalleled feat of derring-do.

The book, still a thrilling adventure story, seems as distant from the dense scholarly pages of *Life and Growth* as the Grand Canyon is from the halls of Yale University. Yet in the years after the Civil War, it was Powell who picked up the enterprise of studying Indian languages. In so doing, he helped reorient the direction of Amerindian linguistics.

Powell and Whitney were nearly exact contemporaries—the former seven years younger than the latter. Like Whitney, Powell too spent his youth as a self-trained naturalist and collector. But Powell's first love was geology, and it was in that field that he made his most lasting contributions to American scientific life.

Powell's story has been well told, and so we won't rehearse too much of it here.[67] After a successful career in the Union Army, and after several spectacular survey expeditions out west, Powell came to Washington in 1873 convinced that the government's haphazard and disparate scientific efforts needed consolidation and regularization. More to the point, Powell believed he was the man to accomplish all this. In 1879, the United States Geological Survey resulted after a great deal of political agitation, although with Clarence King, not Powell, at the helm. Powell had to settle for the Bureau of Ethnology (later renamed the Bureau of American Ethnology) instead. King did not last long, and Powell won his prize in 1881. For the better part of the next fifteen years, Powell presided over the nation's scientific pursuits in the Great West.

The choice to put a geologist at the head of the bureau was not as arbitrary as it might appear. Powell had already discovered the utility of collecting ethnological information as a way of promoting his other scientific research in regions still inhabited solely by Indians. Chief among that ethnological data, and the first he set out to collect systematically as bureau head, was language.

In 1877, Powell published his *Introduction to the Study of Indian Languages* as a way to standardize the way Amerindian linguistic data was assembled and collated. It responded to the "constant direction" needed by investigators who "were frequently calling for explanations." Even in the last quarter of the nineteenth century, much of what constituted the study of Indian languages consisted of missionaries, army officers, explorers, and scientists collecting vocabularies and grammars. Although this kind of enterprise had been going on since the seventeenth century, however, there was still no standardized method for doing it. A generation earlier Bureau of Indian Affairs Commissioner Thomas McKenney, who helped Albert Gallatin to collect Indian vocabularies, complained to him, "I saw enough of those to whom the vocabulary was sent to satisfy me that they are wholly incompetent."[68] Fifty years later, the situation had not improved much. Powell published his *Introduction* to address that problem. And as if there were any doubt about the book's purpose, Powell wrote in his Preface: "It does not purport to be a philosophic treatment of the subject of language. . . . The book is a body of directions for collectors." Fittingly enough, when Powell set about to create a standardized alphabetic representation of Indian sounds, "the author appealed to the eminent scholar, Prof. W. D. Whitney." (The traffic went in both directions. When he was preparing a new edition of the *Imperial Dictionary,* Whitney wrote to Powell looking for help with "the principle nomenclature of our Indian tribes.")[69]

Powell had a sense of the linguistic tradition within which he worked. The scholar Lyle Campbell sees a deep connection between the "theoretical framework" that Powell used and those of DuPonceau, John Pickering, and Wilhelm von Humboldt.[70] Writing in his bureau's 1885–1886 *Annual Report,* Powell acknowledged that "Gallatin may be considered the founder of systematic philology relating to the North American Indians." And he found himself lamenting in terms DuPonceau would have recognized: "In view of the amount of material on hand, the comparative study of the languages of North America has been strangely neglected."[71]

Powell, however, did not see the connection between studying languages and answering historical questions the way his linguistic forebears had. When he addressed one of the biggest of those questions—"Whence Came the American Indians"—he concluded that the study of languages could be of only limited use. "We cannot," he told readers, "trace the languages of the Western Hemisphere to one common body of speech." "Nor can we discover," he went on, "any primitive or fundamental relationship between any one language of the West with any one language of the East." Unable to use the tree model for North American languages, which now governed the philology of Old World languages, Powell was left with only the most general of historical conclusions. Without any demonstrable connection between American and Asian languages, American Indians must have arrived on the continent before the age of "articulate and grammatic speech."[72] Whenever that might have been.

Indeed, by the time Powell took up the task of coordinating the systematic study of Amerindian languages, history itself had changed. More properly, the boundaries around the discipline of history had been drawn to exclude the sort of historical evidence Indian languages might reveal, and to exclude the speakers of those languages from the realm of history as well. Instead, Powell wanted to use language to classify American Indians, rather than to sort out where they came from and how long ago. "The only practicable classification of the tribes," he insisted, "is by language, as all other groupings fail."[73] This was the ultimate goal behind his handbook. Armed with this, Powell sent many of his protégés, known to many as "Powell's Boys," out into the field to gather information about Indian languages.[74] They sent their results—largely vocabulary lists—organized and systematized, back to Powell, who compared the lists as the basis for his grand classification of Amerindian tongues. Classification might give some general shape to the Indian past, but by the late nineteenth century, having a past was not quite the same thing as having a history.

That classification appeared in 1891 in the seventh annual report of the Bureau of Ethnology. *Indian Linguistic Families of America North of Mexico* begins with methodological and historiographic information and moves on to consider issues that might be described as of anthropological concern—agricultural practices, communalism, population. The heart of the report, however, is the alphabetic listing and description of the families into which Powell broke up Amerindian languages—fifty-eight in all. If American Indian languages could not be placed on a branching tree, with some New World Indo-European as its trunk, then Powell could at least group all these languages into an organized taxonomy, borrowing the form and terminology of natural science, complete with families and phyla.

Thus, Powell served as a kind of linguistic Linnaeus for American Indian languages (though he himself bestowed that honor on Gallatin). In this sense, though he clearly built on the work of his antebellum predecessors, Powell moved American Indian languages out of the disciplinary realm of the literary and historical and put them squarely within the concerns of anthropology. As he had said fifteen years earlier in his *Introduction to the Study of Indian Languages:* "It has been the effort of the author to connect the study of language with the study of anthropology, for a language is best understood when the habits, customs, institutions, philosophy . . . embodied in the language are best known." To underscore that the linguist needed to be an anthropologist, Powell concluded, "The student of the language should be a student of the people who speak the language."[75]

Indian Linguistic Families still stands as a triumph, simultaneously a culmination of work that began in the eighteenth century and pointing the way for research in the twentieth. Although Powell's classification was revised several times in the twentieth century—by Alfred Kroeber and Edward Sapir, and by Harry Hoijer who reduced the number of language families from fifty-eight to fifty-four in 1956—it remains a touchstone for the field. Franz Boas predicted as much in 1917 when he wrote, "the classification of North American languages, that we owe to Major Powell . . . will form the basis of all future work." In 1970, Charlton Laird sounded almost mystical in his unalloyed praise for Powell's accomplishment: "The classification of Amerindian speech rests upon one of those rare scientific triumphs so broad and sure that they thereafter require only minor revision."[76]

Whether or not Powell's classification was really as near-perfect as all this would suggest, he was certainly successful in moving the study of American Indian languages into the purview of a larger anthropology and keeping it there. One consequence of this was to narrow the scope of how and why these languages might be studied. As Dell Hymes wrote in a more complaining tone, "a classification intended primarily for ethnological order, conceived as tentative, ignoring grammatical form as evolutionary in nature, based on rough vocabularies, which evidence was never published, became accepted not only as the foundation of further work, which it was, but effectively also as gospel."[77] Powell's work may have represented a dramatic achievement in research on American Indian languages, but it cast a long shadow as well.

Writing just before the outbreak of World War One, Pliny Earle Goddard underscored an ironic result of Powell's *Indian Linguistic Families.* Acknowledging that "the linguistic families of Powell remain largely undisturbed," Goddard went on to call for further research: "There remains a
great amount of linguistic work to be done," especially about "the origins of
languages, and the conditions controlling their development and their dispersion."[78] Ironic, of course, because these were the concerns that had motivated the systematic study of Amerindian languages in the first place. Gallatin and DuPonceau might have used different vocabulary, but they sought
to understand origins, development, and dispersion. By tethering the study
of American Indian languages so tightly to the discipline of anthropology,
Powell helped to finalize the divorce between the study of Amerindian languages and the deliberations of a newly emerging historical discipline.

This proved to have a long-lasting institutional consequence. Powell
codified his Indian language families and their classification at just the moment when fields such as English, Classics, Romance and Modern Languages, and Oriental Studies were forming around the study of particular
languages and literatures, and when these disciplines were achieving institutional permanence through departments and graduate programs. American Indian languages, as Julie Andresen has pointed out, did not become
institutionalized in the same way. They did not get their own departments,
their own faculty, or their own professional society.[79] In an 1885 survey, one
Augustin de la Rosa was the only professor teaching American language at a
North American university, and he at the University of Guadalajara. And as
Richard White remarked recently, "historians have done very little with language, because so few historians know any native languages."[80] When
American Indian languages spoke at all on the campuses of America's new
universities, they did so in order to address anthropological issues.

AS PART OF HIS *Indian Linguistic Families,* Powell also drew a map. The
map placed all the various language families in the geographical regions
where they were spoken. At one level, it acknowledged Powell's intellectual
debts—Gallatin, too, had drawn a map, which Powell had consulted while
drawing his own. Powell's map—actually a very enlarged version of it—
greeted visitors to the Anthropology building at the 1893 World's Columbian Exposition in Chicago. Before they saw any artifacts, any exhibits, any
glass cases, they saw this map. Perhaps more than anything else, this map
embodied how American Indian languages, and the people who spoke
them, were understood.

The World's Columbian Exposition played host to the International

This map represented John Wesley Powell's triumph of classification and a culmination of the linguistic studies he oversaw in the last quarter of the nineteenth century. Courtesy of the Library of Congress.

Congress of Anthropology, and thus the fair served as a great gathering of both anthropological artifacts and of anthropologists. Among the many papers read at the congress, only two dealt with the subject of languages. The first, entitled "The Present State of Our Knowledge of American Languages," was delivered by Daniel Brinton. The second, "Classification of Languages of the North Pacific Coast," was presented by Franz Boas.[81]

It is an intriguing vignette, ripe with symbolic meaning, though who can know whether any of the assembled audience of anthropologists found it so. Brinton, the grand old man of the field, a founder of the discipline and the first university professor of anthropology, aging and near the end of his life, shared the stage with Boas, young and brilliant, and about to supplant Brinton in intellectual importance and institutional influence. These two, and only these two, came to Chicago to discuss Indian languages at the scholarly gathering, which many consider to have been the grand coming-out party for the discipline of anthropology.

Boas, like Powell, saw the study of Native American languages as squarely within the realm of American anthropology, and he made sure it stayed there, both through the work he did on language and through the way he helped give anthropology its disciplinary and institutional shape. In 1911 he published his own *Handbook of American Indian Languages* which has proved enormously important in the study of American Indian languages, and several of his students, mostly notably Edward Sapir, went on to do their own pioneering work.

But Boas's relationship to the study of Amerindian languages is a twentieth-century story and thus beyond the bounds of this one. So we turn instead to Boas's companion at the lectern in 1893, Daniel Brinton.

Brinton remains a fascinating if enigmatic figure in the history of anthropology. As Lee Baker has recently observed, of all the foundational figures of American anthropology—Lewis Henry Morgan, Frederic Ward Putnam, John Wesley Powell—Brinton remains remarkably unknown.[82] This relative obscurity is even more remarkable given that Brinton's career stands at the intersection of a host of intellectual and institutional developments in the era after the Civil War. Moreover, he taught at both a university (Penn) and a public museum (the Academy of Natural Sciences). He was also central to the late nineteenth-century debates over the relationship between race and anthropology. Although Brinton made his living practicing medicine and pursued anthropology as an avocation, he helped make possible the professionalization of the field. He also left a lengthy paper trail, publishing in both scientific and popular journals, and his extensive library remains intact at the University of Pennsylvania Museum. He will visit these pages again.

Like some of his predecessors, Brinton believed that the scientific study of American Indians revealed an essential human unity, although not necessarily an equality. In the 1890s he was perfectly capable of making perfectly vicious comments about the inferiority of black Americans, but as Baker cautions, Brinton's racism needs to be placed in a larger cultural context. By that measure, during an era of especially bitter racism, Brinton was more moderate about race than some, more dogmatic about it than others. For his part, Powell's work in Native America does not seem to have moved him much beyond the widely held prejudices of the day. He warned people in his *Indian Linguistic Families* about the dangers of getting too close to their subject of study: "There is a curious tendency observable in students to overlook aboriginal vices and exaggerate aboriginal virtues. It seems to be forgotten that, after all, the Indian is a savage."[83] In this sense, Brinton's anthropological ideas were firmly rooted in the nineteenth century, and absolutely consonant with his times. They were the ideas about inherent racial and cultural inferiority that Boas would eventually help to displace.

It was surely fitting that Brinton should rise before the 1893 gathering in Chicago to discuss Indian languages. Some of his most serious and enduring work came in the field of Amerindian languages, and he, along with Powell, stood as the foremost student of the subject at that moment. He seems to have had, as Baker puts it, "a passion and unusual skill for classifying and analyzing American languages."[84] Behind this skill and passion, however, lay a set of motivations also rooted in earlier scholarly traditions. The line of linguists who saw in Amerindian languages something of eloquence, literature, and history began with Jefferson and DuPonceau. By the late nineteenth century, it ended with Brinton.[85]

Moving easily between institutions of one kind and another, and moving just as easily across disciplinary boundaries more fluid than they are today, Brinton often called himself an "Americanist." In fact, he titled an 1890 collection of his pieces *Essays of an Americanist*. That moniker both gave definition to Brinton's scholarly interests and underscored the kind of nationalistic, patriotic impulse that lay behind the work of Jefferson, DuPonceau, and others of earlier generations. Almost in terms of obligation, he wrote: "As Americans by adoption, it should be our first interest and duty to study the Americans by race."[86] And like his predecessors, he continued to believe that American Indian languages would be central to the general study of linguistics. Before a crowd at the Historical Society of Pennsylvania, he said of Indian languages: "If they are essential to a comprehension of the red race, not less so are they to the science of linguistics in general." Echoing DuPonceau about the possibilities of work in the American linguistic field, he cried, "What an opportunity is thus offered for the study of the natural evolution of language, unfettered by the petrifying art of writing!"[87]

Yet whereas DuPonceau brought a kind of buoyant optimism about the role American languages—and thus Americans—would play in the development of a new science, Brinton sounded somewhat more despairing. Perfectly aware of the way in which disciplines were being institutionalized in new universities, he complained: "Not an institution of higher education in this land has an instructor in this branch [Amerindian language]; not one of our learned societies has offered inducements for its study." And he was perfectly aware of the way in which the boundaries around the field of linguistics itself were being drawn: "Shall we have fellowships and professorships in abundance for the teaching of the dead languages . . . of another hemisphere and not one for instruction in those tongues of our own land . . . whose structure is as important to the philosophic study of speech as any of the dialects of Greece or India?" Science might be "cosmopolitan" and the field of anthropology "confined by no geographical boundaries," but "the languages of America . . . have every whit as high a claim on the attention of European scholars as have the venerable documents of Chinese lore, the mysterious cylinders of Assyria, or the painted figured papyri of the Nilotic tombs."[88]

Even as he spoke, Brinton saw the nationalistic project behind the study of Indian languages evaporating. Europeans had not flocked to this country to study these languages, and international acclaim did not redound to those Americans who did. As Brinton himself acknowledged before those assembled at the Pennsylvania Historical Society, "We may cast our eyes over the civilized world and count upon our fingers the names of those who are engaged in really serviceable and earnest work in this department."[89]

If the inherent—and, to Brinton at least, the obvious—scientific importance of Indian languages did not persuade, then he offered an almost aesthetic reason instead. "No class of terms," he told his audience in reference to place names, "could be applied more expressive and more American. The titles of the Old World certainly need not be copied, when those that are fresh and fragrant with our natal soil await adoption."[90] Actually, Brinton was quoting, and therefore reviving, Henry Schoolcraft. At the end of the nineteenth century, with Indian languages firmly within the province of anthropology, Brinton, like those at the beginning of the century, wanted them appreciated for their literary qualities.

In a different essay, Brinton told readers that Indians were incomparable "raconteurs," and that "in no Oriental city does the teller of strange tales find a more willing audience than in the Indian wigwam." Refuting those who found Indian languages deficient, primitive, and constricting, Brinton insisted, "It is a singular error due wholly to ignorance of the subject to maintain that the American tongues are cramped in their vocabularies, or that their syntax does not permit them to define the more delicate relationship of ideas." Conversely, Brinton found further evidence of Indians' innate "linguistic and literary ability" in "the work some of these natives have accomplished in European tongues."[91] Perhaps more forcefully than anyone else in the late nineteenth-century scientific world, Brinton argued that Indian languages, and those who spoke them, might be appreciated as more than abstruse, scientific data.

Brinton went on to prove his point about the "linguistic and literary ability" of Native Americans by bringing out a remarkable set of volumes in the 1880s under the heading "Brinton's Library of Aboriginal American Literature." In this project, Brinton harkened back to antebellum scholars who saw an inextricable link between language and literature. The series ran to seven volumes, including titles like "Legends of the Micmac," "Migration Legends of the Creeks," and "Prose and Poetry from the Nahuatl." In the advertising prospectus for the series, Brinton insisted on the scientific value of these works: "The aim of the editor of this series is to put within the reach of students authentic materials for the study of the languages and culture of the native race of America."[92]

In making this literature available to the public in the late nineteenth century, Brinton fought a battle that had largely been lost earlier in the century. After all, as Susan Scheckel reminds us, early in the nineteenth century many "literary nationalists" thought that the "history and myths of American Indians could provide the new nation with a sense of 'primitive' origins."[93] Yet, just as we have seen how the connection between language and nation was severed for American Indians in the first half of the nineteenth century, so too the connection between literature and nation had been erased. As Americans searched to create their own literary and cultural independence, Indian mythic traditions wound up excluded from the effort. In this sense, as Joshua Bellin has noted, "the campaign for literary nationalism . . . was fought not only against Europe's courtly muses but against America's native mythos" as well.[94] Brinton hoped there might still be room for Indian literature within the national canon.

Perhaps the most remarkable connection between Brinton's disquisition and that of earlier writers came in the middle of an 1883 essay, in which Brinton broached the topic of "Indian oratorical display." Echoing Jefferson, perhaps deliberately, Brinton wrote: "Specimens of native eloquence have been introduced into school books, and declaimed by many an aspiring young Cicero."[95] For Brinton, Indians remained eloquent.

Of course, as we have seen, when he wrote that Indian eloquence "has been commented on by almost all writers who have studied" the topic, his verb tense was not quite right. By the end of the nineteenth century, Indians had largely been stripped of their eloquence and children did not learn their elocution by reciting Indian speeches. Few took Logan's speech at face value any more. Perhaps Brinton made a simple mistake; perhaps he too casually had become lost in the memories of his own youth, when the topic of Indian eloquence would have been more familiar. Perhaps he was aggressively trying to rekindle the subject. In any event, Brinton announced himself, if not Logan's mourner, at least the mourner of his speech.

In the end, Brinton's attempt to keep the study of Amerindian languages within the bounds of literary and historical discourse softened his racialist views, as had happened with others of an earlier age. Powell, the insistent scientist, might not have been able to see past the savage Indian, but Brinton at least glanced in that direction. In an essay on "Native American Poetry," he wrote that reading this poetry "elevates our opinion of the nations whom we are accustomed to call by the term savage and barbarous. We are taught that in much of which we are inclined to claim as our special prerogatives, they too have an interest."[96] Brinton wrote this as the Indian wars were coming to their awful conclusion, at a moment when the triumph of civilization over savagery seemed foreordained, and when Indians had been stripped of their nationhood. Remarkable that Brinton could find something more than the easy dismissal most Americans gave to American Indians and their language and literary traditions—that as poets, they could be called "nations" again.

BY 1903, TEN YEARS after Daniel Brinton and Franz Boas shared the stage to talk about American Indian languages in Chicago, Boas was ensconced at Columbia University, in the department of anthropology. Brinton had died in 1899, Powell in 1902, and Boas had displaced them both as the leading American anthropologist. Around Boas gathered a generation of students who would shape most of twentieth-century anthropology in the United States.

In that year, Boas offered his course Anthropology 5, "American Languages," and a young Edward Sapir enrolled in it. Just as Boas had supplanted Brinton as the chief student of those American languages, so too Sapir would break from his mentor over linguistic ideas in the 1920s. Sapir's ideas would move the study of Amerindian languages in new directions.

The particulars of that dispute—a debate between inheritance and diffusion of morphological patterns—do not concern us here. By the time it occurred, however, discussions of Amerindian languages were taking place almost entirely within anthropological circles, and for almost entirely anthropological purposes. With Brinton gone, no one pleaded the case to study American Indian languages for historical or literary reasons.

In 1925, almost exactly one hundred years after Albert Gallatin and Stephen DuPonceau began their correspondence over the nature of Indian languages and how best to study them, Sapir wrote: "the real problems of American Indian linguistics have hardly been stated."[97] True, Boas, Sapir, and other anthropologists in the first half of the twentieth century had brought about a revolution in the study of Amerindian languages, and from that vantage the work of their antebellum predecessors must have looked crude. Still, it seems ironic, given all the effort expended to understand them during the intervening decades, that Sapir felt American scholars were no closer to the heart of the matter than they had been when Jefferson started writing. Ironic, and perhaps a bit hubristic, that Sapir should not acknowledge that work much. Ironic still further that as the twentieth century wore on, students of Indian languages would have to rely on the vocabulary lists, rough grammars, and crude orthographies gathered by eighteenth- and nineteenth-century missionaries, Powell's boys, and dozens of others. Those yellowed pages represent the last witnesses to a growing list of languages for which there remain no native speakers left. DuPonceau had glimpsed this in a letter to the Reverend Eleazer Williams in 1817. "The languages of the American Indians will probably be lost in the process of time," he opined, "and perhaps the period is not far distant when nothing will remain but the memory of them."[98] In this sense, many Amerindian languages had caught up with the "dead" languages of the Old World.

No one left to mourn for Logan, and by the end of the nineteenth century almost no one left to celebrate his language either.

4

THE PAST IS UNDERGROUND: ARCHAEOLOGY AND THE SEARCH FOR INDIAN HISTORY

Archaeology is the most faithful guide for the history of ancient times.

G. A. MATILE, 1867

When we met Edwin James, assistant surgeon of the United States Army, in the last chapter, he was writing his own "History of Indian Languages." In his prefatory remarks, he wrote that a record of Indian languages "would be like ruins and monuments, authentic monuments by which to confirm or correct the statements of history." Roughly fifty years later, Roeliff Brinkerhoff, a founder of the State Archaeological Society of Ohio, gave a speech in which he described "relics [as] the letters of the archaeologist's alphabet."[1] The analogy James and Brinkerhoff used across a half-century span was potent. Language as ruins; ruins as language, two sides of the same historical coin.

The anonymous writer of an 1837 essay in the *North American Review* agreed that language constituted "by far the most enduring 'monuments' which our native tribes possess."[2] And while this writer was impatient with those who focused their attention on archaeological finds, his use of the analogy was a grudging concession to the growing hold of archaeology on the scholarly and public imagination. In the early republic and antebellum periods, archaeology emerged alongside the study of languages as an exciting new pursuit for Americans. And just as the study of Indian languages shifted away from the missionary project toward a historical one, archaeology also began as way to answer historical questions about the Indians. In several ways, James and Brinkerhoff remind us, the two mirrored each other: languages provided an entrée into the "literary" side of Indian history, but those languages themselves were evanescent and disappearing. Ar-

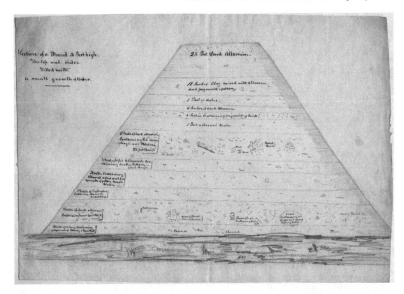

"Section of a Mound 16 Feet High." This pencil drawing by Philadelphia doctor Montroville Wilson Dickeson (1810–1882) shows an unidentified Indian mound in Louisiana or Mississippi, ca. 1843. Dr. Dickeson, a pioneer American archaeologist, was one of many Americans who traveled through the Ohio and Mississippi valleys to study the mysterious mounds that dotted the landscape. Courtesy of the University of Pennsylvania Museum of Archaeology and Anthropology Archives.

chaeological objects had a tangibility and permanence, but were largely mute as recorders of specific history.

The archaeologists of this era traded on a widespread belief in the explanatory power and epistemological transparency of objects, specimens, things. What I have called elsewhere an "object-based epistemology" lay at the heart of much of the intellectual work of the nineteenth century. Rooted in this tradition, archaeologists believed that the objects they found could tell stories about Native Americans in a way nothing else could. Yet we should not belittle the challenge American archaeologists faced. As we saw in the first chapter, the practice of history itself became defined as a textual business in the late eighteenth and early nineteenth century. Those who sought history in recovered objects rather than in texts had proposed something like an alternative way of conceiving of the past. They had to figure out how to make those objects speak in the language of history. No easy feat for archaeologists today, much less for those in the early republic. Given all this, as Curtis Hinsley wryly puts it, "no wonder they kept digging."[3]

Ultimately, though, the development of American archaeology across the nineteenth century roughly paralleled that of language study. American archaeology struggled to establish an identity and legitimacy for itself against the developments of archaeology in the Old World, and in this the drum of scientific nationalism we heard in the last chapter beat here too. In addition, the study of Native America through objects buried underground began as a search for Indian history within the chronological frameworks of the Bible. By the century's end, while archaeology in Europe was seen as a part of the historical discipline, in the United States it became part of the largely ahistorical concerns of anthropology. And just as the development of linguistics had a profound impact on how Indian languages were studied, and thus on how their speakers were perceived, so too the path of Indian archaeology from history to anthropology led to certain ways of understanding the native past and away from others.

American Archaeology Ascendant

The year 1820 marked the beginning of American Archaeology.

Or so wrote Professor Warren K. Moorehead in 1901 as he looked back on "A Century of American Archaeology" in the pages of *Popular Science Monthly*.[4] He was not altogether right, of course. Usually, any look back for archaeology's origins in this country—as with language study—winds up with Thomas Jefferson. In the chapter on "Aborigines" in his *Notes on the State of Virginia,* Jefferson describes the curiosity that led him to trench through an Indian mound "in my neighbourhood." Jefferson went to this mound to resolve the question of whether mounds were "general sepulchers for towns," or whether, as others argued, they were erected periodically after "the bones of all their dead, wheresoever deposited at the time of death" had been recollected. Bones, then, interested Jefferson in his brief description of the excavation.[5]

But Moorehead was searching for more lineal ancestors, for the beginnings of what he recognized as modern archaeology, and he found them in the person and work of Caleb Atwater. Atwater lived in Circleville, Ohio— so named because of the circular Indian earthworks upon which white settlers built their town—and he succeeded briefly in making this unassuming town in southern Ohio the very center of American archaeology. (No longer a hub of archaeological activity, Circleville is today much better known for its splendid annual pumpkin festival.)

Atwater had been at work for some years on the Indian remains, first in and around Circleville, later throughout the whole state of Ohio. In 1820 the

Circleville, Ohio, in 1836, as drawn by G. F. Wittich in 1870. The town took its name from and built itself upon a set of mounds built in concentric rings. No wonder Caleb Atwater became fascinated by American archaeology. Courtesy of the Pickaway County Chamber of Commerce.

American Antiquarian Society published the results of his researches as the first volume of their journal: "Description of the Antiquities discovered in the State of Ohio and other Western States." That Atwater should present his survey of the mound country of Ohio to the public through the American Antiquarian Society in Worcester, Massachusetts, was not simply an accident of publishing. The AAS had been founded in 1812 "to discover the antiquities of our own continent; and, by providing a fixed and permanent place of deposit, to preserve such relicks [*sic*] of American antiquity as are portable."[6] Reverend William Jenks, one of its founders, believed that the AAS ought to focus on three more specific areas: ancient Indian nations, early European settlements, and Indian mounds. The AAS sponsored not only Atwater, but several other archaeologists who excavated midwestern mounds.[7] In this way, the AAS hoped to become for American archaeology what the American Philosophical Society was for the study of Amerindian languages. No mere whim that the Society's journal, whose premier issue featured Atwater's report from the mound fields, bore the title *Archaeologia Americana*.

Atwater's essay is what impressed Moorehead, what he referred to as "the first creditable report along archaeological lines," and one of nearly 150 pages. According to Moorehead, before 1820 "no one had recommended the study of our earth and stone monuments, or the strange relics found in or near them." He gave Atwater credit for "direct[ing] men's eyes towards a strange pre-Columbian culture." Working, "under great disadvantages" in an area that had been wilderness a generation earlier, Atwater was an intellectual pioneer.[8]

In this sense, Moorehead was right. We can recognize in Atwater work that resembles the scientific archaeology which defines the discipline today. Indeed, in searching for means to date his discoveries in the mounds, Atwater tried counting the rings of trees in the vicinity, foreshadowing the later development of dendrochronology, or tree-ring dating.[9] But Jefferson and Atwater did share a common fascination: mounds, large earthen structures, sometimes shaped like a grave, sometimes like an animal effigy, at still other locations built in geometric patterns, obviously erected by human beings and obviously old. Well before archaeologists began to read the landscape in more sophisticated ways for evidence of human activity, these mounds—not surprisingly—drew their first attention. Even to casual observers, it was obvious that the Ohio and Mississippi River valleys, so attractive to nineteenth-century farmers, merchants, and adventurers, had also drawn mysterious groups of people in some distant past.

In fact, interested readers were already well aware of the mounds in the Ohio and Mississippi regions before Atwater's lengthy report. Word about mounds began to filter east in the reports from settlers and missionaries in the western and southern frontiers in the last quarter of the eighteenth century. James Adair includes a mention of mounds in his 1775 *History of the American Indians.* Twice in 1817, shortly before Atwater's publication, *The Port Folio* ran reports from the hinterlands on Indian mounds. One, datelined Chillicothe, Ohio, described the excavation of an Indian burial mound; the other dispatch came from Lexington, Kentucky, and sketched what the author believed to be an extensive fortification, complete with "parapets," "bastions," and "side-curtains." "It appears," wrote C. W. Short, "that the engineer was not unacquainted with the great efficacy of flank defenses."[10]

Volume 1, then, of *Archaeologia Americana,* featuring the lengthiest, most scientific consideration of mounds to date, served as the scientific starting gun for the greatest pursuit of nineteenth-century American archaeology: the hunt for the Mound Builders. Indeed, through most of the century, American archaeology and mounds were virtually coterminous.

The Mound Builders stand, if not precisely as the greatest discovery of nineteenth-century American archaeology, then as its greatest invention. Archaeologists and other scholars of Native American history today generally agree that no such "people" actually existed. The mounds themselves, which differ widely from region to region, are now regarded as having been produced by cultures we call Adena, Hopewell, and, more generally, "Mississippian" cultures. But archaeologists in the nineteenth century chased Mound Builders, illusory as they turned out to be, and so we will chase them as well.

Viewed from the vantage of the nineteenth century, Moorehead was even more right about Atwater's importance to the field of archaeology. Not only did Atwater describe an exemplary method of careful, accurate survey and mapping, and exercise a judicious degree of speculation based only upon available evidence; not only did his work become the touchstone for other mound excavators, but his 1820 report also identified many of the central historical questions that these mounds and their builders raised. In a remarkable way, Atwater managed to sketch the boundaries around the Mound Builder debate in the nineteenth century.

Atwater made it clear in his "Description" that his was a historical undertaking, and he drew a distinction between what constituted historical evidence and what might be considered more scientific proof. Persons who "require proofs amounting to mathematical certainty," he wrote, "need not give themselves the useless labour of perusing the remaining part of this memoir." If not absolute certainty—"the nature of the subject does not admit such proof"—then "a reasonable one" based on the careful study

> of the skeletons of the people themselves; their dress; their ornaments, such as beads, bracelets, badges of office; their places of amusement, burial and worship; their buildings, and the materials used in their structure; their wells; domestick utensils; weapons of offense and defense; their medals and monuments, intended to perpetuate the memory of important events in their history; their idols; their modes of burial, and of worship; their fortifications, and the form, size, situation, and materials with which they were constructed.

This was a thorough, even exhaustive list, designed to impress readers with the sheer extent of Atwater's own research. The archaeological items on this list constituted for Atwater all the historical evidence that could be mustered to explain and interpret the mounds. As he described it, "These are fragments of history, as Bacon would say, which have been saved from the deluge of time."[11] The reference to Francis Bacon is a nice touch. With it, Atwater both drew a connection between his work and that of empirical science, and marked the difference between science and history.

At least one reader understood entirely what Atwater was up to. Writing to him in July 1820, C. S. Rafinesque, ostensibly to report on a mound in Kentucky, philosophized: "The man or men, who will endeavor to collect all the scattered accounts and notices of American monuments, and who will bring them forth in a methodical, comparative, perspicacious point of view, will render a real and important service to the historian of our ancient times and of our predecessors on this luxuriant soil, and even to the history of mankind."[12] Atwater's goal precisely.

The first, most pressing question posed by these mounds was whether they were constructed by the ancestors of the Indians who currently occupied the Ohio and Mississippi valleys—and were now being displaced from them. Atwater's conclusion, based on an examination of skeletons, would seem unequivocal: "The skeletons found in our mounds never belonged to a people like our Indians. The latter are a tall, rather slender, strait limbed people; the former were short and thick."[13]

That conclusion led to an obvious next question: if not related to present-day Indians, then who were these Mound Builders and where did they come from? In answering the question "Who then were the Authors of our Ancient Works?" Atwater began with the Bible, "the most authentick, the most ancient history of man." In fact, this immediate recourse to scripture to answer the question of where Mound Builders had come from was related to Atwater's major purpose. The overarching conclusion Atwater draws from his investigation of mounds addressed the issue of human unity. "If the coincidences between the worship of our people, and that of the Hindoos and southern Tartars," Atwater challenged, "furnish no evidence of a common origin, then I am no judge of the nature and weight of testimony."

To prove a common origin, as we have already discussed, was to prove the story of Genesis correct. For those skeptics "who are constantly seeking for some argument with which to overthrow the history of man by Moses," Atwater compared his data with that from "the most authentick sources" and found a striking similarity of form between the mounds of Asia, Europe and America—"similarity of works almost all over the world"—to indicate "that all men sprung from one common origin." Atwater told his readers that he considered this fact "as strengthening the Mosaic account of man."[14]

On the last page of "Description of the Antiquities Discovered in the

State of Ohio and other Western States," Atwater concluded by reassuring his readers: "The discoveries of the Antiquarian throw a strong and steady light upon scripture, while the scriptures afford to the Antiquarian the means of elucidating many subjects otherwise difficult to be explained, and serve as an important guide in the prosecution of his investigations."[15] In the end, Atwater had used the techniques of a new, more scientific archaeology to demonstrate that these mysterious mounds yielded only information to reinforce the comforting verities of biblical history.

These matters, needless to say, did not get settled in 1820. Atwater leaned toward a theory which had Mound Builders descended from survivors of the flood—he made a particular point of drawing a parallel between the significance of hills and high places in the biblical landscape with the obvious significance of these mounds in the American landscape. Others, like Alexander Bradford, intrigued by the vastly more complex ruins in Central and South America, believed that perhaps the origins of the Mound Builders could be found in Mexico. After laying out for readers eleven indisputable conclusions about these disappeared people, he concluded: "the only indications of their origin, to be gathered from the locality of their ruined monuments, point towards Mexico." Bradford did have to confess, however, that "in progress of this comparison, we find no vestiges in the United States of such edifices as crowned the Mexican and Peruvian terraces."[16]

Still others looked at what came out of the ground and saw evidence for Phoenicians, Welshmen, lost tribes of Israel, giants, pygmies, and a few other equally plausible hypotheses. In 1849, the author of *Peter Parley's Tales*, a popular series of children's books, provided as good a summary as any of the five most current theories explaining Indian origins: (1) that the Indians were a lost tribe of Israel (far and away the most persuasive); (2) that they were misplaced Phoenicians or Carthaginians; (3) that actually, they were Welsh people a long way from home ("the pretensions of the Welsh have been put forth with not a little zeal," as the author put it); (4) that the "Eastern and Western Continents were once united"; (5) that Indians had originally wandered over from the northeastern part of Asia.[17]

Before we giggle too hard and too dismissively at these conclusions, it is worth reiterating that those who treated the subject most seriously strained, like Atwater, to fit their own observations into the understanding of human history as outlined in the Bible and in other classical texts, even if these attempts to reconcile archaeological discoveries with scripture led to some extraordinary intellectual gymnastics. (Indeed, there is still a lively, sometimes bitter, debate among archaeologists over whether the New

World was populated 12,000 years ago or, as some insist, as long ago as 16,000 years).[18]

Rather than dismiss these early researchers, or dissect their theories to determine what was "wrong" with them, however, we should recognize the genuine dilemma antebellum scientists faced. As we discussed in chapter 1, biblical and classical texts were really the only historical resources available to them, and so they worked hard to fit increasingly incongruous data within these increasingly rickety frameworks. The question of just where these Indians had come from had bothered Americans since the seventeenth century, and despite the intrepid work of dozens of diggers, by the middle of the nineteenth century the answer seemed no closer. The most elusive thing of all about the Mound Builders seemed to be that the more people trenched those mounds, the less they seemed to know about them.

Coincidentally, *Peter Parley's Tales* appeared the year after the most extensive and important compendium of research about mounds since Atwater's had appeared. In 1848, Ephraim Squier and Ephraim Davis, a journalist and a medical doctor from Chillicothe, Ohio, published *Ancient Monuments of the Mississippi Valley*, a stunning 300-page summary, complete with elegant illustrations, of all that had been discovered about and in the mounds. The work had been much anticipated and was deemed important enough that it came out as the first volume of the new Smithsonian Institution's *Contribution to Knowledge* series.[19]

Ancient Monuments of the Mississippi Valley quickly became the standard reference work on the topic of mounds, displacing Caleb Atwater's "Description." Though they now stood as the most celebrated students of mounds, and therefore of ancient American history, Squier and Davis acknowledge their scholarly debts, writing that Atwater "deserves the credit of being the pioneer in this department."[20] After making some introductory remarks, Squier and Davis devote eight chapters to descriptions of the mounds themselves, both geographically—"mounds of the southern states," "mounds of the north-west"—and by the function to which the authors believed they had been put—"mounds of sacrifice," "temple mounds," and so forth. The next nine chapters treat the artifacts recovered from these mounds, again by category. Hailed at the time, *Ancient Monuments* still stands as a remarkable archaeological achievement. Since so much of what Squier and Davis documented has subsequently disappeared, first under farm fields and then under suburban expansion, their descriptions constitute the last, best record of some of these mounds. Fifty years after *Ancient Monuments* appeared, Frank Hamilton Cushing gushed to Isaac Hayes: "These two men were amazing considering their day and generation."[21]

Squier and Davis stressed that they had conducted the work recorded in their book personally, thus distinguishing themselves from many armchair archaeologists who speculated on matters archaeological by reading the accounts of others. In this, they echoed their colleagues who studied languages, and underscored the growing empiricism that separated the science of the nineteenth century from that of the eighteenth. They also outlined the rudimentary principles of stratigraphic excavation, and they insisted that archaeology ought to be empirically, rather than theoretically, driven. "Archaeological research," Squier wrote, "to an eminent degree, demands a close and critical attention to the facts upon which it is conducted."[22]

In this sense, archaeology developed alongside the new field of geology. Eighteenth-century diggers had noticed that human accumulation took place in strata, and geologists refined the understanding of naturally occurring layers. Geologists studied natural history based on the principle that that which lay closest to the surface was the most recent, that which lay beneath, older. It remained, then, for archaeologists to apply the same principle to remains left by humans and to read human history by peeling back these stratigraphic layers. The connection with geology was potent. Geology grew, in the early and midcentury, to become perhaps the most popular science in the Atlantic world, practiced by celebrated college professors and countless thousands of Sunday afternoon rock collectors. "Geology and archaeology go hand in hand," English archaeologist D. T. Anstead wrote to a friend in 1861, and for archaeologists, the stratigraphic principle constituted the most important methodological development of the nineteenth century.[23]

One can still sense some of the excitement this break-through generated, and its power as an archaeological tool, in Squier and Davis's prose. "The fact of stratification, in these mounds, is one of great interest and importance," they told readers, a feature "heretofore [ ] remarked, but not described with proper accuracy." Trying to paint a verbal picture, though the book did provide beautiful illustrations, they went on to demonstrate that these layers were not the result of natural processes: "the stratification, so far as observed, is not horizontal, but always conforms to the convex outline of the mound. Nor does it resemble the stratification produced by the action of water, where layers run into each other, but is defined with the utmost distinctness, and always terminates upon reaching the level of the surrounding earth."

This all led to the conclusion about the explanatory power of stratigraphy:

If the stratification already mentioned as characterizing [the mounds] is unbroken and undisturbed, if the strata are regular and entire, it is certain that whatever occurs beneath them, was placed there at the period of the construction of the mound. And if, on the other hand, these strata are broken up, it is equally certain that the mound has been disturbed, and new deposits made subsequent to its erection. It is in this view, that the fact of stratification is seen to be important . . . for it will fix beyond all dispute, the origin of many singular relics.[24]

Stratigraphic digging brought some chronological order to what had been the chaos of artifacts randomly dug up from the ground. Thus was modern archaeology in the United States born.

Squier and Davis had some self-conscious sense that they were moving archaeology in a new direction. They complained that archaeology had been influenced too much by "the poet and the romancer," and that "while every other branch of research has enlisted active and enlightened minds in its elucidation, the archaeological field has been left comparatively unoccupied." They drew a sharp distinction: poets and romancers had muddied the scientific waters, and "if these monuments were capable of reflecting any certain light upon the grand archaeological questions . . . then they should be carefully and minutely, and above all, systematically investigated."[25] Squier and Davis clearly wanted to answer historical questions through the archaeological method, but they already hint at the divide that would grow through the nineteenth century between history—still after all, a "literary" pursuit—and science.

Squier and Davis dedicated Ancient Monuments to the aged Albert Gallatin. The dedication acknowledged a scholarly debt to be sure. But it also underscored that just as Gallatin's work constituted a singular achievement in the study of Amerindian languages, so too Ancient Monuments represented the apex of American archaeological achievement in the era before the Civil War. Squier and Davis may have felt that "the archaeological field has been left comparatively unoccupied," but they were in fact part of a generation of investigators writing and publishing about Indians archaeologically in the 1840s and '50s, a generation that included Caleb Atwater, Henry Schoolcraft, Lewis Henry Morgan, and Samuel Haven. Haven's magnum opus, Archaeology in the United States, was largely a summary of archaeological research to that point with, as one reviewer put it, "comparatively few observations or opinions of his own."[26] Still, the book did its job ably, and it constituted an important contribution to the archaeological discussion. Appearing as it did in 1856, it also served to bring an era to an end. It may well be the case that the few decades before the Civil War marked the height of public interest in the archaeological questions related to American Indians. For literate Americans in the antebellum period, Indians were everywhere in the print culture—in books, the journals of learned societies, and popular magazines.

The Civil War brought this era to an end, most obviously because of the disruptions it caused precisely in the geographical areas then of primary archaeological interest. In the postwar period, which might aptly be labeled the "Age of Indian Wars," it also became clear—Little Bighorn notwithstanding—that the military conquest of the Indians was no longer a question of whether, but of when. The postwar period proved Albert Gallatin's 1836 observation prescient: "So long as the Indians were formidable, their mode of warfare and their excessive cruelty and ferocity made them objects of execration. . . . That state of things is at an end; the natives have ceased to be an object of terror, and they are entirely at our mercy."[27] As Indians receded as an urgent and immediate threat to most white Americans, so too the field of American archaeology ceased to enjoy the public visibility it once had.[28]

As it happens, Samuel Haven served as librarian for the American Antiquarian Society. It had been founded in large measure to stimulate and publicize archaeological research on those mysterious mounds. Tellingly, volumes 4, 5, and 6 of *Archaeologia Americana*, published between 1860 and 1874, contained much about the history of colonial America, and nothing about American Indians, or indeed about archaeology at all. By 1883, the Reverend George Ellis of the AAS Council acknowledged that the organization "cannot probably maintain its ancient prestige in the broad field of American Archaeology."[29]

Digging for the History of Progress

Before he described the bones he dug out of his neighborhood mound, Jefferson complained: "I know of no such thing existing as an Indian monument: for I would not honour with that name arrow points, stone hatchets, stone pipes, and half-shapen images."[30] The refrain was as common as it was damning. There were no ancient monuments in the United States, none to compete with the ruins that littered the European landscape and served as such romantic evocations of past history. Jefferson himself had fallen in love with those ruins and recreated one—the Maison Carée—as the new Virginia Capitol in Richmond.

It remains a remarkable confluence of national desires. In the early republican period, Americans yearned for raw material out of which to con-

Fort Rosalie, Adams County, Mississippi. This pencil and watercolor sketch by Montroville Wilson Dickeson shows the remains of a fort built by the French in 1716 on top of an ancient mound, ca. 1843. The most obvious question posed by mounds was, who built them? By the middle of the century the answer was just as obvious: Mound Builders. Courtesy of the University of Pennsylvania Museum of Archaeology and Anthropology Archives.

struct a stirring and romantic past for their own continent, quite apart from that of Europe. And even as white settlers streamed into the territories west of the Appalachians during the early republican period, they found a landscape that had obviously been settled before. Here was evidence that the continent was not so entirely new, in all the wrong ways, after all—ruins that, while they were not as elaborate as temples and castles, had the advantage of being utterly mysterious. The desire to use mounds as a way of filling up the pages of the continent's pre-Columbian history linked archaeology to the process of nation-building.

When excavators dug up Indian sites, scientific inquiry and nationalistic pride intersected, just as they did through the study of languages. Americans might struggle, especially in areas like painting, architecture, and literature, to create a culture different from but equal to that of Europe. Archaeology, like language, seemed at first an area where Americans could compete with or even out-do their European counterparts. "America is one of the most important Ethnological regions of the world," an anonymous author trumpeted in 1848, and went on "but its archaeology possesses a still higher interest."[31] It might well have been true, as English critic Sydney

Smith snidely quipped in 1818 in the pages of the *Edinburgh Review*, that "in the four quarters of the globe, who reads an American book?" But the study of Indian artifacts and monuments in the antebellum period commanded serious attention on both sides of the Atlantic. When none other than eminent British naturalist John Lubbock reviewed four books on American archaeology—including *Ancient Monuments* and *The Archaeology of the United States*—in London's *Natural History Review*, the Smithsonian thought it an important enough event to reprint the essay in its 1862 *Annual Report*.

No one trumpeted American archaeology as a point of nationalistic pride more loudly than William Pidgeon. In 1858 he published a bizarre, if quite popular, book entitled: *Traditions of De-Coo-Dah and Antiquarian Researches*. The book claimed to be Pidgeon's study of mid-western mounds aided by De-Coo-Dah, an almost clairvoyant Indian informant whom Pidgeon had befriended. In fact, it isn't at all clear that Pidgeon even visited many of the mounds he described, much less that he used an informant to help understand them.[32] No matter. Pidgeon aspired to more than merely dry accuracy.

Right away Pidgeon took on the invidious comparisons that depicted the European landscape, rich in history, against the historically barren American landscape: "Foreign travelers have not infrequently complained that America presents nothing like ruins such as are seen in other quarters of the globe: no dilapidated walls, moss-covered turrets, or crumbling abbeys." In his booster's role, Pidgeon assured his readers that "the time is not far distant when the reproach so often flung at this country, that we have no antiquities, will lose even the appearance of truth."

Not content with this assertion, Pidgeon went on to glorify the mounds in terms overheated even for this era: "the world will look with interest and awe on some of the mightiest monuments of antiquity which stand upon the surface of the earth, as they are opened to view in the western country. The grandeur of Egyptian ruins and pyramidal tombs will cease to attract the undivided attention of those who look after records of the earliest times." After all, "what are moss-clad turrets, or crumbling abbeys, that bear on their bosoms the impress of era and nationality, compared with our everlasting artificial hills, that have outlived history, tradition, and era . . . ?" America only needed "to awake her story from sleep, to string the lyre and nerve the pen, to tell the tale of her antiquities, as seen in the relics of nations, coeval perhaps with the oldest works of man."[33] A tremendous expectation to place on mounds Pidgeon himself may or may not have seen.

Pidgeon, needless to say, did nerve up his pen and write a history of the Mound Builders as fantastical as any European myth. Regardless of the liberties it took with available facts, his account was predicated on an important consensus: the Mound Builders, whoever they were and wherever they came from, were now an extinct race of people and in no way related to the current indigenes. Whatever else might be the subject of scientific and historical dispute, that much seemed clear.

Indeed, it seemed impossible to most Americans to attribute to contemporary Indians anything archaeological that betrayed the least bit of sophistication or aesthetic appeal. An 1872 article in the *Dubuque Times* assured its readers that some recently discovered statuettes found in a railroad cut could not have been carved by the local tribes: "The question arises, By what people were these idols set up? Certainly not by the race of the Indians who have lately occupied that territory." Likewise, the *Atlanta Constitution*, in reporting on some new finds eroding out of the Chattahoochee River in 1886, waxed poetic about the "extinct race" of Mound Builders while insisting that "the known indolence of the race found here by white man forbid[s] the conclusion that he was the builder" of the mounds.[34]

It is worth asking why Americans seemed so certain, in the words of J. D. Baldwin, that "no savage tribe found here by Europeans could have undertaken such constructions as those of the Mound-Builders." Most obviously, Americans needed Mound Builders to be different from contemporary Indians in order to justify the opinion of the latter as backward, savage, and otherwise lost to civilization. Alexander Bradford put it clearly in 1843. Because the Mound Builders had already vanished at the time of contact and the continent "was inhabited by savage hordes . . . the time had arrived when a new race, and the Christian religion, were appointed to take possession of this soil."[35]

Of course, Americans needed to maintain these opinions to soften whatever qualms some might have felt about the process of conquest and expansion most of their countrymen enthusiastically endorsed. Alice Beck Kehoe has made this point emphatically. "The history of American archaeology," she argues, "is a remarkable example of a post hoc objectification of the doctrine of Manifest Destiny." In this sense, archaeology provided a scientific and "objective" rationale for the destruction of Native Americans being carried out so zealously in the nineteenth century, helping to validate, in Hinsley's opinion, "social groups engaged (or enmeshed) in industrial growth, capital accumulation, and colonial expansion."[36]

The Mound Builders served a related purpose as well. They were offered as evidence in the continuing struggle to demonstrate that the

North American continent had a history, natural and human, comparable to Europe. As Baldwin also told his readers, "It can be seen . . . that the Mound-Builders had a certain degree of civilization which raised them far above the condition of savages." Maya, Aztec, and Inca ruins impressed certainly, and many Mound Builder connoisseurs ascribed the mounds to some connections with those civilizations. But Americans were searching for something that would make the United States itself a historically rich landscape, and Peruvian Incas did not suffice. As Curtis Hinsley has noted, the "relationship between historical time and the national landscape" was the center of an urgent debate in the early republic.[37] That desire to inscribe on the landscape of the United States the vestiges of lost civilizations and ancient empires led to the projection of almost any historical reference onto the mounds—Israelites, Phoenicians, Welsh, Atlantans, or some completely fictitious group. "Ancient Egypt," William Pidgeon told his readers, "has also left her impress here."[38]

Using archaeological evidence to prove that the Mound Builders were an extinct race, unrelated to contemporary Indians, might have provided Americans with a convenient rationale for their continental expansion in the nineteenth century. But the mysterious Mound Builders also sat at the center of the negotiations between archaeology, biblical chronology, and a progressive view of history. In this role, Mound Builders probably played their most significant part in America's intellectual history.

The editor of the American edition of English naturalist John Lubbock's hugely popular book *The Origin of Civilization and the Primitive Condition of Man* worried in the preface about what he called the "grave question" of social degeneration: "was primeval man a developed and superior being who has retrograded and degenerated into the savage state?"[39] This question had real urgency for Victorians on both sides of the Atlantic. After all, evidence that human groups could "de-evolve" would fly in the face of the confident notion that human history moved in a linear direction toward greater and greater progress. Lubbock made the stakes clear: "Is there a definite assured law of progress in human affairs—a slow, gradual ascent from the lower to the higher? . . . If the past history of man has been one of deterioration, have we but groundless expectation of future improvement?" Happily for Lord Avebury, as Lubbock became later in his life, the archaeological evidence demonstrated that although there might be the occasional and exceptional slippage back into barbarism, on the whole human progress marched forward.[40]

It is not clear that mounds were on Lubbock's mind when he wondered about the laws of progress and degeneration. His book, and the even more influential *Prehistoric Times,* which first appeared in 1865, were great, global summaries. In the latter work, Lubbock relied almost entirely on the researches of Atwater, Squier and Davis, and Henry Schoolcraft for his discussion of North American Indians. Indeed, he continued to draw on these same sources in the seventh edition of the book, which appeared just after his death in 1913—a comment both on the enduring nature of those scholars, on the persistence of the Mound Builder idea itself, and perhaps on how much Lubbock kept up with current scholarship.

In fact, the American situation presented a more complicated version of the problem of degeneration. As Kehoe, among others, has pointed out, nineteenth-century archaeology in both Europe and America, far from building theory around evidence, was fairly well predicated on proving the idea of progressive development in the first place. Americans, however, needed to use archaeological evidence to demonstrate that Indians had made very little progress at all. Bruce Trigger has put it this way, "It was generally agreed that the archaeological record supported claims that Indian cultures had not experienced major developmental changes . . . and that Indians were perhaps incapable of them."[41] Archaeology in the nineteenth century could prove progress or stasis, depending on what a specific cultural context demanded.

Lubbock's consideration of the idea of degeneration, and of its implications for a Victorian worldview, echoes the sentiments of Alexander Bradford, published almost exactly thirty years earlier. And for Bradford, the question of social degeneration was posed most certainly and most immediately by American archaeology.

Bradford wrote his *American Antiquities* in the midst of the ferment of activity that percolated around mounds and Mound Builders in the 1840s. As he cast his glance across the state of archaeological research, he too found it a "grave question whether any portions of our race, however abused, have not retrograded from a more advanced stage of knowledge and intelligence." As he looked around the world, Bradford saw "vast regions . . . occupied by tribes in this state of barbarism." But, he asked, "is it certain that such was their original condition?" No idle musings, these, because they led directly back to the most important historical issue of all: "Historically, no such period of common and universal degradation has ever existed if we place any reliance upon the ancient authorities, or upon that most venerable of all records, the Bible."[42]

This, then, was the final reason Americans in the antebellum period needed first to invent the Mound Builders and then to sever them from any connection to contemporary Indians. Not only did the Mound Builders help justify the dispossession of the Indians, not only did they populate the American landscape with a race of ancient and wondrous people, but by insisting that Mound Builders did not degenerate into hopelessly unprogressive Indians, Americans could hold on to the legitimacy of the Bible as a historical source. Remarkable cultural baggage to cart around for a people who, in the end, never really existed.

OF COURSE, AS THE nineteenth century wore on, the evidence mounted that there was no mysterious, extinct race of Mound Builders, and that in fact, contemporary Indians were almost surely the descendants of those who built the mounds. John Wesley Powell played a central role in banishing the Mound Builders from American archaeology. The 1882 Second Annual Report of Powell's Bureau of Ethnology contained an article by Henry Henshaw that focused on the animal carvings from the Mississippi mounds. Henshaw used the essay to go after Squier and Davis and the whole notion of Mound Builders. These carvings had been initially interpreted as exotic, tropical beasts, and thus proof of a vast Mound Builder empire reaching across the whole of the North American continent. Henshaw, however, demonstrated that they merely depicted local fauna. "The theories of origin for the Mound Builders suggested by the presence in the mounds of supposed foreign animals," he wrote dryly, "are without basis." When Samuel Kneeland wrote to French archaeologist le Metayer de Guichainville in 1885, he reported only two "plausible theories" about the Mound Builders. Powell's had them as the ancestors of modern Indians; the other was that the Mound Builders "with the Mexican, Central American & Peruvian races were a distinct and extinct race."[43]

In 1881, Powell had made Cyrus Thomas the head of the Bureau's mound project, and Thomas commanded a small group that worked with remarkable energy across mound country from Illinois to Arkansas and from North Carolina to Iowa. In 1894, Thomas produced an account of the division's work in the twelfth Annual Report of the Bureau of Ethnology. Running to over 700 pages, Thomas's "Report of the Mound Explorations by the Bureau of Ethnology" may well have marked the last time the Mound Builders appeared as a people in a scientific report, largely because Thomas's report so thoroughly dismantled the notion of their very existence. And while Thomas disagreed with Squier and Davis fundamentally, he certainly stands as their archaeological successor. No one reading this almost deadening prose would confuse Thomas with a poet or romancer. American archaeology now belonged entirely, from its methods to the language of its discourse, to the world of social science.

Thomas's report stands as a culmination of a shift that moved American archaeology away from historical explanation and toward anthropological concerns. Archaeology, like the study of language also under Powell's influence, tried to establish classifications horizontally across space, rather than vertically through time. Archaeologist Bruce Trigger has pointed out that "the systematic study of cultural variation in the archaeological record was oriented primarily toward defining geographical rather than chronological patterns."[44] Language and relics—still two sides of the same coin, but now an anthropological rather than a historical one.

Powell and his Bureau of Ethnology played a central role in dispelling what has become known as the Mound Builder "myth," although by no means did the Mound Builders disappear from scientific discussion immediately: through the 1880s and 1890s Stephen Peet, a minister and the founder and editor of the *American Antiquarian,* kept the Mound Builders alive in the pages of his journal, and kept alive as well the insistence that they were not related to Indians. Although Peet still wondered "who this people were, whence they came, and whither they went," he was positive about their relationship to the present indigenes. "We may say," he wrote in 1880, "in reference to those who erected the mounds in the Mississippi valley, that they were probably not Red Indians." In the face of mounting evidence to the contrary, Peet persisted. As he compared Indian relics and Mound Builder remains he concluded: "We think enough contrast between the . . . relics has been shown . . . so we cling to the term Mound-builders and Indians."[45]

"Cling" is a nice choice of word because with it Peet captured, inadvertently or otherwise, that the whole Mound Builder notion was indeed crumbling under the weight of archaeological evidence. In the bureau's 1890–1891 *Annual Report* Powell acknowledged the appeal of the myth even as he dismissed it:

> It is difficult to exaggerate . . . the force with which the hypothetic "lost race" had taken possession of the imaginations of men. For more than a century the ghosts of a vanished nation have ambuscaded in the vast solitudes of the continent, and the forest-covered mounds have been usually regarded as the mysterious sepulchres of its kings and nobles. It was an alluring conjecture that a powerful people, superior to the Indians, once occupied the valley of the Ohio and the Appalachian ranges . . . swept away before an invasion of copper-hued Huns from some unknown region of earth, prior to the landing of Columbus.

Alluring to be sure, and it made the study of archaeology similarly engaging. Once Powell and other postwar scientific archaeologists succeeded in slaying the Mound Builders, both in connecting them to the Indian groups already on the continent at the time of contact and by explaining the mounds in definitive, if more prosaic, ways, Americans lost interest in them. Taken away from poets and romancers, the history that archaeology revealed may have been more accurate, but it didn't satisfy American needs nearly so well.

As I have suggested, the trajectory of the Mound Builders in the scientific imagination was also connected to a shift in the public interest in American archaeology more generally. What had been a subject that attracted much popular attention in the antebellum era now became a subject reserved increasingly for anthropological specialists. Dull prose, I suspect, was not the only reason for this shift in audience. Americans had needed Mound Builders—indeed, had set about inventing them—to satisfy their own historical yearnings. Through the Mound Builders, Americans populated the continent with a fantastic empire built by a lost race, proving that the "new world" did have a history after all. The invention of the Mound Builders enabled Americans both to have a "new world" that was not burdened with the baggage of a familiar, well recorded past, and to use the landscape as a blank canvas upon which they could paint the historical scenes that most suited them.

Whither American Archaeology

That it should have been some of "Powell's boys" who finally did in the Mound Builders was almost an inevitability. According to Irving Hallowell, a "new era" in American archaeology began in the 1880s, initiated by developments at Harvard University and at the Bureau of American Ethnology (BAE).[46] The crescendo of interest in mounds and their builders, which had swelled through the 1840s and 1850s, now died down, and after the Civil War, American archaeology shifted in important new directions. By the 1880s, twin torches had been passed: from institutions like the American Antiquarian and the American Philosophical Society, which had fostered American archaeology in its incipient period, to the federal government and Harvard University; and from gentlemen-scholars like Squier and Davis (both dead in 1888) to people—scientific professionals now—like John Wesley Powell, first director of the BAE, and Frederic Putnam, whose influence extended to many institutions in addition to Harvard. Reverend Ellis of the AAS, who acknowledged in 1883 that the society would no longer

MONUMENTAL GRANDEUR
OF THE
MISSISSIPPI
VALLEY!
NOW EXHIBITING FOR A SHORT TIME ONLY,

WITH SCIENTIFIC LECTURES ON

American Ærchiology.

Dr. Dickeson, late Professor in Philadelphia College of Medicine ; Member of the Academy of Natural Sciences, and Fellow of the Royal Society of Copenhagen, &c., &c., will Lecture THIS EVENING on the

ANTIQUITIES & CUSTOMS OF THE UNHISTORIED INDIAN TRIBES,

who dwelt on this Continent 3,500 years ago, and also on the leading peculiarities in the construction of those *Mounds, Tumuli, Fossæ,* &c., with the Geology, Mineralogy and Botany of this beautiful country.

Dr. D. has devoted twelve years of his life in these investigations, having in that time explored the whole Valley of the Mississippi, and opened over 1,000 Indian Monuments or Mounds, and has now a collection of 40,000 *relics* of those interesting but unhistoried Native Americans.

During the entertainment, the Doctor will unroll a most magnificent *Scenic Mirror*, covering 15,000 feet of canvass, illustrating the Monumental Grandeur of the Valley, with the splendid scenes that occur upon the *Father of Rivers.*

His Lecture, which accompanies each moving of the Tableaux,' abounds in invaluable information, and is worth alone, double the price of admission.

THIS GORGEOUS PANORAMA,
WITH ALL THE

ABORIGINAL MONUMENTS
Of a large extent of Country, once roamed by the RED MAN, was painted by the

Eminent Artist I. J. EGAN, Esq.,

AND COVERS OVER 15,000 FEET OF CANVASS!
It has been pronounced by our Celebrated Artists to be the most

FINISHED AND MAGNIFICENT PICTURE
Ever presented to

THE AMERICAN PUBLIC.

Each View and Scene is taken from DRAWINGS MADE ON THE SPOT, by

Prof. M. W. DICKESON, M. D.,
Who spent TWELVE YEARS of his Life in opening

Indian Mounds.

SECTION I.

Marietta Ancient Fortification—A grand view of their Walls, Bastions, Ramparts, Fossæ and Walls, with the relics therein found—Circleville Aboriginal Tumuli—Cado Chiefs in full costume—Youths at their War Practice—Hanging or Hieroglyphical Rock—Colossal Bust at low water mark, used as a metre by the Aborigines—Portsmouth Aboriginal Group in a Storm—Cave in the Rock, Stalagmitic Chamber and Crystal Fountan, Descended and Mummied Bodies in their burial places—Magnificent effect of Crystallisation—Terraced Mound in a snow storm, at sunset—Twelve gated Labyrinth, Missouri—Indians at their piscatory exploits.

SECTION II.

Bon Hom Island Group—Distant view of the Rocky Mountains—Encamping Grounds of Lewis and Clark—Louisana Swale Group, with extensive Wall—Lakes and Sacrificial Monuments—Natchez Hill by Moonlight—Indian Encampment—Distant view of Louisana—Indians preparing supper—The Tornado of 1844—Destruction of Indian Settlements—Horrid loss of Life—Louisana Squatter pursued by Wolves—Humorous Scene—Prairie with Buffalo, Elk, and Gigantic Bust on the ledge of a Limestone Rock—Spring Creek, Texas—Fort Rosalie—Extermination of the French in 1729—Grand Battle Scene—Mode of Scalping.

SECTION III.

Chamberlain's Gigantic Mounds and Walls—Natchez above the Hill—Indians at their Games—Baluxis Shell, Mounds—Ferguson Group—The Landing of Gen. Jackson—Lake Concordia and Aboriginal Tumuli—Huge Mound and the manner of opening them—Cado Parish Monument—De Soto's Burial at White Cliffs—Mammoth Ravine—Exhuming of Fossil Bones—Temple of the Sun by sunset.

Exhibition to commence at 8 every evening, and at 3 o'clock every Wednesday and Saturday afternoon.

Admission - - - - - - - - 25 cents.
Children under 12 - - - - - 12½ "

During the week a FREE ENTERTAINMENT will be given in the Afternoon, for the examination of the *Indian Museum.*

PRINTED AT THE MERCURY OFFICE—NEWARK, N. J.

Broadside for a lecture by Montroville Wilson Dickeson. American archaeology enjoyed a tremendous public appeal in the mid-nineteenth century. Courtesy of the University of Pennsylvania Museum of Archaeology and Anthropology Archives.

play a central role in American archaeology, went on to suggest moving the society's collection of archaeology artifacts, fittingly enough, to Harvard's Peabody Museum and to the National Museum in Washington.

These institutional shifts accompanied two others as well. The first was theoretical. In trying to evaluate the archaeological evidence coming out of the ground, Americans turned after the Civil War to chronological and evolutionary ideas developed by European archaeologists, especially Danish ones. J. J. A. Worsaae's "three-age system"—the Stone Age, the Bronze Age, and the Iron Age—of human progress appeared to English readers in 1849 when his book *The Primeval Antiquities of Denmark* received its first English translation. (After 1860 or so, the Stone Age would be subdivided into "Paleolithic" and "Neolithic" phases.) These theories proved a powerful influence on American archaeologists. In referring to the Danish finds, the Reverend Stephen Peet told his *American Antiquarian* readers: "Here the first data of science were gathered and . . . the foundation of what may be called Pre-historic Archaeology was laid."[47] In fact, European ideas about archaeology proved so persuasive that they exerted a retroactive influence on the American scene. In a lecture on the founding of the Peabody Museum, Frederic Ward Putnam asked his audience, "How did Mr. Peabody take an interest in Archaeology at a time when no interest of any extent was felt in this country?" and then went on to answer that question, "Presumably he had heard about it in Europe, if he was in England at the time of the lively discussion and interest in Paleolithics."[48]

Adopting the three-age system from the Europeans caused yet more hand-wringing about the retarded state of American science. In 1879, writing in the first volume of the *American Antiquarian,* Stephen Peet had reminded readers that "the science of archaeology in America is in its infancy"—ignoring or oblivious to the fact that Americans had been digging with some kind of system since the early republic—and he had gone on to make the invidious, if familiar, comparison: "European archaeologists have made much more advancement than we in America."[49]

But beyond the rewriting of the history of American archaeology, this European influence was additionally problematic. As we shall see, just as the study of Amerindian languages could not be accommodated by the branching tree of Indo-European, neither did the three-age system work altogether well to explain American archaeological finds.

The second change might be called geographical. In the latter half of the nineteenth century, the very phrase "American archaeology" ceased to have one obvious meaning. What had been synonymous with digging done on the North American continent by the end of the nineteenth century as-

sumed a new cosmopolitanism. Americans began sponsoring and participating in excavations back in the Old World, and by the late nineteenth century the exciting archaeological action was no longer in the New World, but
in the Old, no longer in the Mississippi Valley, but in the Tigris-Euphrates
region. This work, done by English, French, German, and American excavators, captured the public's attention, and commanded the serious institutional support. Recognizing this, Peet changed the name of his *American
Antiquarian,* which in its first two volumes called itself "A Quarterly Journal
Devoted to Early American History, Ethnology, and Archaeology," to the
American Antiquarian and Oriental Journal beginning with volume 3 in
1880.

There is no question that the three-part ladder of social progress developed by the Danes grew out of their own nationalistic impulses, what Bruce
Trigger calls Danish "patriotism." The schema that began with the Stone
Age, progressed to the Bronze Age, and culminated with the Iron Age allowed Danish archaeological finds to be placed in an evolutionary sequence
different from that which was organized around Roman history. The area
called Denmark, after all, had been beyond the realm of Roman influence,
and thus outside the realm of well-ordered history. The Danes of the 1830s
and 1840s created a "controlled chronology that did not rely on written
records."[50]

Despite its roots in Danish pride, the explanatory power of the three-
age system quickly persuaded archaeologists in other parts of Europe. Scottish scholar Daniel Wilson picked up on the system in his interpretation of
Scottish archaeological sites. Wilson himself wound up in North America—
at the new university in Toronto—and helped transplant the three-age system to American soil. After the Civil War, then, the debate over whether
American archaeological finds proved or disproved the European three-age
theory drove much of American archaeology. As Clark Wissler put it some
years ago, in the latter part of the nineteenth century the goal "was to locate
archaeological objects . . . and compare them typologically with archaeological objects in the Old World."[51] Putnam was one who embraced the European explanatory model. Several times he gave a lecture entitled "Paleolithic Man in Eastern and Central North America." In another lecture, this
one entitled "Periods of Prehistoric Man," he followed the three-age system
exactly, dividing the "Stone Age" into a Paleolithic and a Neolithic, and he
went on to compare the excavations of shell mounds in Denmark with those
in New England.[52]

Peet was another of those who believed that America too had its three
ages: "The bronze is indeed associated with the works of Mexico; the copper

with the Mound-builders of the Ohio Valley; the stone, rude and polished, is also associated with the fire beds and shell beds and bone heaps of this continent." Glancing over this evidence, Peet concluded: "the European system is confirmed," and he went on to say that "the archaeology of Europe" could well "serve us in America." Yet even Peet acknowledged that the American archaeological evidence looked a bit distorted when viewed through the lens of the three ages. In fact, America seemed to present a mirror image of European development. "The succession in time is exactly reversed," he told readers, and continued, "the latest of all in America are identical with the earliest or most ancient in Europe." Nearly ten years later, he was still wondering "whether American archaeologists are to accept these conclusions [about the European three ages] as applicable to the continent which we inhabit."[53]

There was another, homegrown system by which to evaluate social evolution, and Peet tried to wrestle the two into some compatibility. Lewis Henry Morgan had posited his own three-age system ranging from savagery, proceeding through barbarism, and culminating in civilization. He further subdivided the first two categories into lower, middle, and upper. Morgan's system relied on five criteria in evaluating where a certain group fell on his scale. As Peet summarized them, "the means of subsistence, geographical surroundings, the condition of art and architecture, the tribal organism and religious symbols." Using these "keys," Peet believed that "Mr. Morgan leads the way from historic to pre-historic races and gives us tests by which by which we may divide and sub-divide them."[54] This was surely a more sophisticated way of evaluating social organization than one based solely on tools. But, from an archaeologist's point of view, it depended on too fuzzy an evidentiary basis. How does one dig up the "tribal organism" after all or find "the means of subsistence?"[55] In the end, the Danish system proved more persuasive in large part because it relied on the kind of "objective" data that archaeologists could recover most easily.

Peet tempered all his analysis with the caution that Americans needed to do more archaeology in order to sort these questions out. That qualification summarized the thrust of much of the archaeological research undertaken in the latter part of the nineteenth century. The goal of discovering some evidence of an American Stone Age sent excavators off in search of human remains associated with extinct megafauna. Such a discovery would demonstrate that humans had made it to the New World before the last Ice Age. Henry Mercer, for example, son of a prominent Philadelphia family and a graduate of Harvard, spent several months exploring Paleolithic cave sites in Europe before returning to the United States to look for Paleolithic humans in caves from Maine to Tennessee. Mercer also published a long essay examining the authenticity of an artifact known as the "Lenape Stone." Etched on the stone, apparently, was a depiction of an Indian alongside a woolly mammoth. A startling image, were it genuine, and Mercer concluded that it probably was not. Likewise, the Smithsonian's Thomas Wilson wrote to Putnam in 1888 about the "campaign" he was organizing "which will last all summer in search of Paleolithic man."[56]

Once archaeologists began looking, of course, Ice Age men, Paleolithic men, "drift men," as these elusive people were variously called, started to turn up everywhere. One William Seymour of Brooklyn and head of the Long Island Archaeological Club wrote a lengthy report to Putnam about his own discoveries. "Such evidences of prehistoric man," he informed Professor Putnam, "are more numerous in the drift of Long Island than in any other section." He dismissed those who still challenged the authenticity of this evidence: "Their day is nearly over, for evidences of pre-glacial man are rapidly accumulating."[57]

The search for an American Stone Age after the Civil War made the banks of the Delaware River near Trenton, New Jersey, briefly a center of the archaeological world. There Charles Abbott, employed irregularly as a field assistant by the Peabody Museum since 1875, claimed to have discovered lithic evidence to link early Americans with the last glaciation. For the better part of the last quarter of the nineteenth century, American archaeologists debated vigorously, and often bitterly, the significance of Abbott's "Trenton Gravels." As Frederic Ward Putnam put it to his boss at the American Museum of Natural History in New York, "No question has ever arisen in American archaeology that has caused a more earnest discussion than the antiquity of man in the Delaware Valley."[58]

In brief, Abbott claimed to have found crude stone tools, similar morphologically to the earliest European stone implements, in a river deposit of sufficient age as to make them contemporary with the Ice Age. The scientific argument that ensued over the finds arrayed an increasingly angry and contentious Abbott, and a few supporters, against much of the archaeological community, including Powell's boys at the Bureau of Ethnology. And while, in the end, Abbott's gravels did not prove to be what he claimed them to be, it is worth remembering that the Trenton Gravels did influence the thinking of a large number of people about the question of human antiquity in America. Abbott's research figured prominently in the lengthy essay entitled "The Prehistoric Archaeology of North America," contributed by Henry W. Haynes as part of Justin Winsor's definitive *Narrative and Critical*

History of America, and Putnam continued to defend the finds, and those of Ernest Volk in the same area, well into the twentieth century.

Abbott wrote prolifically, often for popular magazines. Over one hundred of his essays appeared in places like the *American Naturalist* and *Popular Science.* He elaborated his ideas about the American Stone Age most thoroughly in his 1881 book *Primitive Industry.* There, he argued that a Stone Age race of people had preceded the Inuits, and that "Paleolithic" Americans had been displaced by "Neolithic" ones. Like Peet, Abbott believed that the three-age system could be applied to American archaeological finds, and with the discovery of the Trenton Gravels he had the material to prove it.

In retrospect, the discovery of the Trenton Gravels feels almost inevitable and overdetermined. The pages of Peet's *American Antiquarian* were filled with discussions of Paleolithic and other prehistoric discoveries, so eager were archaeologists to establish that there had indeed been an American Stone Age to correspond with the European one. One suspects that if Abbott had not made his finds, someone else, as the saying goes, would have invented them.

For our purposes, however, it does not matter that Abbott's finds did not ultimately pass scientific muster.[59] Abbott's rocks stand for us as a crystallization of the whole discussion of whether or not the three ages of Europe could be found in the North America. At that level, the Trenton Gravels lead to the consideration of two larger sets of questions.

First, by linking the age of human beings more firmly with geologic strata, the concept of the Stone Age implicitly suggested that human beings were a considerably older species than the Bible would have it. J. D. Baldwin recognized as much in *Ancient America:* "Doubtless the antiquity of the human race is much greater than is usually assumed by those whose views of the past are still regulated by medieval systems of chronology."[60] So too did John Orne, an audience member at one of Putnam's lectures, who wrote in smug tones thanking the latter: "Such information consisting of the latest results of archaeological investigation into the primitive history of our race cannot fail to weigh [ ] upon the minds of those, who, relying on certain cherished records, limit the origins of the race to one pair, and the antiquity of it to 6000 yrs."[61]

For others, however, who by the mid-nineteenth century had grown to accept that the earth might be older than a scant few thousand years, the idea that the age of human beings lay outside that chronology proved too much. In two books that appeared in the 1870s, James Southall tried to rescue the Bible from this onslaught of Ice Age Paleolithic people. He opened *The Epoch of the Mammoth* by sounding every bit the rational scientist: "It is purely as a question of science that I propose to discuss [the age of human beings]." If science proves that humans are older than the biblical chronology, so be it. If, on the other hand, "the two records agree, it is only another wonderful testimony to the endurance and vitality of the Hebrew books." It will comes as no surprise that Southall did indeed find that science harmonized with religion on this question. Science, as Southall reminds us, is "fickle," and in a strained bit of logic he went on, "It is evident . . . that Science is considerably unsettled and often in error, that the opinions of to-day are in a great many cases not the opinions of to-morrow."[62] Hence, claims that human beings predate the Bible are not to be trusted.

Southall demonstrated conclusively, or at least to his own satisfaction, this "main fact: *that human history commences about four thousand five hundred or five thousand years ago.*" This point he drove home repeatedly. Along the way, however, he took on what he now saw as his main adversary, the Stone Age: "We have thus proved (as we believe) that the present races of mankind do not date back further than several thousand years ago . . . we see no traces of a Stone Age." Three years later, he was just as emphatic. Not only were "the evidences for the antiquity of man in America [ ] comparatively meager, and not well substantiated," but "the system of the Three Ages set up by the Danish archaeologists is to be rejected as scientifically unfounded."[63]

Southall fought a losing battle. Whatever believers might salvage of biblical history, a 5,000-year antiquity for humankind did not survive the nineteenth century. English archaeologist John Henslow put it clearly in 1861: "The *facts* are beyond dispute, that the works of man have been *plentifully* extracted from geological strata prior to the last catastrophe."[64] Through the course of the twentieth century, scientists pushed the age of the human species back further into the past, and while there remains some question about exactly when the New World was populated, it surely took place more than 10,000 years ago.

There is, of course, a deep irony in all this, even if it went largely unnoticed. As we have discussed previously, the first generation of American archaeologists worked mightily to understand American Indians, ancient and modern, within the historical frameworks provided by the Bible and other classical texts. Whatever the unresolvable intellectual dilemmas of their work, theirs was an attempt to marry the empirical evidence coming out of the ground with a biblical view of the world's history. The three-age system, and the search for the American Paleolithic in the postbellum period, dissolved that marriage, and in that dissolution we can see two failures for those who pursued American archaeology. On the one hand, the attempt to fit the archaeological evidence of Native America into the biblical narrative did not work. On the other hand, Americans themselves, Morgan's attempts notwithstanding, had developed no competing system of social evolution as compelling as the Danish one.

Second, the Danish three-age system equated social progress with technological advancement, and in this sense it is as much an artifact of its age as the stone tools it categorized are of theirs. Through this conceptualization, archaeology provided empirical, objective proof that human progress had reached its height with the technologically superior West.[65] But as we have already discussed, the ideological thrust of American archaeology was to demonstrate the inherently unprogressive nature of Indians. Sorting out this apparent conundrum sent American archaeology in a slightly but crucially different direction than it followed in Europe.

Charles Abbott certainly found evidence of progress when he looked at Indian arrowheads. To readers of the *American Naturalist,* he announced that there was "an unquestionable indication" that "the art of arrow-making had been progressive." How and where that progress had been made remained an open question: perhaps it had occurred before Indians settled the New World, perhaps after. "In either case," Abbott finished, "the progress had been made."[66] But this was progress on a small scale, within a single of the three ages. Stephen Peet put his finger on the larger-scale problem when he saw in America the mirror image of European progress: "In America the most civilized was the soonest removed, and the rudest remained the longest."[67]

Here, then, was the flip side of the metahistorical question posed by the notion of degenerated Mound Builders. If degeneration offended the sensibilities of some mid-nineteenth-century social theorists, then could it be possible that some groups remained frozen in their primitive state of social development and demonstrated no progress at all? This was certainly one implication of Peet's observation—that the "rudest" survived without change into the period of European contact.

In fact, by searching for—and more importantly, by not finding—any evidence that Native Americans had made progress through the European three ages, archaeologists simply reconfirmed commonly held notions about the essentially unprogressive nature of American Indians. Peet recognized this, as he struggled to mesh the European system with Morgan's: "the stone age . . . would include savagery as well as barbarism, for the relics of the fisherman are as thoroughly stone age as are those of the village residents of the interior, and the agriculturalists, and hunters may be regarded as having the fullest use of these relics. . . .The question is, can we take the relics and classify them so that we can say that one belongs to the fisherman, another to the hunter, another to the agriculturalist, and another to the villager." These finer gradations of social progress were elided by the three-age system. Thus, as Joan Gero has suggested, by relying only on the "objective" evidence of material remains, and the technological schema through which they were organized, archaeology not only shaped the answers to questions about human antiquity, but also formulated how questions got asked in the first place.[68]

This in turn allowed Indians to be placed outside the flow of history that carried Europeans and Euro-Americans forward in the direction of limitless progress. Unlike European archaeology, which pushed the idea of linear progress backward in time and helped unify the history of the recent past with that of ancient times, American archaeology reinforced the idea that only Europeans had a history, as defined in these progressive terms. Native Americans, meanwhile, floated in some temporal limbo and were removed from it only when Europeans arrived and initiated the tragic but inevitable historical process of extinction.[69] In Europe, archaeology organized around the three ages created historical continuity and thus became a part of historical understanding. In the United States archaeology grew away from history, as it became a formal discipline over the course of the nineteenth century, and underscored that European arrival represented a triumph of progress over stasis.

Stephen Peet sounded almost doleful as he surveyed the different relationship archaeology had to history in the United States and the rest of the world. Through archaeological discoveries, he told readers, "in fact, history has been almost everywhere lengthened." And he went on:

> But the strange thing about American history is that it dates its beginnings with a very modern event . . . and confines its history mainly to the white race. If the archaeologists have brought about such results elsewhere, may they not break through the barriers which surround them and carry back our history so that it may compare with that of other nations?[70]

Peet had it exactly right: America before contact was put outside the realm of history, and not even the science of archaeology nor these kinds of patriotic appeals could link Indian history with American history in the minds of nineteenth-century Americans.

New Archaeology in the Old World, Old Archaeology in the New

In the year that Squier and Davis both died—1888—the Babylonian Exploration Fund provided support for the first American excavations in the Near East.[71] The coincidence has a nice, resonant symbolism. Of course, Americans had been interested for some time in the archaeological excavations going on in the Old World. The American Oriental Society, for example, had been founded in the 1840s complete with its own journal. Still, only in the latter part of the nineteenth century did Americans sponsor and participate actively in the archaeology of the ancient Near East and Mediterranean.

Rather than recount the history of these American expeditions, which historian Bruce Kuklick has already done, I want to notice several significant issues about them. First, as we saw with the postwar shift in the focus of philology and language study, by looking back to the Old World as the center of scholarly interest, Americans put themselves at an obvious disadvantage. Europeans had not taken up the study of American archaeology, or Amerindian languages, with as much enthusiasm as some antebellum Americans had expected. Depending on how one chooses to look at this, the trajectory of American archaeology either reflects the growing cosmopolitanism of American scholars, who now had the resources and the confidence to participate in European intellectual projects, or it reflects the failure, despite initial hopes, to create a new and lively field of intellectual pursuit that centered around the study of Native America—a field of which European scholars would be jealous.

Either way, by turning their attentions back to the Old World, Americans had to compete against archaeologists who were closer to the sites, and therefore had easier logistical problems to negotiate, who had been there longer, and who, in certain cases, enjoyed the advantages of access that colonial rule provided. In many cases, Americans who wanted to play the game had to do so according to rules set by their European colleagues and competitors.

Yet while the attentions and energy of American archaeologists moved from mounds to ziggurats, the intellectual motivation for this work remained the same. In the wake of Darwinian biology and German "higher criticism," Christian religious belief found itself under dramatic assault in the late nineteenth century. Into this crisis of faith stepped the archaeologists, many of whom believed that by discovering the physical remains of Old Testament stories they would undergird the Bible as a reliable document and help save Christianity from the corrosive effects of scientific doubt. As Kuklick has put it: "By the 1880s, scholars of the Near Orient in the United States saw their studies in the front lines of a defense of the Old Testament."[72] With the archaeology of ancient America now contributing to the crisis of religious skepticism, Near Eastern archaeology spoke even more directly to debates over the veracity of the Bible as a reliable historical source. Indeed, James Southall thought that the archaeological proofs of biblical truth coming from the Old World might, by extension, bolster his contention that the Bible also explained the origin of Native Americans.[73] By the end of the nineteenth century, American expeditions to the Near East in defense of the Old Testament took on this urgent, almost crusading excitement. As a result, those who sought to reconcile science and religion no longer took much interest in the archaeology of ancient America.

At the same time, whatever might have been the case in the antebellum period, by the turn of the twentieth century discoveries made in midwestern mounds, Florida shell middens, or even southwestern pueblo sites simply could not compete for newspaper and magazine space with the spectacular finds coming out of the ground in Egypt, the Near East, and the Mediterranean basin. North American Indian sites did not produce the monumental architecture, breathtaking arts and crafts, or ancient writings that archaeologists in the Old World seemed to be discovering every season. In an age when American art museums avidly collected the art and architectural objects coming out of the Old World and even from Central and South America, not much coming out of the ground in North America could compare.[74]

That acknowledgment points to another significance of the move by American archaeologists to the Old World. American archaeology in the Near East and Mediterranean was inextricably bound up in an emerging institutional nexus, which included new museums and newly expanding universities. For the American builders of these institutions, Old World archaeology provided a happy confluence of urgent intellectual questions and stunning objects to exhibit to the public. The goal for excavators was to answer those questions and to come back with archaeological trophies.

The antiquities of the ancient world became defined as "art" in the schema of the new art museums. Which antiquities and from where, of course, depended on their availability. The Metropolitan Museum of Art's first major bequest came from Baron di Cesnola and constituted his cache of Cypriot relics. The Boston Museum of Fine Art (MFA), on the other hand, went after Egyptian material through the joint sponsorship of excavations with Harvard—Harvard got the prestige of publishing the results of the project; the MFA got to keep the goodies.[75] Art museums from Brooklyn to Cleveland to Detroit all pursued roughly similar strategies.

Although American Indian artifacts did not make the leap into the category of "fine art"—and would not until the last quarter of the twentieth century—they were displayed prominently at world's fairs and international expositions. In the American ethnological displays at the 1893 World's Columbian Exposition, for example, North American archaeology accounted for half of the exhibition, in Franz Boas's description; the other half, according to Boas, was "the archaeology of Central America; and the ancient culture of Peru." Significantly, though, for Boas the American displays at the fair were an opportunity not so much to highlight archaeology per se, but to underscore archaeology as a constituent part of a larger anthropology. In assessing the displays, he felt "that the strong side lies wholly in a full representation of American anthropology."[76] The year 1893 simply underscored in a dramatic and public way that American archaeology belonged wholly and properly within the realm not of history or art, but of anthropology.

At the same time, several of the newly emerging research universities made oriental, biblical, classical, or Near Eastern studies centerpieces of their plans for institutional growth and academic prestige. Several more tried to get into the business driven by the same impulse and, for a variety of other reasons, were not successful. By the turn of the twentieth century, according to Kuklick, five universities had come to prominence in this field: Chicago, Harvard, Johns Hopkins, Pennsylvania, and Yale. All had helped establish that dominance in part through sponsoring archaeological expeditions.[77] Some of these universities established their own museums to house the collections they accumulated. Yale eventually deposited its antiquities as part of its small but comprehensive art gallery. Chicago built its own oriental museum.

What needs to be noted here is that the archaeology of ancient America, like the study of Amerindian languages, did not become institutionalized in the same way. Whole departments had been established to support Old World archaeological and related research, and in addition, such scholars might find homes in departments of history, classics, and art history besides. Yet, just as we saw happen in the field of American Indian languages, by the end of the nineteenth century, American archaeology had become a subset of anthropology. As a result, those archaeologists who worked on American sites found jobs almost exclusively in departments of anthropology, and thus would come in the twentieth century to share their institutional home with people interested in Indonesian folklore and African kinship patterns.[78]

Perhaps more than anyplace else, the University of Pennsylvania felt the tension between Old World interests and the efforts of American archaeologists to establish a place for themselves in the institutional nexus of the late nineteenth century. Part of its plan to use Near Eastern studies as a path to academic prestige included a new museum. Of all the university museums to be built in this period, none was larger or more ambitious than the one that grew at 33rd and Spruce Streets on Penn's campus.

Penn's museum was largely the brain child of Provost William Pepper and his collaborator Sara Yorke Stevenson. Pepper and Stevenson envisioned nothing less than an American version of the British Museum—a comprehensive storehouse of archaeological artifacts of all the world's great civilizations and of ethnological artifacts from the world's non-Western cultures. The late-nineteenth-century tension between those who wanted to pursue the sexier, headline-grabbing work in the Old World and those who wanted to continue the nearly one-hundred-years effort to answer questions about American antiquity, played itself out in the early years of Penn's museum. When the university began to build its museum it did include an American section in it, but perhaps not wholeheartedly. The 1893 Report from the museum's board records that in the annual budget, the Egyptian and Mediterranean Section received nearly $2000; the Babylonian Section nearly $6000, while the American and Prehistoric Section got $331.20.

Differences over the scale, scope, and focus of the museum's collecting and excavating activities caused board member C. Howard Colket to resign in 1894. Daniel Brinton resigned in that year too, citing the same complaints. Writing to Sara Stevenson, Brinton announced that he was "not in unison with the policy adopted in regard to the Museum." "The original plan," he went on, "was to confine it to archaeology and ethnology," by which Brinton meant principally American archaeology and ethnology.[79]

These tensions flared again over what kind of material should appear in the pages of the museum's *Bulletin*. Through the *Bulletin*, the museum communicated with an educated and interested public, "the intelligent laymen, such as are represented by the contributing membership of the Department," according to Stevenson. Additionally, the museum used the *Bulletin* as a source of barter in the professionalizing world of science. Stewart Culin, who took responsibility for overseeing the *Bulletin*, could report that after four years of publication, issues of the *Bulletin* had been exchanged for "scientific books and publications numbering some 5000 titles."[80]

That the *Bulletin* hoped to appeal both to the public and to professionals did not mean a consensus about what those audiences should read. Under Culin's guidance, the *Bulletin* concentrated on things American. This did not please Robert Brock, who, as it happened, provided the funds to publish the *Bulletin*. As he wrote with some exasperation to Stevenson in 1902:

> There seems . . . to be a misapprehension as to the "Bulletin" being devoted solely to American Archaeology. . . . I think that I have told you, as I have told Mr. Culin frequently, that there is no part of the work of the Museum in which I had so little interest as the American work, and it is therefore ridiculous to suppose—this being the case—that I am willing to undertake the expense of the "Bulletin" solely for that work.[81]

Culin, Stevenson, and Brock seemed to have worked out an agreeable compromise early in 1902, but the *Bulletin* ceased publication shortly after this contretemps, and the museum went without an official journal until 1910.

At its most mundane, the tension over the divergent paths taken by American archaeology at the turn of the last century cost Penn's museum a board member or two, the prestige of Daniel Brinton, America's first professor of anthropology, and its journal. But the pettiness of these institutional squabbles masked the larger issues at stake. Among other things, the infighting at the Penn museum reflected the larger struggles over the public attention archaeologists working in the American field could command, the support—institutional and financial—they could generate, and the prestige that work could garner in the increasingly professionalized world of university-based research.

Certainly, archaeological work in the American field continued to go on. As we have already seen, John Wesley Powell made the Bureau of Ethnology the most important sponsor of work on mounds and on other American Indian sites as well. Likewise, Harvard and a few other museums and universities continued to pursue questions of American archaeology. Most significantly, by the last quarter of the nineteenth century, work in the Southwest attracted numbers of researchers with remarkable energy and talent, but also considerable play in the public. "Cliff dwellers" joined Mound Builders in the last quarter of the nineteenth century as a mysterious, unknown group of ancients who lived in North America before Columbus.

The imbalance at Penn might have been exaggerated, but by and large, for the institution-builders who reshaped the American university at the end of the nineteenth century—Gilman at Hopkins, Pepper at Penn, Harper at Chicago, to name just three who enthusiastically sponsored excavations in the Old World and the creation of departments and museums to support them—institutional glory was to be found in the Near East, not in the Ohio River Valley.

As a consequence, archaeologists with little or no institutional connection wound up doing much of the archaeological work that was done in this country by the turn of the twentieth century. Clarence Bloomfield Moore, for example, did pioneering work on the archaeology of Florida.[82] He strikes us today as an archetypal gentleman-scholar. Complete with family money to fund trips to Europe, Central and South America, and up the Amazon, in addition to his extensive excavations in the inhospitable wilderness that once was Florida, Moore played this role as if sent straight from central casting. Moore's researches are still regarded respectfully by archaeologists and remain important to those who work on the Southeast. Yet Moore worked largely on his own. Without a professional position, he did not perpetuate his own work through the training of students, nor did he establish any institutional framework to continue his research agenda.

Moore remains known among specialists in the field. Samuel Kneeland, I suspect, does not. A Harvard-trained physician of some distinction, he also pursued a wide range of natural science interests, including archaeology, with tremendous energy. He was exactly the sort of person who might have played a major role in the archaeological debate in the antebellum period. Yet, though he taught zoology at MIT for several years, he never could find a regular position in an institution that would permit him to be a naturalist full-time. Early in 1886, he consoled a New York friend similarly unlucky: "I have lived in New York . . . and know well how hard it is to get literary or scientific employment . . . it is a fierce struggle for existence." Later in that same year, Kneeland wrote that he had been turned down for a job at the Met.[83] The list of American archaeologists who found themselves on the margins of American intellectual and institutional life could go on.

No career better illustrates the difficulties that faced American archaeologists who found no home in the new institutional worlds of the late nineteenth century than that of Charles Abbott. We saw earlier that Abbott was at the center of debates over just how old the first Americans might have been. In 1889, Abbott was appointed to be the Penn museum's first curator, although the museum at that point had no permanent home and virtually no objects. In fact, Abbott was named the curator of the American section, and he saw his role as assembling an American collection. Abbott sent a flyer to Philadelphia-area doctors in 1890 asking for donations of objects "illustrating the physical and industrial faculties of the native races of both North and South America." These donations were intended, the circular continued, for the museum of "American Archaeology."[84]

Abbott's career at the university museum was as sad as it was brief. He, like Brinton and others, left or was forced out because the museum's ambitions were larger than Abbott understood or accepted. He tried to cajole Putnam at Harvard into giving him some sort of permanent position there, but to no avail. Yet Abbott was an important, highly regarded archaeologist in the late nineteenth century. We might view his inability to find adequate institutional support for his researches—either at Harvard or at Penn—not only as testament to what surely seems like an irascible and grating personality (after all, when have these qualities posed an obstacle to university advancement?), but as an example of the clash between those from an older generation of what we would now call "amateur" scientists and the new, professionalized world of the research university, as it emerged in the late nineteenth century. Whatever the case, Abbott's career illustrates that although studies of American Indian archaeology were among the oldest of the nation's intellectual pursuits, by the end of the nineteenth century they had not become institutionalized in the new American research university the way that other disciplines had.

A final analogy with the study of American Indian languages: in 1885, the *American Journal of Archaeology* first appeared, and devoted most of its pages to detailing archaeological research in the Old World. That it should do so comes as no real surprise, given the interests of its founders and of the Archaeological Institute of America (AIA), for which the magazine continues to serve as the official organ. The AIA and its journal stand as part of that growing institutional web that supported the turn of American archaeologists to the Old World. Putnam had been there at the AIA's founding in 1879, along with other Boston and Cambridge luminaries, but as he complained in a letter to fellow Americanist Lewis Henry Morgan, "from that day (now over a year) I have not heard a word about the Institute from headquarters . . . I [have been] left out in the cold."[85]

More significantly, however, in the first article in the first issue, Charles Eliot Norton sketched the biography of J. J. Middleton, "The First American Classical Archaeologist." Norton's purpose was not simply to resurrect the forgotten Middleton and his 1812 volume *Grecian Remains in Italy*, but in so

The Peabody Museum of American Archaeology? Even at Harvard's Peabody, archaeological discoveries from the Old World crowded out American archaeology by the late nineteenth century. Peabody Museum, Semitic Gallery, ca. 1893. Courtesy of the Peabody Museum, Harvard University.

doing to rewrite the history of American archaeology in order to create a lineage for the growing number of American excavators now working in the Old World. According to Norton, Middleton's book "form[s] the cornerstone of the growing library of American treatises on classical archaeology, while its author's name properly stands at the head of the fast lengthening list of American investigators of the 'monuments of former men' in the Old World."[86] The history of language study had been recast at about this moment in just the same way to trace it back to Germany.

By the time Norton wrote his essay, at the moment when Americans were preparing to enter the Near Eastern and Mediterranean archaeological fields in a serious way, most regarded the Indian "problem" as all but solved. Conquered now, and presumed on the road to extinction, American Indians present and future held a waning interest for many Americans. So too their past.

THERE WERE SOME in the late nineteenth century who continued to believe that the archaeology of America held just as much importance and interest as that of the Old World, that it was central to a complete understanding of American history. Not surprisingly, among those who felt this way were John Wesley Powell and Daniel Brinton. Powell, while drawing a passionate, if not altogether successful, agricultural metaphor, complained: "Our archaeological institutes, our universities and our scholars are threshing again the straw of the Orient for the stray grains which may be beaten out." Meanwhile, he went on, "sheaves" of material "are stacked all over this continent; and they have no care for the grain which wastes while they journey beyond the seas."[87] Just as the self-styled Americanist championed the literary aspects of Amerindian languages, so too Brinton trumpeted the value of American archaeology. In a letter to Harvard's Jeffries Wyman just after the war, he wrote: "American archaeology will in time rank equal with that of Egypt and the Orient."[88]

Another of those, perhaps more interestingly, was poet Walt Whitman. Late in his life Whitman tried to sing the song of American archaeology: "We have our schools and expeditions for Greek exploration," he wrote. But why did Americans not "give our own evidences a chance to show themselves, too?" Plaintively, he asked, "Why not open up our own past—exploit the American contribution to this important science?" Whitman was living on Mickle Street in Camden, New Jersey, when he wrote that. He wrote it in 1888. Across the Delaware River in Philadelphia, the Babylonian Exploration Fund was gearing up for its first expedition.

5

THE ART AND SCIENCE OF DESCRIBING
AND CLASSIFYING: THE TRIUMPH OF
ANTHROPOLOGY

The classification of tribes is well nigh accomplished for a large part of North America.

JOHN WESLEY POWELL, 1890

In this chapter, we will begin at the end. As the nineteenth century turned into the twentieth, anthropology emerged as a lively new "science," created from a synthesis of several related but autonomous fields. Harvard librarian and historian Justin Winsor saw as much when he observed in 1888 that out of archaeological and ethnological work in the nineteenth century "has risen the new science of Anthropology, broad enough in its scope to include not only archaeology in its general acceptation, but to sweep into its range of observation various aspects of ethnology and geology."[1] In fact, Winsor had it only partially right. In the end, anthropology served as the umbrella under which gathered four studies, archaeology, language, ethnography/ethnology, and "somatology"—the four "legs" of anthropology's "chair" in the oft-used metaphor. These were the researches around which anthropology coalesced as an academic discipline in the 1890s, and they remain the heart of anthropology today.

Needless to say, there is nothing magical—or even altogether logical—about this disciplinary arrangement. That anthropology arose as it has reflects a set of historical contexts, institutional contingencies, and personal rivalries as much as some intellectual inevitability. As Dell Hymes famously asked over a quarter century ago: "If anthropology did not exist, would it have to be invented? If it were invented, would it be the anthropology we have now? To both questions, the answer, I think, is no."[2] What Hymes wondered, reduced to a Gertrude Steinian form, was whether there was a there,

154

there, any longer in anthropology. And in the wake of the cultural and political shifts of the 1960s, it wasn't at all clear that there was.

In fact, as he surveyed his intellectual landscape in 1836, nearly one hundred fifty years earlier, C. S. Rafinesque saw what we might call anthropology organized in a different way. What he described as the "new science" of ethnography, which undertook "to describe nations," encompassed several subsidiary branches, including: "Anthropology or the knowledge of physical mankind, Philology, or the comparative study of human speech and languages; Besides the nameless branch attending to the moral ideas, arts, institutions, manners, civilization, governments and religions of mankind; which might be called moral ethnography."[3] Looked at from Rafinesque's point of view, Hymes's question becomes not merely the hypothetical grapplings of a discipline in crisis, but a historical question about how and why the field came to look the way it did.

These unsettling questions would not have occurred to American anthropologists in the late nineteenth century. Whatever their methodological differences, whatever the differences in the materials they studied, archaeologists, linguists, ethnographers, and physical anthropologists in this country all shared the same subject: Native Americans. In the United States at the turn of the twentieth century, Native Americans served as the glue that held together the incipient anthropology. Conversely, anthropology became the sole disciplinary home for the study of Native Americans. By the end of the nineteenth century, there could have been no American anthropology without Indians to give it some semblance of disciplinary coherence, and there was virtually no serious study of Indians that was not anthropological. At a disciplinary level, the two were bound together inextricably.

This chapter then charts how the boundaries that defined anthropology by the end of the nineteenth century came to be drawn in the particular way they were. Some of this has already been foreshadowed by our examinations of developments in archaeology and language study, both of which ended up as anthropological subfields by the turn of the twentieth century, although they each had arrived on the intellectual stage independently and with different aspirations. My task, then, is to revisit some of these developments in language study and archaeology, and add to them an examination of the way Native Americans were described through the genre of ethnography, of how physical anthropology emerged as a way to measure their capacity for cultural achievement by measuring their bodies, and of the way museums became the first disciplinary home for anthropology.

Further, by considering how anthropology and the study of Native Americans came to be coterminous by the end of the nineteenth century, I want to make a reciprocal argument as well. Anthropology took on its particular aspect by the end of the nineteenth century both through what was included as its concerns and what was not. Most important among the latter, of course, was history. The discipline of anthropology grew at the same moment that the discipline of history became formalized and institutionalized. As we have already discussed in the first chapter—and as we will examine more fully in the next—that formalization largely excluded Indians from the realm of history. Rejected by the discipline of history, Native Americans were embraced entirely by anthropology, and thus what we do know about Native America we know largely because of the work of anthropologists. As a result, however, by the turn of the twentieth century American intellectual life was filled with anthropological Indians and largely devoid of historical ones.

The Literature of Ethnography and Ethnographic Literature

The American world of letters needed James Fenimore Cooper. It was not simply that he was among the first American writers who enjoyed a tremendous success both in the United States and abroad. (Indeed, so wide was his fame and so quickly did it spread that Russians like the poet Alexander Pushkin and the diplomat Alexander Griboedov were reading Cooper's novels almost as soon as they appeared). Or that Cooper managed to combine tremendous public success with wide critical acclaim. More than that, at several levels—his use of American history, American themes, American landscapes—he was seen, then as now, as the progenitor of an American literary tradition.[4]

If there was a consistent criticism made of Cooper's work, peppered in among the accolades, however, it concerned the way he drew his Indian characters. An anonymous review of *The Prairie*, while gushing in its enthusiasm for the novel, paused to remark: "Mr. Cooper is not apt to idealize his characters, but he has presented the aborigines of this continent in far too flattering colors . . . . Mr. Cooper has given us Cato and Coriolanus dressed in blankets and moccasins." Nearly fifteen years later, in an 1852 essay, the historian Francis Parkman echoed this almost exactly when he asserted that the "permanency of Cooper's reputation must . . . rest upon three or four finely conceived and admirably executed portraits." And then he quickly added, "we do not allude to his Indian characters, which it must be granted, are for the most part either superficially or falsely drawn; while the long conversations which he puts into their mouths, are as truthless as they are tiresome." No more eloquent Indians, not even in works of fiction.

Cooper might have even conceded the charge, at least a little. Writing to the French Duchess de Broglie in 1827 he described two of the actual Indians upon whom he based characters in *The Prairie*. "I knew Ongpatunga ... personally," Cooper wrote, "He was a chief of great dignity and celebrated for his eloquence. Peterlasharoo ... was also an acquaintance. This man would have been a hero in any civilized nation. He is the model of ... Hard Heart, the principle Indian character of the 'Prairie.' " At roughly the same time, he confessed to Charles Gosselin that while his description of the Sioux in *The Prairie* was "in the main correct enough," it was also "a little poetic, as it should be."[5]

In fact, Jared Sparks, himself a progenitor of the historical profession in the United States, had said nearly the same thing about Cooper's Indians as early as 1828, but Sparks pointed an accusatory finger. "The author," Sparks chided, "has been led into these extravagances by the authority of Mr. Heckewelder."[6]

The Mr. Heckewelder in question—John—was an English-born Moravian missionary. As a missionary, he came to spend a number of years living with or near the Delaware Indians who had been displaced from Pennsylvania into the Ohio territory in the late eighteenth century. After his return from the missionary field, he spent the last years of his life recording his experiences and the knowledge he had acquired, establishing himself as a nationally recognized expert on Indian customs and language. At the behest of the American Philosophical Society, he published "An Account of the History, Manners, and Customs of the Indian Nations Who Once Inhabited Pennsylvania and the Neighboring States." It appeared in 1819, four years before Cooper published *The Pioneers*, the first of the Leatherstocking tales, and it sealed Heckewelder's reputation as an expert on the topic of Indians—Sparks chose exactly right when he used the word "authority" to describe Heckewelder.

Heckewelder's "Account" remains a fascinating, remarkable work. For over 350 pages, Heckewelder describes for his readers all aspects of Indian life, at least as he observed them: Chapter 8, Education; Chapter 24, Food and Crockery; Chapter 37, Funerals; Chapter 41, Computation of Time.

The "Account" is also as partisan as it is thorough. Heckewelder had lived with the Lenape who had been displaced from eastern Pennsylvania and relocated in Ohio, and he wrote as their advocate. Taking sides in the war between the Iroquois and the Lenape, Heckewelder writes, "the former

. . . have, by their intercourse with the whites, become an industrious and somewhat civilised people . . . while the latter have always been oppressed and persecuted, disturbed and driven from place to place."

In Heckewelder's rendering, the Lenape become an exemplary, virtuous people. They treat their elders well: "There is no nation in the world who pay greater respect to old age than the American Indians." Husbands are just as attentive to their wives: "If a sick or pregnant woman longs for any article of food, be it what it may, and however difficult to be procured, the husband immediately sets out to endeavor to get it." Even on the charged subject of female labor, and the accusation that Indians treated women badly by making them work too hard, Heckewelder redeems their reputation: "There are many persons who believe, from the labour that they see the Indian women perform, that they are in a manner treated like slaves. These labours, indeed are hard, compared with the tasks that are imposed upon females in civilised society, but they are no more than their fair share, under every consideration and due allowance, of the hardships attendant on savage life." Indians even had a great sense of humor: "Genuine wit, which one would hardly expect to find in a savage people, is not infrequent among them."[7] Heckewelder had gone to the Ohio territory to proselytize among the Lenape. By the end of "An Account," it is not at all clear who had converted whom.

Heckewelder spends much time in the "Account" dispelling popularly circulating ideas about Indian "cruelty," citing even Columbus, among others, as having attested to their "kindness." Against these, he also enumerates numerous examples of white cruelty, concluding with an apologia: "I admit that the Indians have sometimes revenged, cruelly revenged, the accumulated wrongs which they have suffered from unprincipled white men; the love of revenge is a strong passion which their imperfect religious notions have not taught them to subdue."[8]

That Cooper, who himself had little personal experience with Native Americans, should have drawn so much of his material from Heckewelder's unstintingly positive description of the Lenape would probably have been enough to provoke many of his critics. Worse than this, Cooper may well have borrowed his ideas about Indian-white relations from Heckewelder as well. Heckewelder's explanation for the faults and vices the Indians clearly did have was as simple as it was damning: "All these nations and tribes," Heckewelder wrote in the introductory chapter, "by their intercourse with the white people have lost much of the honourable and virtuous qualities which they once possessed, and add to their vices and immorality." And he tacked on a further thought sure to gall readers in the new nation: "especially within the last forty years." He returned to this point toward the very end of the "Account," when he reiterated that much of what could be called Indian brutality occurred because "they have been excited by unprincipled white men."[9]

Heckewelder made these statements not as armchair speculation nor as ideologically driven polemic, but as the results of empirical observations he himself had made. He told his readers at the outset: "The sure way to obtain correct ideas, and a true knowledge of the character, customs, manners, etc. of the Indians . . . is to dwell among them for some time."[10] Heckewelder's conclusions came from his firsthand experiences, observations that formed a data base no other commentator on the subject could match. Here was *his* claim to authority.

That claim, however, underscored a central dilemma for the study of Native Americans. While many who did dwell on the subject agreed that more research needed to be done on Indians, it seemed frustratingly common that those who did that research came away with a more complicated, more sympathetic view of Indians, and conversely, a more outraged sense of how they had been treated by Euro-Americans. For many, like Heckewelder, empiricism crashed up against a popular dogmatism, and the result, for critics like Jared Sparks, was the depiction of Indians who were too good, and white settlers who were too bad. From the pages of the "Account," these Heckewelderian delusions clouded Cooper's vision as he wrote the *Leatherstocking Tales*.

Scholars have known for some time about Cooper's reliance on Heckewelder's work, and they have debated how Cooper used it and other kinds of sources in the construction of his fiction.[11] Without entering too deeply into those scholarly waters, I want to suggest that it was not simply Heckewelder's portrayal of the Delaware that intrigued Cooper. More profoundly than sympathetic descriptions and characterizations in Heckewelder's "Account," Cooper was drawn to Heckewelder in his self-appointed role as the Delaware's historian. Heckewelder wrote with a sense of history and of historical processes unfolding, a sense that resonated with Cooper.

We met Heckewelder the historian in chapter 1 and saw how he was driven by the familiar sense of imminent extinction. He lamented, "Alas! in a few years, perhaps, they will have entirely disappeared from the face of the earth." Heckewelder thus offered his "Account" as a historical record of those doomed to disappear, and himself as a historian on their behalf. As we quoted him earlier: "They have no historians among them . . . no convenient means of making their grievances known to a sympathizing world. Why, then, should not a white man, a Christian . . . plead their honest cause, and defend them as they would defend themselves?" Believing that the Lenape "have so much degenerated," since the period of their sustained encounters with whites, "that a delineation of their present character would bear no resemblance to what it was before," he offered a glimpse into their more perfect past: "It is therefore the history of early times, not of the present, that I have written."[12]

In sum, Heckewelder presented his readers in the early republic with a carefully drawn cultural portrait, based on his own researches, of a people he simultaneously acknowledged no longer really existed. The difference between his pristine Lenape and the shabby, threadbare people that anyone might observe themselves in the first quarter of the nineteenth century simply charted the distance the Lenape had traveled on a historical path of degradation and degeneracy. Their encounter with corrupting Euro-Americans had set them on that path, and once this historical process had been set in motion, it would grind forward with grim, predictable inevitability. Eden would be—indeed, had been—lost; the fall would be complete.

There is much here that resonates with the eschatology of the seventeenth and eighteenth centuries, and with the tradition of jeremiad—not surprisingly given Heckewelder's religious orientation. At the same time, however, it is this historical outlook with which Cooper sympathized. As he wrote in a letter to Sir Edward Waller, also included as part of Cooper's *Notions of the Americans*, "As a rule, the red man disappears before the superior moral and physical influence of the white."[13] It is this sense of historical process that drives the action in his *Leatherstocking Tales*.

In 1839 Cooper initiated a correspondence with historian George Bancroft. He introduced himself to Bancroft, "as a sort of historian myself, though in a very humble way."[14] Just what sort of historian warrants some consideration. Cooper did not write historical fiction, in the way we think of that genre today, so much as he attempted to write history in fictionalized form. As Susan Mizruchi has observed about American historical fiction, nineteenth-century historical fiction, and Cooper's work preeminently, needs to be seen as having a "metahistorical dimension," and as participating "in a cultural dialogue on how history should be viewed and written." In this sense, Cooper used literature as a way of exploring the nature and meaning of history, as a way of conceptualizing, rather than transcending, history, as William Kelly has put it. An anonymous reviewer in the *Edinburgh Review* in an essay on George Catlin saw a clear link between Cooper's historical project and that of the painter's. With Native Americans fast on their way to extinction, the reviewer wrote, all we will have left of them are "some histories of his race in the novels of Cooper, and the present descriptive volumes of Mr. Catlin."[15] At the same time, as several scholars have pointed out, it simplifies matters far too much to read the *Leatherstocking Tales* as a parable of triumphalist expansionism, of destiny manifesting itself as a weaker, historically doomed people make way for a conquering, superior one. Terence Martin has argued that Cooper was "ambivalent" about the westward expansion that he watched unfolding in the antebellum period. Similarly, as Michael Schnell has observed, Cooper did not believe that history "is unquestionably progress." Rather, Cooper saw history as operating cyclically, a "vestigially religious version of history," in Schnell's view. Nations rise, and nations fall as these cycles run their course. Thus Schnell reads Cooper's use of the frontier and of frontier characters not as "progress into a new age, but the repetition of an old age, not a hopeful break with the past, but a foreboding of coming repetitions of past catastrophes." Cooper, almost alone among observers of Thomas Cole's *The Course of Empire*, recognized its cyclical view of history and sympathized with its gloomy comment on contemporary American society.[16]

The engine driving these cycles, for Cooper and implicitly for Heckewelder as well, was the clash of cultures. As Schnell notes, Cooper was certainly not alone in believing that history was "a story of repetitive and inevitable ethnic conflict." That conflict, in turn, ruined what Cooper saw as the "utopian phase" of the historical cycle, "when society and nature achieve their optimum balance." Here, then, was the source of Cooper's ambivalence: the "triumph" of white progress over Indian savagery, inevitable though it was, also signaled the beginning a new phase in history's cycle, one that threw out of balance the relationship between society and nature. Victory in that battle with Indians may merely have foreshadowed a kind of historical defeat in Cooper's "vestigially religious" view of history, where "nations are saved or destroyed regardless of their deserts."[17] That same sense of historical process informs Heckewelder's study of the Lenape and explains why he chose to write about "the history of early times," rather than the present. In Heckewelder, Cooper found someone who saw history the same way he did.

Here, then, may be the deeper source of the critical complaints Sparks and others brought against Cooper's Indians. Cooper's sympathetically rendered Indians served as an important vehicle through which Cooper could comment upon the cyclical nature of history and could demonstrate that history was not simply an easy story of progress. Drawing from Heckewelder's tragic sense, Cooper included Indians in the process of American history and in so doing made American history something other than whiggishly triumphant.

HAD HE WRITTEN HIS "Account" twenty years later, Heckewelder might well have called it an ethnography. But, for Heckewelder, writing in the early years of the nineteenth century, the very word *ethnography* was unavailable. The term defined as "nation description" only migrated from German into English usage in the 1830s. So too did the related words *ethnographic* and *ethnographically*. The first record in English of the term "ethnology," with which ethnography would become inextricably linked, did not occur until 1842.

Having moved from Germany to England, the word *ethnography* and its cousins moved quickly across the Atlantic to the United States. By 1836, the American Philosophical Society had already established a "Committee on Ethnography," and in his report to that committee, Stephen DuPonceau defined the term for those who might not have heard it before: "Among the learned of America & Europe," he reported, "Ethnography is now classed as a separate science. It consists of the knowledge of the habits, manners & customs of the different nations of the Earth."[18] In this report, DuPonceau even recommended sending an "ethnographer" on a future APS expedition. Likewise, "ethnology" apparently began to circulate in the early 1840s, and it too found its way to the United States almost immediately.[19]

The point of this brief etymological excursion is to underscore that in the antebellum period, before the practice of ethnography had become established, no single textual form had a monopoly on how Indian cultures could be seriously and legitimately described. Missionaries, travelers, students of languages, and even novelists all might do so, and expect their work to be evaluated by other students of Native American cultures. Jared Sparks may have disagreed with the portrayal of Indians by Cooper and Heckewelder, but he felt the need to reckon with both in the pages of the *North American Review*.

Further, tracing the history of these words serves to remind us that before there could be a practice of ethnography, there had to be a word for it, and that the practice did not arrive fully formed on the scene as soon as the word had. In fact, it does not exaggerate too much to say that at one level the history of ethnography/ethnology in the second half of the nineteenth century is of codifying certain forms and rules, and in so doing establishing ethnography as the single authoritative way to describe native cultures in writing, displacing the other forms we have discussed.

James Clifford reminds us that ethnographic writing, indeed any kind of writing about other cultures, is invariably "complicated by the action of multiple subjectivities and political constraints beyond the control of the writer."[20] Clifford is most concerned with the creation of what he terms

"ethnographic authority." Heckewelder and his "Account" come closest perhaps to a "protoethnography." The list of topics he considers anticipates the
kind of subjects future ethnographers would attempt to describe. More
than that, intensive "fieldwork" and a working familiarity with native languages, which would number among the hallmarks of the professional
ethnographer in a later generation, lie at the heart of Heckewelder's work
and as we have already mentioned are central to establishing the authority
of his "Account."

By the turn of the twentieth century, the ethnographic genre had coalesced around a set of fundamentals. Among those Clifford identifies are
(1) field work and language competence, mentioned earlier; (2) an ethnographer both scientifically trained and personally heroic; (3) ethnographic
powers of observation that were almost preternaturally acute; (4) an ethnographer who tended to study a particular research question, usually by examining a particular societal institution; (5) an increasingly sophisticated
theoretical framework into which those observations were synthesized.[21]

The result, more often than not, wound up being curiously ironic. On
the one hand, ethnographers created a kind of immediacy for readers
through their texts—"You are there because I was there," as Clifford puts
it. At the same time, ethnographies tended to keep natives at a certain kind
of distance. Ethnographers borrowed the dry, often passive language of
science to describe their human subjects, and as a consequence the particularities of the humans under observation tended to vanish. Since ethnography's purpose was to elucidate large generalizations and abstractions, individuals became synecdoches.

Take, for example, the textual fate of the Pawnee.

In the 1830s, John Irving, Washington's less talented literary nephew,
went west to Pawnee country searching for the "real" Indians of his imagination. He found instead "straggling Indians, in the frontier towns" who
had "so degraded an air as to attract but little attention." Pages later, Irving
wonders, "where are the braves of the nation?" and answers his own question in Heckewelderian terms: "they have come within the blighting influence of the white man."[22] Across the two volumes of Irving's *Indian
Sketches: Taken during an Expedition to the Pawnee Tribes,* any encounter
between whites and Indians inevitably became cultural contests that Indians were bound to lose. Irving even spun a metaphor that underscored
that loss of balance between society and nature. As he comes to a clearing in
the woods, felled trees still on the ground, Irving spots a lone Indian: "Let
him look upon the forests and read his own fate; . . . alike they have lived
and flourished in the wilderness of nature, and alike they are disappearing

before the approach of civilization."[23] Civilization and destruction went hand in hand on the prairie.

And so it went in the antebellum period. *Indian Sketches: Taken during an Expedition to the Pawnee Tribes* was described by critic Philip Hone as one of so many books which "a New Yorker could read comfortably in the evening before a fireplace sitting in bath gown and slippers by his astral lamp."[24] Much of the writing that centered on Indians, whether the product of missionary work like Heckewelder's, fiction like Cooper's, or travelogues like Irving's, tried to make some historical sense of the events and situations it described and recorded. These authors did so, more or less, by conceiving of ethnic conflict between whites and Indians as the primary motive force in history, and of the cost of progress as the loss of a balance with nature. The preface to an 1888 edition of Irving's *Sketches* acknowledged that what the book described belonged to "that time" when the Pawnee "lived in their pristine simplicity"—a time when they remained "uncontaminated by the vices of lawless white men."

In 1880, nearly a half century after Irving went out west to find the Pawnee, John Dunbar described them for readers of the *Magazine of American History* in two articles. Gone, in these pieces, is any of the romance, emotion, and literary ambition Irving tried to infuse, however successfully, into his book. Gone too is any sense of personal voice—either of individual Pawnees or of Dunbar as the author. In its place, stiff, almost stilted descriptions of Dress, Lodges, Agriculture, Trade, Medicine, and several other themes. As Dunbar described his purpose: "The facts given have been carefully arranged with a double view; to specify such traits and usages as best mark them as a tribe, and also to afford data for comparing them as to their characteristic usages with other of the prominent Indian families of the country."[25] Hardly the stuff a New Yorker, or anyone else, might curl up beside the fire to read.

History as well vanished from the new ethnography. The final of Clifford's characteristics of ethnography was the synchronic snapshot, rather than "long-term historical inquiry." Ethnographic fieldwork, after all, might be an intensive experience, but it was generally, though not always, short. As a consequence, just as individual natives stood for entire groups, in ethnographic writing a particular moment in time came to stand for an entire society's history. Dunbar, after all, might well have used his observations to measure the Pawnee's change over time. He had several earlier sources upon which he could have drawn—Irving had seen the Pawnee, so had Lewis and Clarke even earlier. Instead, Dunbar skips over the nineteenth century, a period of rapid, intense change for the Pawnee, blithely writing, "the history of the tribe since the accession of the Louisiana may be passed over briefly."[26]

In passing over this history briefly, Dunbar includes almost no discussion of the interactions between the Pawnee and white America. These relationships, of course, had been at the core of Cooper's, Heckewelder's, and even Irving's writings. Whatever his literary sins, Cooper attempted to draw real Indian characters in his novels, and he used Heckewelder to do so. Those characters, in turn, participated in a great, if ultimately tragic, historical process, one that lay at the heart not simply of their own history but of American history writ large.

By contrast, Dunbar's ethnography, devoid of both individuals and history, put Pawnees at a social distance and at a temporal one as well. They emerge not as a current or present presence, but as a collection of "noteworthy features," a tribe existing in some ill-defined historical moment, without any immediacy for the readers of the *Magazine of American History.*

In an 1888 letter to Thomas Janvier, ethnographer Adolphe Bandelier complained: "it remains to show that Fenimore Cooper's Indian is a fraud. Understand me: I have nothing personal in view. Cooper has no more sincere admirer than I am, but the cigar-store man, and the statuesque Pocahontas . . . as they are paraded in literature and thus pervert the public conceptions about Indians—these I want to destroy."[27]

Such were the consequences of the new ethnographic authority.

EVEN AFTER THE CIVIL WAR, critics still debated the nature of Cooper's Indians. John Esten Cooke, writing in 1874, nearly twenty-five years after Cooper's death, felt the need to defend the author against the charge that his savages were somehow too noble.[28] By that time, however, Cooper's reputation was already in eclipse. It would vanish almost entirely from the American literary firmament with the publication of Mark Twain's essay "Fenimore Cooper's Literary Offenses," a witheringly funny indictment that charged Cooper, among other things, with violating fourteen out of the eighteen rules governing romantic fiction, including "that the personages in a tale shall be alive, except in the case of corpses, and that always the reader shall be able to tell the corpses from the others." It took many years for Cooper and his *Leatherstocking Tales* to recover from that.

Whether or not Cooper stands guilty of crimes against literature is something for literary critics to debate. Rather, the dismissal of Cooper and his Indians, which culminated with Twain, helps mark a crucial delineation. Cooper had used Indians in his fiction as a way of writing a certain kind of history. The emergence of ethnography as the genre of describing Native Americans contributed to their removal from the realm of history and into the realm of science. In the second half of the nineteenth century, ethnography became both an established practice and the only form of writing about Native Americans that had authority and legitimacy. Neither fiction with Indian characters, nor western travelogue, nor missionary reports—all of which continued to be written in great volume during the second half of the nineteenth century—could claim any longer to represent Native Americans with the "scientific" accuracy of the newer ethnography. More than that, through ethnography Indians were treated as scientific subjects, rather than historical ones.

Ethnology Ascendant

J. Barnard Davis called himself a "country fellow."

As two English learned societies—one called ethnological, the other anthropological—contemplated a merger, Davis complained about having to pay two membership fees, and about having to trudge into London for two different meetings. Naturally, he hoped these two groups would indeed merge.

Recognizing, perhaps, that his support for this union might sound cranky or merely cheap, Davis made his case to readers of London's *Anthropological Review* by sketching a history of the two words. Ethnology probably traced its use back to the French, he wrote in 1868, while anthropology originated in Germany with Blumenbach. No matter. Both, he insisted, really described the same pursuit—the scientific study of humankind—and the time had come to end the semantic parsing: "The science has acquired the denomination of *Anthropology* in every part of the continent, in America, and in Britain."[29]

In fact, events in England in the late 1860s had been presaged to some extent in the United States a quarter century earlier. Writing to Secretary of War W. L. Macy in 1846, Albert Gallatin felt the need to clarify things. "The modern appellation 'Ethnological,' " he explained, "has been substituted for that of 'Antiquarian.' " The confusion Gallatin hoped to resolve was over what the difference was between the American Antiquarian Society and the American Ethnological Society (AES), which had met for the first time in 1842, and of which Gallatin was a founding member. "The object of both," he told Secretary Macy, "is the same."[30]

As we shall see, however, the way in which anthropology supplanted ethnology as the label for the field and for the disciplinary home of those who studied Native American groups was not simply a matter of substituting one word for another in the interests of disciplinary clarity.[31] Just as the move from some genres of writing toward ethnography signaled a shift away from historical concerns, so too the replacement of ethnology with anthropology marked a move from a concern with the relationship between race, history, and the Bible, to a concern with culture and with theories of culture. Mr. Davis notwithstanding, the two proved not to be entirely synonymous.

SECRETARY MACY MIGHT HAVE been tempted to ask: why then bother to start another society? In fact, the two organizations did not have identical goals. As we have seen, while the Antiquarian Society wanted to focus its researches specifically on the natives of the United States, the Ethnological Society had even larger ambitions: "The object of this Society," so Article II of its founding charter reads, "shall comprise inquiries into the origin, progress and characteristics of the various races of man." And in case there was any ambiguity about the need for such an organization, members proudly proclaimed, "The ground marked out for the operations of the Society, is unoccupied by any institution in the United States."[32]

Ethnology was "the science of the age," according to Ephraim Squier, and the AES would be at the forefront of this new field of inquiry. Yet, if the AES distinguished itself as embarking on a new intellectual project, it was surely motivated by familiar-sounding nationalistic impulses. Indeed, the society itself as much as admitted to trying to keep up with developments in Europe. Part of its founding justification came because "the establishment of similar societies in England and France, shows the general sense of the importance of ethnological investigations." One writer, reviewing the first volume of the AES's *Transactions*, boasted that "in this department of literature our countrymen are not behind those of any country in Europe. Except," the writer had to concede, "the Germans." Squier was even more buoyant when he claimed, "it is a matter of just pride to know that America has furnished some of the most distinguished, if it may not indeed be claimed that she has furnished the greatest number." Ethnology was not only the science of the age, Squier went on, but "it is, and must continue to be . . . an *American* science."[33]

The AES made good on its promise to consider humankind in a comparative perspective when it published John Russell Bartlett's *The Progress of Ethnology* as an appendix to the second volume of its *Transactions*. Bartlett attempted a great, global synopsis of all that was then known about different groups. Beginning in North America, Bartlett took readers to South America, Africa, the "Eastern Archipelago," and Asia in under two hundred pages. In truth, however, the vast majority of the society's energies were spent in New World researches, for reasons we have seen before. Squier explained why ethnology must be an American science: "for nowhere else on the globe is afforded so wide and so favorable a field for researches of this nature."[34]

Squier was an enthusiastic convert to the "science of the age" and an active participant in the American Ethnological Society. He provides a link between the incipient field of archaeology and the newer ethnology. He and his archaeological partner presented to the Society in 1848, showing off some of their finds from the Ohio mounds, and the AES's *Transactions* underscored the connection between the two by suggesting that "for the extension of Ethnological Science . . . the explorations of Messrs Squier and Davis . . . should be extended to other portions of the country."[35] As one who moved between fields of study himself, Squier made as good an attempt as any at positioning this new ethnological science within its intellectual milieu. Ethnology, Squier wrote, is "the study of man in [a] comprehensive sense . . . the ultimate of all other sciences; it begins where the rest stop . . . the existence of Ethnology as a science presupposes a general high attainment in all other departments of knowledge."[36] Not simply a way to study human progress, ethnology itself, fittingly enough for the age, was predicated on that progress in the first place.

Still, as a definition of this new science Squier's remains a bit vague, and so we will turn to the Englishman James Cowles Prichard, president of the Ethnological Society of London, who in a speech in 1847 distinguished for his audience the difference between ethnology and natural history: "It is distinct from natural history, inasmuch as the object of its investigation is not *what is*, but *what has been*." To clarify, he added, "natural history is an account of the phenomena which nature at present displays . . . Ethnology refers to the past." Having rooted ethnology in the study of the past, Prichard made it absolutely clear what past: "Ethnology is the history of human races."[37]

We should pause to notice the two things Prichard has linked in his definition of ethnology: race and history. While Robert Bieder has argued that American ethnology developed "in sharp disagreement with certain European thinkers," Americans did share this concern with the history of human races.[38] In the 1830s and 1840s, race replaced nation as the translation of "ethnos," and determining the history of those races sat at the heart of the ethnological pursuit. Squier was more specific about why ethnology was destined to be an American science: "Within the boundaries of our own country *three* at least of the five grand divisions into which the human family is usually grouped, are fully represented."[39]

Here, then, begins the scientific study of race, and—it goes almost without saying—of the justification of racism by science. As we have discussed already in the first chapter, it is well known and well documented that the new racial scientists carried with them a priori assumptions about racial hierarchies, and about the superior and inferior races. Europeans were no better in their use of science to buttress racism, but in America these questions had a particular charge. After all, the United States might be home to "three at least" of the world's five races, but two of them had been enslaved or decimated by the third.

That the science of race developed in order to "prove" the racial inferiority of blacks and Indians there can be no doubt. Rather than review that sad and vicious scientific history, however, I want to turn to a related issue that made race central to the new ethnology.

It must have been a coup for the American Ethnological Society to feature in the second volume of its *Transactions* an essay by Samuel Morton. Morton, a Philadelphia physician, pioneered the field of anthropometry—the scientific measurement of the human skeleton—in the United States. More exactly, Morton measured skulls and their cranial capacity, filling them with mustard seed and lead shot, and he gave his first public lecture on the subject in 1830. When his *Crania Americana* appeared in 1839 it was recognized immediately as a scientific tour de force. In the course of his researches, Morton collected hundreds of skulls and probably examined many more. He wanted to compare skulls from all over the world, although this task proved complicated. As William Ruschenberger, of the Academy of Natural Sciences, wrote to Morton in 1833: "The difficulty in obtaining skulls is much greater than you would suppose, from the prejudice existing with sailors and even officers against anything of the kind being brought on board ship."[40] It comes as little surprise, therefore, that his frame of reference was American, and most of his work was done on Native American skulls. As he put it: "A primary object with me had been to compare the osteological conformation of our aboriginal tribes with each other, and also with the other races of men.[41] By the time he died in 1851, he had amassed a charnel of roughly seven hundred skulls, the majority of them from the New World.

His research seemed unimpeachable and his conclusions unarguable. There in countless charts and tables was the evidence to prove that the five human races—Morton identified the Caucasian, Mongolian, Malay, Amer-

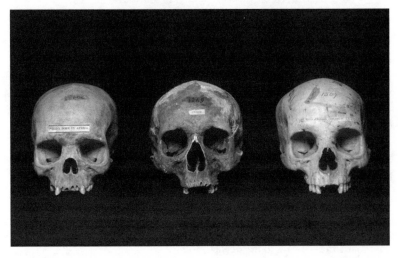

These are just three of the roughly 1,600 skulls that came to comprise the Morton Collection. Though they were assembled and studied in order to establish and prove hierarchies of racial superiority, the skulls remain a remarkable resource for the study of comparative anatomy, and are hauntingly beautiful as well. Courtesy of the University of Pennsylvania Museum of Archaeology and Anthropology.

ican and Negro—differed significantly in their brain capacity, and that Caucasians had the biggest brains underneath those noblest brows. These are Morton's most famous, or infamous, conclusions.[42]

Morton's work invariably intersected another nineteenth-century "science" of even lower repute: phrenology, and for that reason he had fallen from scientific grace long before Stephen J. Gould reexamined the skulls for his book *The Mismeasure of Man*. In response to a query about the "actual value" of Morton's research, Ales Hrdlicka, the curator of physical anthropology at the United States National Museum, wrote in 1911: "He started . . . on the premises of phrenology, which later in the century had to be abandoned as entirely groundless. This is about all, I believe, that can be said."

However, before dismissing phrenology entirely, we ought to remember the advice Morton received as he worked on *Crania Americana* from J. E. Doornek: "I think you ought to contemplate the most prominent manuals of phrenology as far as they ought to be considered to belong to and to form a part of physiological anthropology."[43] In this sense, physical anthropology in the United States had its origins in what we now call the pseudo-science of phrenology and to an even greater extent in the racialized work Morton did on Native American skulls.

But Morton was not only interested in establishing a racial hierarchy based on brain size. He wanted to use anatomy as a way of establishing the relationships between races across both time and space, to use anatomy to construct "the history of human races."

Squier briefly explained the theory upon which this history was predicated. "Except by interbreeding," he wrote, "the great races of men have *physiologically* retained their essential features from the earliest periods with which we are acquainted."[44] Skulls never change, and thus measuring those recently removed from their owners provides a transparent window onto the racial history "from the earliest periods." Morton too operated with this assumption, for example, in his examination of "upwards of four hundred American crania." These examinations led Morton "to regard all the American nations, excepting the Esquimaux, as people of one great race or group. . . . The Indian in all his numberless localities, is the same exterior man, and unlike the being of any other race." Having established that, Morton went on to weigh in on the question of who might have peopled the New World in the past. "Both Europeans and Asiatics may in former times have visited this continent," Morton conceded, but then challenged: "where are now these intrusive strangers?" The skulls revealed that "if they ever inhabited this continent, they have long since been swallowed up in the waves of a vast indigenous population, which, in its present physical characteristics, preserves no trace of exotic intermixture." Squier and Morton both used what we might see as a corollary to the "ethnographic present." Contemporary skulls could be used without any reservation or qualification to draw conclusions about members of races at any point in the past.

Those conclusions, in turn, led to an even more important one. "In other words," Morton explained, "I regard the American nations as the true *autochthones*, the primeval inhabitants of this vast continent." In saying this, Morton took sides in the debate that we touched on in chapter 1 between those who believed in the Adamic descent of all human beings, as described in the Bible—the monogenesists—and those who saw the different races as having each a separate origin—the polygenesists. Morton laid his cards on the scholarly table: "I believe [the different races] have originated from several, perhaps even from many pairs, which were adapted, from the beginning, to the varied localities they were designed to occupy."[45]

Morton did not hesitate to make the equation between the physical dimensions of his skulls and the mental and moral capacities of their owners. Not only were all Indians the same anatomically, but they shared essentially "the same moral and mental attributes." Squier, a tremendous admirer of Morton's, was well aware of these implications of ethnological research, and

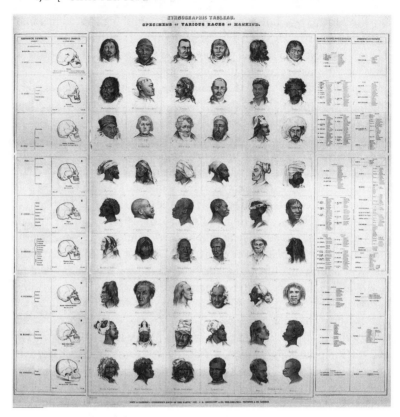

"Ethnographic Tableau," from Josiah Nott and George R. Glidden, *Indigenous Races of the Earth* (1857). This "tableau" distilled the mid-nineteenth-century connection between ethnography and the scientific study of race into a convenient, easily read chart. Courtesy of the Library Company of Philadelphia.

of how controversial they might be. Polygenesis, what Squier called "the doctrine of a diversity of origin in the human race," still resided on the margins of general acceptance, and "has yet so few open advocates" because it "is generally esteemed so radical a heresy that investigators . . . hesitate in pushing their researches to their ultimate result."[46] He was less confident about the connection between crania and morality. "Analogy," he offered, "would imply that, *psychically* the same law holds good." But, he went on, "if we assent to this, we must deny the power of mental development; deny that in his higher nature man is capable of infinite progression."[47] Racial science, as a part of the new ethnology, seemed to challenge both the notion of human progress, and the foundation of biblical history. No wonder scientists wanted to tread gingerly.

Ethnology, then, as it emerged in antebellum America, purported to be a scientific umbrella, covering a synthesis of old and new research, but largely addressing a familiar set of questions: who were the Native Americans, and how were they related to other peoples/races of the world; how long had they been on the continent, and where did they come from? Morton and his skulls stood as the most exciting new research on these topics, but he believed that his work only underscored the conclusions of others. All Indians constituted one great race not only because they were "linked by a common physiognomy and complexion" but also "by the structure of their languages and by their archaeological remains. . . . All point to one vast and singularly homogeneous race." And he finished his thought by reminding his readers that "when I speak of their being of one race or of one origin, I allude only to their indigenous relation to each other, as shown in all those attributes of mind and body which have been so amply illustrated by modern *Ethnography* [my emphasis]."[48]

As neat as you please, Morton tied together the study of language, archaeology, the incipient field of "physiological anthropology" based on his own work on skulls, and ethnography with an ethnological ribbon. By the mid-nineteenth century, then, ethnology did indeed seem to have triumphed as the "science of the age."

What's in a Name? Ethnology Becomes Anthropology

We can surmise that at just the moment—1868—when "country fellow" Bernard Davis complained about having to pay two sets of dues to keep up his interests in the scientific study of human beings, Ephraim Squier was stewing about something similar. By 1871 at any rate, Squier announced himself as the president of the newly formed Anthropological Institute of New York.

The American Ethnological Society, with which Squier had been so involved, did not survive the Civil War with anything like its original vitality or sense of purpose. While anthropology, he wrote, had "profound lessons" to teach "senators or kings," and was helping separate true religion from "ritualistic dogmatism," the former growing "all the loftier and purer from the dissociation," Squier thundered in the first issue of the Anthropological Institute's *Journal*: "To these grand results we may ask, 'What has The American Ethnological Society contributed?' Absolutely, for twenty years, nothing!" From the ashes of the Ethnological Society, Squier would raise the Anthropological Institute.[49]

As it turned out, the first volume of the *Journal* turned out to be the last, and the Institute did not have much of an active life. Its significance for us, therefore, lies not so much with what it accomplished as with the name Squier chose for it: "anthropological" rather than "ethnological." Although his institute did not last long, Squier correctly sensed a shift in the scientific winds. Anthropology, not ethnology, would be the science of the postwar age.[50]

Squier spent a fair bit of time in the *Journal*'s pages defining his new institute and in so doing trying to draw the boundaries that separated anthropology from ethnology. "The particular objects of this society," he began, "are the study of man in all his varieties." More specifically, he continued: "Its special object will be the study of the history, condition, and relations of the aboriginal inhabitants of America." He then went on to state that "the physical characteristics, religious conceptions, and systems of men, their mythology and traditions, their social, civil, and political organizations and institutions, their languages, literature, arts, and monuments, their modes of life and their customs are within the objects of the Institute."[51]

All of this sounds as familiar as it does ambitious. In fact, nothing here much distinguishes anthropology from the claims made for ethnology nearly a generation earlier. Several pages later, Squier conceded as much: "Anthropology, which is only a more comprehensive name for the Science of Man than Ethnology, has really risen to the rank of a recognized science."[52] Squier made no comment about the irony that ethnology had announced itself as a "comprehensive" way of studying human beings a generation earlier and was now being supplanted by a yet more comprehensive approach. Nor did he evince any bitterness that this turn toward anthropology represented a turn toward European intellectual developments, despite the nationalistic hopes that ethnology would be an American science.[53] But Squier was right that anthropology's disciplinary stock was rising.

In addition to reports on "Sculptured Rocks from Ohio," and on the "Indians of Oregon," that lone volume of the *Journal of the Anthropological Institute* also contained an essay by French anthropologist Paul Broca outlining "The Progress of Anthropology in Europe and America." Like Squier, Broca used his essay to attempt some differentiation between ethnology and anthropology. He reminded readers that "our science" had been subordinated to other studies like geology, philology, and paleontology, and that "it was impossible that anthropology should reach the present height before these auxiliary sciences had attained their maturity." This too, of course, reads almost exactly like the way Squier had described ethnology in the 1840s.

Broca went on. "Ethnology," he wrote, "studies man only as a member
. . . of races and peoples. Ethnography studies him besides, as one of the inhabitants of the earth . . . subject to the general laws which govern the whole
of nature." And here he pointed toward a crucial distinction between the
old science of humankind and the new: "While the stand-point of our studies is chiefly that of the natural history of man, that of the Ethnographical
Society is chiefly his psychology and history."[54]

It is worth pausing over that sentence and comparing it to Prichard's
definition of ethnology from a quarter of a century before. Prichard had insisted that ethnology should be "distinct" from natural history, while Broca
suggests that anthropology is synonymous with "the natural history of
man." As such, anthropology could make itself more "scientific" by borrowing the well-established intellectual apparatus of natural history, its classificatory schemes and terminology, and applying them to human groups. But
Prichard has also noted that "natural history is an account of the phenomena which nature at present displays," while both he and Broca agreed that
"Ethnology refers to the past." By extension, therefore, the anthropology
Broca defined for American readers concerned itself with what human
groups at "present display," not with their history.

Without making too much of Broca's essay, we can say that he anticipates an important implication in the shift from ethnology to anthropology
in the United States. The former arose as part of a larger fascination with the
historical questions posed by the very existence of Native Americans in the
antebellum period. The latter wanted to develop a more rigorous set of scientific frameworks and traded in that interest in historical issues in the bar-
gain. Ethnographers, in particular, worried about particularities; anthropologists reached for general theories. In the mid-nineteenth century, as
James Clifford has observed, those two enterprises, although related, remained distinct. By the end of the nineteenth century, they merged to form
a central core of anthropological research—ethnographic detail used as the
raw data upon which to build larger theories about human cultures and societies.[55]

Like all shifts of intellectual history, of course, this one was neither immediate nor complete. Ethnology continued and continues to be used as a
term to define certain kinds of studies and is sometimes used interchangeably with ethnography. In some quarters, as the nineteenth century wore
on, however, it did become almost entirely associated with the study of race,
which retained much scientific authority in some quarters, even as it grew
to become increasingly malodorous in others. This was certainly true in the
antebellum and Reconstruction South, where "proving" things about race

had a particular urgency. After Morton's death, Americans continued to measure every aspect of other human beings that could be measured with great enthusiasm, looking to prove everything from intellectual inferiority to criminal behavior. In 1852, for example, one Peter Browne attempt a classification of humans "by the hair and wool of their heads." Stephen Peet, editor of the *American Antiquarian,* reviewed the history of ethnology in 1885 in such a way as to make it seem only a science of measuring things. According to Peet, ethnology began with the study of (1) skin color, moved to (2) facial angles, to (3) face studied frontally, to (4) shape of the eyes, to (5) shape of the pelvis and the proportion of the limbs, to (6) shape of the skull, arriving finally at (7) the capacity of the skull.[56]

Indeed, it may well be the case that in some quarters "anthropology" became the preferred term precisely in order to steer the study of human beings away from race—the ethnos—and toward a broader, more generic man—anthropos. Henry C. Wright, for example, published *Anthropology; or the Science of Man* in 1850—an early use of the word in the United States. His purpose, however, was not so much to introduce a new science to readers, as to denounce the biblical defense of slavery. Only separated from race and slavery could the study of human beings move forward in any scientifically meaningful way, although in 1850 Wright for one was convinced that "the American Republic rushes to its destiny and will soon be numbered with the things that were. Thank God!"[57]

The republic did survive the catastrophe Wright predicted, and not too many years after it was over, the American Association for the Advancement of Science replaced the discussion of "Ethnology" in its *Proceedings* with a discussion of "Anthropology." In the postbellum world of science, all things concerning the study of humankind would be undertaken increasingly by anthropologists.

Anthropology at the Bureau of Ethnology

Late in 1887, Franz Boas wrote to John Wesley Powell from New York City about the formation of a new ethnological society. Powell wrote back asking, "May I be allowed to make a suggestion? In England and America the term ethnology is gradually being restricted to the study of the classification of peoples . . . while the term anthropology is being used by scholars as the proper name for the general science of mankind."[58]

Nothing in that modest semantic quibble seems remarkable—ironic perhaps given that Powell was then at the head of the federal Government's Bureau of Ethnology. Organized in 1879 (it would change its name to the Bureau of American Ethnology in 1892), the bureau stands as the most important institutionalization of ethnology as an autonomous endeavor at the very moment when anthropology was emerging as the broad, "general science of mankind."

As we have noted already, the general outline of the bureau's history has been well sketched and does not require much discussion here. Founded in the years following the Civil War as part of a larger reorganization of federal efforts to promote scientific research, the bureau looms as significantly as it does in the history of late nineteenth-century American science largely because of Powell's energy and zeal. Although he had desperately wanted to be named to head the new Geologic Survey (he would have to wait until 1881 when Clarence King stepped down), Powell took charge of the bureau, made it a dynamic research concern, and publicized its efforts widely. By the time his tenure at the bureau came to an end, Powell had made it one of the major centers of anthropological research in the country and made himself perhaps the most influential American anthropologist.

Powell brought to the bureau considerable experience in geology and related natural sciences. The world of nineteenth-century natural science in which Powell was steeped remained concerned with systematics—collection and classification. Just as plants or animals or rocks could be classified and grouped into rational arrangements, so Powell believed that the tribes of Native Americans could also be so ordered. If the bureau had an overarching agenda and purpose under Powell's leadership, that was it. As William McGee, who succeeded Powell, put it when he took over the bureau at the turn of the twentieth century: "The Bureau was instituted in 1879 largely for the purpose of devising a practical classification of the Indian tribes."[59]

For Powell, then, the scientific study of Native Americans—it was from the beginning really a Bureau of American Ethnology—was indeed a new branch of natural history. As Otis T. Mason, a curator at the United States National Museum, put it in an 1882 lecture, "Anthropology is the natural history of man in its widest sense."[60] What Powell needed, then, was a core around which to organize his classificatory system of native groups—a human analogy to the taxonomies that organized the plant and animal worlds.

As we have already discussed in chapter 3, he hit upon language and its use for classifying a language's speakers. From the publication of *Introduction to the Study of Indian Languages* (1877) to the release of his *Indian Linguistic Families* (1891) Powell made language study central to the bureau's mission of classifying American Indians.

Powell was not the only one who saw the connection between language and anthropology, of course. Horatio Hale called language the "true basis of anthropology," largely for two reasons: first, because he believed that it was "the only test of the affinities of races" and second, "its not less important position as the only sure test of the mental capacities of any race."[61] As we have seen, the connection between language and the study of Indians reaches back into the eighteenth century. Still, from his position as head of the Bureau of Ethnology, Powell did as much as anyone to make Native American linguistics a subset of anthropology. When anthropologist Clark Wissler wrote in 1943 that "the study of languages was the first major objective in anthropological research," he was in fact paying homage to Powell and acknowledging just how influential he had been.[62]

Powell contributed something else crucial to the development of anthropology, aside from the focus on language. From his post at the bureau, he helped impose a new rigor and system on those who actually did the fieldwork. Just as he worked to create a uniform orthography to record Indian languages, he wanted all his workers to gather information according to the same method. In this sense, Powell brought methodological rigor to the emerging discipline of anthropology, creating a real science out of a motley set of practices.

His attempts to professionalize what had up until then been a disparate collection of adventurers, missionaries and others met with the approval of one young and aspiring anthropologist. Franz Boas, who looked to Powell both as a teacher and as a possible sponsor, wrote in 1887: "I have read with interest your remarks on the requirements of an ethnologist and heartily concur with them. I believe they are acknowledged by all scientific ethnologists as the basis and elements of our science." Boas agreed with Powell on another point as well: "Your complaint of the deficient character of the work of most explorers is only too well founded." A year later, he wrote again—one senses almost seeking approval—to detail for Powell his own field methods.[63] These letters smack of the sycophant, as Boas tried mightily to win Powell's support for his own work, but they take on a greater significance when we remember Boas's own role in training the first generation of professional anthropologists in the United States.

Although Powell may largely be remembered now for his contributions to anthropology as an administrator, and for his work on Indian languages, he did fancy himself to be reaching toward grander anthropological theory. Above all, Powell believed in human progress, if not a version of human perfectibility. That progress resulted from what he described as "the exercise of human faculties in activities to increase happiness." These "anthropic" activities would be the focus of anthropology's work, distinguishing it from the study of humankind's "biotic" functions. Those "anthropic" functions had set human beings on a course of "cultural progress," even if "by steps so minute that it was left to modern science to discover it." In fact, Powell merely acknowledged what "civilized men have always recognized . . . that activities are teleologically developed, and that happiness is increased thereby."[64] That anthropological research had already proven this truth, or would do so in the future, was a distinction Powell probably would not have recognized. For Powell, anthropology served only as scientific reinforcement for what "civilized men have always recognized."

In 1881, Powell wrote a brief memorial sketch of Lewis Henry Morgan. In it, Powell spent some time lauding Morgan's contributions to anthropology, especially Morgan's 1870 book *Systems of Consanguinity and Affinity of the Human Family,* saying that it "marks a most important epoch in anthropologic research."[65]

It was a fitting gesture. Powell owed a great intellectual debt to Morgan and Morgan's ideas about human progress. As we have discussed earlier, Morgan conceptualized a set of stages through which human groups moved, although in some indeterminate chronology: savagery to barbarism to civilization. Morgan relied, as Idus Murphree has analyzed it, on the interpretation of a collection of traits—technology, governing institutions, property, and the family—to map groups on the ascending line of cultural progress. Morgan's theories married developments in geology, paleontology, and Darwinian evolution to human culture, and "made the development of culture a natural process embracing the whole family of man."[66] In this way, Morgan too believed in a kind of teleological progress for human kind, and he was convinced that those who had not yet reached the stage of civilization would ultimately arrive there.[67]

Morgan was central to the development of the anthropological idea of "primitive society," and Powell was certainly not alone in falling under his influence.[68] As his biographer Carl Resek describes, Morgan's Rochester home became a "clearing house for proposed and past research in ethnology." Frederic Ward Putnam, Otis T. Mason, and Horatio Hale all joined Powell in making pilgrimage trips to Rochester to talk with Morgan.[69] Morgan's publication in 1877 of his magnum opus *Ancient Society* sealed his place at the apex of American science, and in 1879, the year that Powell assumed leadership of the Bureau of Ethnology, Morgan was elected president of the American Association for the Advancement of Science. Looming as he did at the forefront of American ethnology, Morgan provided the theoretical frameworks in which a new generation of researchers would work in the last quarter of the nineteenth century.

As Curtis Hinsley has noted, Morgan's "legacy" to this generation was the tripartite classificatory scheme—a way to order humanity in categories—and the criteria by which to evaluate the categories in which different human groups belonged. Language worked wonderfully well to help with this classification because Powell and others believed that it was essentially a reflection of the stage of social evolution the speakers had reached. Here were the rudiments of a taxonomic system by which to arrange the American Indians.[70]

Hinsley is surely right to remark that this scheme—like so much nineteenth-century natural science—reflected a set of aesthetic considerations about neatness and order, and that the stages of social evolution dripped with Euro-centric cultural assumptions. More importantly for our considerations, following Morgan's lead, Powell moved the study of American Indians away from the parsing of racial types, which had consumed Morton and others, toward understanding Indians as living representatives of one particular stage of social development.

Yet, while Powell believed in human progress measured against some long event horizon, he saw Indians as largely static within their particular category, and the work he directed through the bureau reflected that predisposition. In this sense, to classify the Indians meant to remove them from what Hinsley calls "historical probings."[71] Powell himself thought a great deal about history and how it moved. Committed to an ever upward, ever onward view of progress, Powell railed against whatever remained of a cyclical view of history: "The course of human events is not an eternal round," he wrote in one essay. In another, he seemed to be arguing with his predecessors from the early republic when he wrote that the anthropologist "no longer looks into antiquity for human perfection, but he looks into the future of the world's history for the establishment of universal justice."[72] The Indians might get there yet, but Powell never said when or how.

WILLIAM DWIGHT WHITNEY, America's pioneering linguist, also wrote about "The Value of Linguistic Science to Ethnology." Yet, though Whitney and Powell shared research interests and though each admired the work of the other, Whitney had slightly different ideas about what the value of language to ethnology would prove to be. Whitney believed that only through language could ethnologists reach the elusive questions of culture—although he did not use the word in his essay: "Language is an outward picture of the internal life of a community; in it their capacities are exhibited, even their outward circumstances reflected." That much, at least, was

H. S. Poley, *Typical Ute, Chief Piah*, ca. 1894. As objects of ethnographic study, Indians no longer had the individuality that artists like Charles Bird King had tried to capture. They became specimens illustrating what was "typical." Courtesy Denver Public Library, Western History Collection.

consonant with other anthropologists who looked to language as a part of a "general science of mankind." But Whitney, much like his antebellum predecessors, continued to insist that language study "is a historical science." He went on to say that the study of language "alone can convert what would otherwise be a barren classification into something like a true history."[73]

Powell, of course, used language precisely for classification—although he might have bristled at the suggestion that the results were "barren"— and not for history. In helping to make linguistics a constituent part of the new anthropology, Powell also helped ensure that it would be an ahistorical, synchronic study. Anthropology, as it grew under Powell's guidance at the Bureau of American Ethnology, promoted, in Bruce Trigger's phrase, a "flat" view of native history.[74]

Indian languages, or more precisely the anthropological study of them, would tell no "true history."

The Museum Makes Anthropology

Looking back from the vantage point of 1890, Thomas Achelis thought 1868 marked the moment when "the term Anthropology . . . began to gain the rights of citizenship." This was the year, Achelis remarked, when the anthropologist Bastian took the helm of what was then called the ethnological department of the royal museums in Berlin.[75]

Whether or not 1868 is the right date in an etymological sense, Achelis made an astute observation. The post–Civil War period saw a proliferation of museums across the American urban landscape. Most were either museums of art or comprehensive museums of natural history, and it was in the latter that Native American objects usually found themselves on display. In fact, of course, Native American objects had been part of Charles Willson Peale's museum in early national Philadelphia, but this new era of museum building helped generate the collection and display of anthropological kinds of material on a whole new scale.

The ways in which the discipline rooted itself in this new generation of museums contributed to the success of anthropology in the debates over how to define the proper study of humankind during the latter half of the nineteenth century.[76] In turn, it was in these new museums that anthropology coalesced institutionally, as its four constituent parts came together under one roof to form a single field.

That the scientific study of Native Americans should find its institutional home in natural history museums comes as little surprise. We have already noticed that several of the important figures who made Native Americans their object of study—Powell preeminently among them—started out as natural scientists of one flavor or another. Likewise, nineteenth-century natural science was a museum-based enterprise as much as anything else, dependent as it was on the collection, classification, and careful study of specimens. With war still raging, Louis Agassiz, the nation's most celebrated naturalist, anticipated these museum developments in anthropology in a letter to Tom Cary. "Every day," the Swiss scientist wrote, "the History of Mankind is brought into more and more intimate connection with the Natural history of the Animal creation, and it is now indispensable that we should organize an extensive collection to illustrate the natural history of the uncivilized races."

Agassiz drew a line at once stark and simple: the "uncivilized races" belonged properly in the natural world and should be studied and displayed in that way. He went on to describe how human artifacts should be collected so as to turn them into natural history "specimens": "To make the most instructive collections relative to the natural history of mankind two classes of specimens should be brought together, one concerning the habits and pursuits of the races, the other concerning the physical constitution of the races themselves."[77] In his imagination, Agassiz has already joined two of anthropology's parts within a new museum collection: the objects associated with ethnology and the anatomical specimens associated with the study of race. Treating the study of humankind in this way, Agassiz proved prescient that anthropology would treat the "uncivilized races" as part of a natural history, a history conceived of differently from the history of civilized races.

Agassiz did not have to wait long nor look too far afield to see how museum developments might contribute to the study of humankind. Late in 1866, with a gift of $150,000, George Peabody endowed an institution at Harvard that would bear his name: The Peabody Museum of Archaeology and Ethnology. Fittingly enough, with a permanent building still under construction, the museum's first display, approximately fifty objects, occupied a case in Agassiz's own Museum of Comparative Anatomy, also at Harvard.

The terms of Peabody's gift made it clear that he envisioned a museum devoted to American research. Worried about the "gradual obliteration or destruction of the works and remains of the ancient races of this continent," Peabody hoped his museum would preserve some of these artifacts. He was also particularly interested in the question of human antiquity in the New World and instructed that "especial attention be given" to finds "of human remains or implements of an earlier geological period than the present."[78]

In 1872, in an act symbolic and symptomatic of the way intellectual boundaries were being redrawn, Agassiz transferred all the "ethnological and archaeological collections" from the Museum of Comparative Anatomy to the Peabody, although the latter still did not have its own facility.[79] That would have to wait until 1877, when the long-awaited, much-anticipated museum opened to the public. By the time those doors opened, the Peabody was in the charge of the man who would turn out to be its longest serving and probably most influential director, Frederic Ward Putnam.

We have briefly met Putnam earlier. His importance to the development of anthropology in the late nineteenth and early twentieth centuries
lies at least as much in his ability to shape institutional developments—
from Harvard's Peabody, to the World's Columbian Exposition, to the
American Museum of Natural History in New York—as in any of his particular researches. From his various institutional positions, he did as much
as anyone to create anthropology within the museum context.

Putnam too came to the scientific study of humankind after a training
in natural science. More than that, he had been a student of Louis Agassiz's.
As he told anthropology's father figure, Lewis Henry Morgan, in 1880, he
believed that his "zoological studies and methods of research" along with
the "work I had with Prof. [Jeffries] Wyman, both in human & general
anatomy have prepared me for my archaeological & ethnological research
in a better manner than if I had gone to them directly."[80] Putnam's career,
and his self-awareness of it, underscore that by the last quarter of the nineteenth century almost no one could conceive of studying "uncivilized
races" in anything other than natural history terms.

The building Putnam entered every day when he went to work was in-
scribed with the name: "Peabody Museum of American Archaeology and
Ethnology." Even as the stonecutters completed those letters, Putnam and
others were already referring to the Peabody as an anthropological institution. The 1877 *Annual Report* proudly claimed that the Peabody remained
"the only museum in America specially devoted to anthropology," a characterization Putnam echoed a few years later in a public lecture on "Archaeological Explorations by the Peabody Museum." As he said emphatically to
Morgan, he might not be "a student in zoology" any more, but "*I am one in
Anthropology.*"[81]

Putnam brought all the ideas of nineteenth-century systematic natural
science with him through the doors of the Peabody. He fretted, as all who
worked in museums then did, about the proper classification and arrangement of the objects in his care. Writing in 1881, and proud of his "new and
permanent cases," Putnam explained that objects had been arranged "to
show both their ethnological and archaeological bearings; the object of this
arrangement being to exhibit as far as possible the present condition of a
people, and to trace its history." Several years later, and nearly ten years after
the museum opened its doors, Putnam elaborated the principles behind the
Peabody's displays: "In their care and arrangement a natural classification
has been attempted, grouping together objects belonging to each people. By
this method is brought out the ethnological value of every object in the Mu-

seum." The goal here, he went on, was "so that in the mind of the student each is put into the great mosaic of human history."[82]

Ethnology provided our understanding of "present conditions," archaeology our understanding of past conditions. What we should notice is that the foundation for that "natural classification" of peoples was doubtless based on the linguistic researches we have examined earlier, and which reached one apex with Powell's classificatory tour de force in 1891. Language, it bears repeating, defined Native American tribes and marked their extent on the map, and in this sense, language joined the other three, more obviously object-based parts of anthropology—bones, archaeological artifacts, and ethnographic objects—in the museum.

At the same time, the history that the archaeological specimens displayed illustrated the broadly defined evolutionary categories pioneered first by the Danes, and then given an American spin by Morgan. (It is worth remembering that the Danish three-age system was worked out by Thomsen in a museum context.) This conception of history implied comparison, so that the artifacts taken as metonyms for the people who produced them could be measured against each other. George Peabody had instructed that the Peabody also collect such comparative material, and Putnam took this charge to heart. By the end of the nineteenth century, the Peabody's galleries offered visitors a number of opportunities to compare the cultural production of groups from North and South America, Europe, and even more far-flung places.[83]

In the Peabody's *Annual Report* for 1881, Putnam also proudly announced that the museum's library too had been rearranged to reflect the museum's conception of anthropology. The books could now found under "the four great divisions of Anthropology: archaeology, ethnology, philology, anatomy."[84] Thus, by the last quarter of the nineteenth century, anthropology's disparate parts had cohered inside the galleries and library of the Peabody Museum.

IN 1894 PUTNAM WROTE a letter to Morris K. Jesup, who ran the American Museum of Natural History and had hired Putnam to be the curator of the American Museum's Department of Ethnology. In the letter Putnam "respectfully" suggested "that the name of the department be changed from archaeology and Ethnology to Anthropology." He also proposed a visit: "It is my earnest desire that you should visit the Peabody Museum and thus better understand some of the plans I have made for the anthropology dept. of the American Museum."[85]

With his work at the Peabody, Putnam proved instrumental in defining anthropology as the umbrella study of human kind, and he made the Peabody the exemplary institution for that study. Putnam made, or thought he had made, the Peabody the model for all other museums to follow. What remained for him, as a restless, ambitious institution-builder, was to export his vision of anthropology around the country. And this he attempted, with varying degrees of success in New York, Chicago, and Berkeley.

In Chicago, of course, he was put in charge of organizing the anthropological displays and conferences at the 1893 World's Columbian Exposition, a task that occupied him for the better part of four years. Historian Robert Rydell has explored the anthropological side of this mammoth event in some detail, and his conclusions are worth reiterating. In addition to the formal displays in the anthropology building, Putnam also helped design the "anthropology" on display at the Midway Plaisance. There Putnam recruited groups of live Indians to be put on display. While Putnam assured people that the "presentation of native life [would be] in every way satisfactory and creditable to the native peoples, and no exhibition of a degrading or derogatory character will be permitted," he also made it clear that one intention of these live displays, less than four years removed from the massacre at Wounded Knee, would be to demonstrate to Indians "the material advantages which civilization brings to mankind." Apparently, degradation was in the eye of the beholder. Emma Sickles, one of Putnam's staff at the fair, objected to the way these Indians were being treated. In a letter of protest to the *New York Times,* she complained that Putnam's exhibit "has been used to work up sentiment against the Indian by showing that he is either savage or can be educated only by Government agencies." She was fired.[86]

While Putnam busied himself preparing for the great fair, he also began agitating among wealthy businessmen in Chicago for the creation of a grand, comprehensive museum of science. This, he told the audience at Chicago's Commercial Club in 1891, was an opportunity that "must not be lost. . . . For the city to longer remain without such a museum seems impossible."[87] Chicagoans, including Marshall Field, were persuaded, and thus the Field Museum of Natural History was born.

After the fair closed, Putnam attempted to shape the way anthropology would be institutionalized in the new Field Museum. He was quickly thwarted. Unable to negotiate his way through various institutional thickets, including relationships with key figures at the new University of Chicago, Putnam left Chicago in the spring of 1894. As he put it to his young protégé Franz Boas, "So I have wiped my hands of the whole Columbian

Interior of the Anthropological Building, World's Columbian Exposition, Chicago, 1893. The World's Fair in Chicago served as the grand coming-out party for the new discipline of anthropology, and it helped launch anthropological collections in natural history museums. This is some of what those millions of visitors saw. Courtesy of the Chicago Historical Society.

Museums business, which has been a dirty piece of work on the part of many."[88] The grass did not grow. By June he had taken the post of curator at the American Museum in New York.

In each of Putnam's attempts to build new institutions to support anthropology, he tried to graft the Peabody's definition of the field onto the local institutional circumstances. That definition began by putting linguistics, archaeology, ethnology, and physical anthropology underneath the heading of anthropology. Further, with its institutional basis in museums, Putnam's anthropology could be both studied and illustrated by comprehensive museum collections following the principles of natural history. Those collections, in turn, told the reassuring story of social evolutionary progress, while insisting both on the superiority of Western civilization and on the very great cultural distance between us and them.

Putnam described all this to his New York boss Morris Jesup in 1896: "A year ago we established the new department of Anthropology in order to illustrate the history of man in the same way as we are showing the history of animal life . . . we learn how the civilization of today has been developed from the primal arts and primitive aspirations. . . . Thus we are the better able to appreciate our achievements as a people, and to understand the cause of our failures as we struggle on, in our particular environment, for the higher development of man."[89] Under Putnam's influence, anthropology, the new study of humankind, became fully a part of the natural sciences, reflecting many of the assumptions and intellectual foundations of that field that developed during the nineteenth century. Looking back on twenty years of his own career as an archaeologist, he still credited his training with Agassiz as central to making a real science out of what had hitherto been mere theorizing.[90] A small irony, perhaps, that having started his career at the first and only museum devoted specifically to American archaeology and ethnology, Putnam should work so hard in New York and Chicago to make sure that anthropology was included in larger museums of natural history.[91]

Yet if Putnam's museum-based anthropology threw its arms around linguistics, physical anthropology, archaeology, and ethnology, it was less sure of its embrace of fine art. He insisted on drawing a line of distinction between anthropology and art. In a speech to the American Anthropological Association meeting in Berkeley, Putnam seemed to endorse the idea that a comprehensive archaeological and ethnological museum ought to include things usually considered art. Referring to the classical antiquities gathered by the expeditions sponsored by Phoebe Hearst and displayed in Berkeley's museum, he said approvingly that these were "just as much archaeology as the collection of Indian arrowheads and hatchets here. It is just the same." He went on: "A beautiful Greek statue should no more be thrown out of the anthropological museum than a tomahawk should be thrown out. The statue illustrates what one group has done, and the tomahawk what another has done. We must study them all." This comparative project—the ability to compare objects illustrating "the beginnings of things" in all countries—is what makes us "truly archaeologists or ethnologists."[92]

There may have been more than a little politicking in Putnam's applauding remarks about Phoebe Hearst's museum. He was, after all, trying to woo Hearst as a patron in order to put his own stamp of influence on developments at Berkeley (a flirtation that proved ultimately unsuccessful there). In any event, in a letter to Charles Bowditch, Putnam took a different position about the relationship between art objects and anthropological ones. He complained somewhat wearily: "Even here at Harvard it was a long time before I could make it apparent that a Museum of Anthropology was not a museum of art."[93]

Putnam's concern with the difference between anthropology and art struck at the core of the struggles over how this new discipline's boundaries would be drawn and over how it would be given visual representation in the galleries of museums. In an 1888 address, the Smithsonian's George Brown Goode noted that "as a matter of convenience museums are commonly classed into two groups—those of science and those of art." But, he suggested, that division was too simple and no longer reflected the increasingly complex ways in which knowledge was shifting. He went on to describe a space between science and art: "Between is a territory which no English word can adequately describe—which the Germans call Kulturgeschicte— the natural history of civilization, of man and his ideas and achievements." And suggesting an unmet opportunity for museum builders, he concluded: "The museums of science and art have not yet learned how to partition this territory."[94] With those remarks, Goode seemed to call for the creation of new, separate museums of anthropology—neither science nor art, but both, and something altogether different at the same time.

Having made that statement, Goode implied that Putnam's Peabody Museum had not occupied this elusive space between science and art, at least not in the way Goode envisioned it. In fact, for those, like Putnam, who were giving institutional shape to the field of anthropology in the late nineteenth century, the issue was whether Goode's Kulturgeschicte and their anthropology were really synonymous. The answer at Berkeley, and at the University of Pennsylvania's new museum, seemed to be an enthusiastic yes. Beautiful Greek statues, Indian tomahawks—all part of an expansive anthropology, "the natural history of civilization, of man and his ideas and achievements."

This tension between art and science was connected to the tension between Old World and New World archaeology that was felt at Penn's museum.[95] When the doors of Penn's new museum swung open to the public in 1899, visitors found material from both the world of classical antiquity and the contemporary "primitive" world. Statues and tomahawks—not to mention "ethnological objects of Asiatic origin; material from central and South America . . . and collections recently brought from Borneo and adjacent islands—were all on display.[96] Significantly, when it opened, the new museum bore the name: Free Museum of Science and Art.

Filling that territory mapped by George Brown Goode often proved contentious, at least at Penn. But the pettiness of these institutional squabbles masked larger issues at stake. The infighting at Penn reflected the larger struggles over how intellectual boundaries would be drawn. Would anthropology resemble Goode's broad idea of Kulturgeschicte? Or would it focus on the worlds of the "primitive," leaving beautiful statues and other such things to the art museums? Would it have a largely American focus, which implied the world of "science," or would it embrace the world, and by extension the category of "art"?

Even Putnam felt some of this pressure at the Peabody. By 1889, Putnam found the Peabody crowded by the collections of Harvard's as-yet-to-be-completed Semitic Museum. Late in the year, he wrote a polite, if slightly testy letter to President Eliot wondering just exactly when those things might be removed from his museum.[97]

Penn's museum, and its model of trying to encompass both science and art, were unusual. In the main, anthropology did not develop in this country into the kind of Kulturgeschicte that Goode described. Having grown from roots in the natural sciences, American anthropology stayed committed to science, rather than art, and anthropological collections grew, by and large, as part of larger museums of natural history at the turn of the twentieth century. Otis Mason, curator of ethnology at the United States National Museum, had to respond to this question in his 1895 annual report: "Give a list of the new Genera and Subgenera, Species and Subspecies described in the papers referred to in your bibliography." He did so by saying: "The Curator of the Department of Ethnology . . . has endeavored for some years, to insist upon the application and methods of natural history, in the description of Ethnographic specimens. It is his opinion that objects connected with human activities may be arranged into families, genera, species."[98]

In turn, collections of Greek and Roman material, of Egyptian and Near Eastern finds generally wound up in the large, comprehensive art museums built during this period. Putnam had succeeded in holding the line: museums of anthropology did not become museums of art.

The distinction between science and art also reinforced a distinction between those human groups, ancient or living, who had history and those who did not. The archaeology done in the Old World was allied to writing the history of those regions and of those civilizations. These expeditions, with their spectacular finds, established specific chronologies of rulers and events and fleshed out historical narratives that culminated with the contemporary West. Indeed, many departments of history included, and still do include, historians of the classical world—even some archaeologists. In this sense, the civilizations being uncovered in the Old World could be understood along the same historical time line as the modern West. Small wonder that their material productions came to be defined as art.

Modern "primitives," on the other hand, had "culture," anthropologically defined, rather than history. Thomas Achelis, musing on the relationship between history and the "science of ethnology" in 1890, saw it as a great
geography lesson: "Geographically, the earth would be thus divided between the two rival sciences. All of Oceania would fall to Ethnology; also
America before its contact with European civilization; and the greater part
of Africa; isolated parts of Asia; and Europe in the prehistoric period. All the
rest belongs to history."⁹⁹

Most of the world, therefore, existed not in the same time as the ancient
Roman and Greeks, but in some vaguer natural time. These people did indeed change over that time—from barbarism to savagery after all—but
without any temporal specificity. The stages of cultural development central to the new science of anthropology functioned as the human equiva-
lents of geologic ages. The cultural production of these people, whether
tomahawks or creation stories, could be of scientific importance, but because they were not rooted in the specifics of historical context, they could
not rise to the category of art.

Franz Boas and the End of the Beginning

In another report to Morris Jesup at the American Museum of Natural History, Frederic Ward Putnam reported enthusiastically on the local significance of the museum's Department of Anthropology: "The importance of
the Department in connection with the educational institutions of the City
is exemplified by Dr. Boas' position at Columbia University. . . . The question naturally arises if this connection with Columbia University should
not be in some way extended to the other colleges and educational institutions of New York. . . . With such a great Museum as this, rich at it is in many
of its departments, it would seem useless for the colleges of the city to maintain museums of their own."¹⁰⁰

Putnam's report underscores one of anthropology's triumphs. By the
1890s American anthropology had established itself institutionally in the
Bureau of American Ethnology and especially in several important museums. It had successfully established itself intellectually as the home of four
subfields: linguistics, ethnology, physical anthropology, and archaeology.
What held all this together was its subject matter: Native Americans.

Ironically, while the second of these culminations had depended on the
first, the institutional nexus in which anthropology had incubated would
not survive much past the 1890s. The intellectual foundations of American
anthropology proved eminently and easily portable. By the early years of
the twentieth century, the discipline had packed its bags and moved to new

digs in the departmental structure of American colleges and universities. Certainly, natural history museums continued to have anthropological divisions or sections, and several universities maintained lively and important museums. But in the main when Putnam imagined for Morris Jesup that the American Museum might be the engine for anthropology's growth at all of New York's educational institutions, he got the future of the field exactly backward.

By choosing to spend so much of his time shaping the institutionalization of anthropology at museums in Chicago and New York, Putnam seems to us to have been oblivious to one of the critical lessons of his work at Harvard. The Peabody, having been established before the term "anthropology" was even in much widespread use, served as the base from which the university's department would ultimately grow. As Roland Dixon put it when reviewing these developments at Harvard: "In most branches of knowledge that are pursued in Harvard University, laboratories, museums, and libraries are the outgrowth of teaching and research. In anthropology, the order is reversed." Obscured, perhaps, in Putnam's plain sight, the relationship between the Peabody and Harvard's department of anthropology, rough although it may have been, proved more seamless than at other places. Indeed, as Curtis Hinsley has pointed out, the history of anthropology at Harvard "stands actually alone, as an institutional model unreplicated."[101]

Putnam surely understood the importance of doctoral degrees in the professionalizing academic world. Harvard's anthropology department had produced more of them than any other single place by the early years of the twentieth century. Furthermore, Putnam's museum-based vision of anthropology seems to have meshed quite happily with the courses offered to undergraduates and graduate students. "General Anthropology," as it was offered at the end of the nineteenth century, included "Somatology (Physical Anthropology); Archaeology; Ethnology; Ethnography," and was taught in the "lecture room and laboratories of the Peabody Museum."[102]

Still, perhaps because of his own training and experiences, perhaps because his own intellectual world had been shaped by the assumptions of nineteenth-century natural science, Putnam seems not to have envisioned that anthropology, having coalesced in museums, would leave the museum world behind. Putnam reported proudly to Morris Jesup that Franz Boas was spreading the American Museum's influence by teaching courses at Columbia University. He does not seem to have recognized that Boas took the future of anthropology with him when he moved from Central Park West to

Morningside Heights. Anthropology in the twentieth century made its home in university departments, not in the halls of great museums.

Likewise, the Bureau of American Ethnology, the other institutional setting in which American anthropology formed in the last quarter of the nineteenth century, found itself increasingly anachronistic in the new world of research universities and academic departments. It granted no doctoral degrees, nor did it offer professorships, and while important work continued to be done under its auspices, the Bureau lost the centrality to the development of American anthropology it had once enjoyed. As Curtis Hinsley has noted, by the turn of the twentieth century, with the real intellectual action in anthropology moving to the university, the BAE, "child of a past world, was left without respectable program or purpose."[103]

The trajectory of Franz Boas's career in the United States traces almost perfectly the institutional path that anthropology took in the late nineteenth and early twentieth centuries. Indeed, it is fair to say that he had a great deal to do with shaping those changes. Boas's influence on the field is a twentieth-century phenomenon and outside the scope of this study.[104] A quick review of his career here, however, serves as a way of encapsulating many of the issues we have been discussing.

Early on, trying to find a foothold in the emerging science of anthropology, Boas sought the patronage and support of Major Powell and his bureau. Their relationship, to judge from their correspondence, remained cordial, if stiff, and Boas never established a long-term career with the Bureau of American Ethnology.

Some years after Powell's death, from his office at Columbia, Boas wrote to Smithsonian Secretary C. D. Walcott outlining his own thoughts about what had become of the bureau. "The development of the work of the Bureau," he offered, "has been very largely determined by two facts." Both revolved around the bureau's head and driving force, Major Powell: "it was his plan to present the whole field of American ethnology in a limited number of volumes dealing with particular aspects of the general problem. This plan was the outcome of the philosophic attitude of Major Powell," Boas believed, "who saw in the development of the American Indian an expression of the general laws of the evolution of society."

The other issue was Powell's commitment to "the creation of a number of Handbooks of the American Indian." The project of assembling this "general cyclopedia of Indian tribes" limited the scope of what the bureau did and "the question of the organization of field work for the purpose of an exhaustive study of the whole field . . . has never found adequate expression." Child of nineteenth-century natural science, Powell envisioned his Indian surveys much like his geologic ones, producing encyclopedic data on subjects that were essentially static.

But Powell had got it fundamentally wrong, Boas gently asserted. "With the recognition of the fact that ethnological phenomena are," he went on, "in the same way as geological or biological phenomena, the result of definite historical happenings, the general plan that Major Powell had in mind became untenable, and a breaking down of the definite aim that he had in mind may be observed as setting in at a period of not many years after the establishment of the Bureau."[105]

To suggest that the Bureau of American Ethnology had lost its course just a few years after it set out might simply have been Boas's sour grapes. But he was surely right that Powell made no room in his theories to consider "ethnological phenomena" as being caused by "definite historical happenings." In pointing this out, Boas underscored his own efforts to view cultures as having the capacity to change and adapt over time—to have, in other words, their own history. History and psychology, as Regna Darnell has observed, were the twin "hooks" upon which Boas hoped to hang the descriptive data collected by workers in the field.[106]

This recognition that cultures might change historically also meant that Boas could conceive of a future for Native Americans other than total and imminent extinction. Thus, he suggested to Secretary Walcott, the Bureau of American Ethnology might "contribute material of the greatest value" in helping deal with "the important problems relating to the modern needs of our aboriginal population, as well as of the races and peoples of modern immigration."[107] There might also have been a biting irony in these remarks. The very intellectual foundation of the bureau, as Boas well knew, had been laid upon the assumption that ethnology was not really central to contemporary social and political problems. It was established to save a thorough record of people about to drown in the onrushing tide of history.

Unable to make a career under Powell, Boas next turned to Putnam and to museum work. Here too, as is familiar to many, he found himself frustrated and thwarted. Chicago seems to have been unalterably hostile to his particular visions and ambitions; New York not much better.

More than this, Boas's own ideas about anthropology grew in the 1890s away from museum concerns. Just as Powell proved an imperfect mentor, so too Frederic Ward Putnam stands at the end, rather than at the beginning of an intellectual tradition. As Joan Mark has noted, Putnam represents a culmination of developments that had been percolating through the second half of the nineteenth century; he did not point the way toward the future of the discipline in the twentieth. And just like Powell, Putnam seemed unable to envision anthropology as anything more than the natural history of American Indians, as something "which might throw light on the problems of everyday society."[108]

Thus, Boas seems to have lost faith in the capacity for museum collections and displays to embody the study of anthropology. He became among the first to recognize that the visual language that anthropology tried to speak in museums, as David Jenkins has pointed out, "ultimately had less scientific efficacy than the visual languages developed, for example, in geology." As early as 1887, Boas was publicly complaining about the way most anthropological displays were put together, saying, "classification is not explanation."[109]

Though he wrote that in the context of a debate over museum practice, his contribution might well have stood for his critique of the entire anthropological enterprise as it matured both in museums and at the Bureau of American Ethnology. With its roots so thoroughly grounded in nineteenth-century natural history, anthropological classification was taken to be the highest goal of study. Restless to break out of these intellectual constrictions, Boas, by the early twentieth century, came to rest institutionally at the university. From his post at Columbia he exerted an enormous influence over the development of anthropology in universities around the country in the first half of the twentieth century.

Despite all the changes Boas did produce on the field of anthropology, however, he did not significantly alter the ahistorical outlook that developed in the last quarter of the nineteenth century. Nor did he manage to connect the study of anthropology with the study of history. In 1893, Boas presaged the idea of the "ethnographic present," the notion that in dealing with primitive peoples the past and present could inform one another seamlessly. Describing some of the anthropological exhibits at the World's Columbian Exposition, he wrote: "The meaning of the ethnographic specimens is made clearer by the presence of a small colony of Indians who live near their native habitations near the Anthropological building."[110]

Indeed, James Clifford sees the 1920s, by which point Boas was firmly ensconced as the nation's most influential anthropologist, as the period when the genre of ethnography based on participant observation crystallized and became a central part of academic anthropological training. That form of cultural description, equal parts literary and scientific text, was predicated on the notion of the "ethnographic present," the idea that the moment of fieldwork could stand in for any moment in the life of the people being studied. The assumption of this ethnographic present was that cultures did not change historically over time. As Clifford puts it: "To introduce long-term historical inquiry would have impossibly complicated the task of the new-style fieldwork. . . . It was all too easy to exclude diachronic processes as objects of fieldwork."[111] But perhaps it asks too much of Boas to have transcended the process by which Native Americans had been divorced from the study of history.

Otis Mason, a central figure in anthropology at the Smithsonian in the last quarter of the nineteenth century, drew the distinction between history and anthropology more starkly, though perhaps with less theoretical sophistication. "The historian regards the actions of men," he told readers of the *American Naturalist*, "so does the anthropologist." But, he went on, "the former pays most attention to the conduct of individuals, or the voluntary and incidental conduct of masses; while the latter scrutinizes those actions that are tribal, inherited; not so much what a people did, as what they did habitually; not so much what they are doing as what they are accustomed to do." In a lecture delivered two years later, Mason reiterated the point, if a bit tautologically: "Biography, as such, is not anthropology, unless it connotes generic data. History, the biography of political societies, is only anthropological so far as it is not merely biographical."[112]

We have seen the discussion of the relationship between biography and history before, and Mason has boiled it all down: those who exist in history have the individual identities that can be captured in biography, and they have agency, choice, and volition. Those who exist anthropologically are, quite literally here, creatures of habits. For the new anthropologists of the late nineteenth century, Indians did not exist as individual actors in historical dramas, nor did they emerge from the pages of ethnographies as individual characters of the sort Cooper had introduced to American readers only a few generations earlier. Rather, they had become undifferentiated parts of tribal groups and little more than the sum of the inherited patterns of their behavior.

IN THE MID-1930S Robert Lowie sat down to write *The History of Ethnological Theory*. Lowie was a student of Franz Boas and stands as an important member of the generation of anthropologists Boas launched upon the field in the early twentieth century. Published in 1937, the book's appearance underscores that ethnology still had some independent freedom of movement within anthropology's big tent.

Like many of his predecessors, however, Lowie felt a need to begin his *History* with a definition. "At times," he wrote, "ethnography shares its subject matter with literature, but," he chastened, "its attitude is distinct." The ethnographer, Lowie wrote, "renounces aesthetic impressions except as a by-product; he does not select his facts for literary effectiveness since his duty lies in depicting the whole of cultural reality."[113]

Many today, I suspect, would be skeptical that any amount of anthropological fieldwork—much less the relatively short durations that constituted ethnographic work in the early twentieth century—could successfully capture "the whole of cultural reality." That to one side, what strikes us here is that Lowie felt the need to draw a sharp distinction with literature. One hundred years, give or take, after the *Leatherstocking Tales* initiated the debate between ethnography and fiction, Lowie carries it on still. He was right, of course, by the time he wrote. Serious ethnographers, those trained professionally in university departments of anthropology, had largely given up "aesthetic impressions" although some, like Margaret Mead and Ruth Benedict, did achieve a remarkable "literary effectiveness." But as we have seen, history sat as the fault line between literature and ethnography. In Cooper's tales, Indians could have a role in the historical process; in the science of ethnography they did not. Lowie also reminds us that in the process of moving away from literature to anthropology across the course of the nineteenth century, Native Americans lost more than aesthetic consideration. They lost historical consideration as well.

6

NATIVE AMERICANS AND THE PROBLEM OF HISTORY, PART II

The continent is an open book; we can read in it not only history, but prehistory.

STEPHEN PEET, 1889

Early in 1908, Clarence Alvord wrote to Stephen Peet inviting him to join the Mississippi Valley Historical Association (MVHA). The MVHA had been founded the previous year to serve the professional interests of historians in the Midwest and South specifically and of American historians more generally (it would transmogrify into the Organization of American Historians in 1965).

Peet, who was nearing the end of his days, must have been flattered, at least a little, by the invitation. He had founded of the *American Antiquarian* in 1878 and had served as its editor ever since. Yet he felt slighted by the professionalizing world of archaeologists and anthropologists. He complained to W. H. Holmes in 1906, for example, that the Bureau of American Ethnology and the journal *The Anthropologist* had systematically ignored his work. Holmes's reply was less than generous.

So it must have come as some solace to be asked to join the MVHA. In his letter, Alvord described specifically why he had written: "The question of the Indians in the West and of the various mounds, etc., which they have left us, is one that should not be longer neglected." And he went on in a way that, by this point in our story, sounds thoroughly familiar: "It is strange how we Americans with our practical understanding have permitted those remarkable remains of a former civilization to pass away without any adequate study."[1]

In fact, the perplexities of Native America remained for scholars just as perplexing at the end of the nineteenth century as they had been one hundred years earlier. In 1890, Smithsonian scholar Thomas Wilson wrote to

George Brown Goode, the assistant secretary of the Smithsonian, about his own ambitions "to study and discover the origin of our Indian peoples, who were their ancestors, from what country and by what means and what way they came." That litany might well have been written in 1790. Despite the time, effort, and resources expended on pursuing just those questions during the nineteenth century, Wilson surveyed the field and found the scholarly soil "almost virgin."[2]

To judge from Wilson and Alvord, it would seem that the intellectual pursuits centered around Native Americans over the course of the nineteenth century had yielded little of any enduring interest, that they proved to be excursions down blind alleys, and were recognized as such. Looking back from our vantage point, that might well be true. Yet as I hope the preceding chapters have demonstrated, the study of Native America drove the development of several scholarly discourses, before it became the center around which anthropology coalesced. This represented a reorganization of both America's intellectual life and of the institutions that helped shape that life. In short, without those blind alleys the nation's intellectual life would have evolved differently than it did.

The emergence of anthropology as the only disciplinary home for the study of Native Americans represented as well a shift, as I also hope has been evident, in the framework which governed that research. That shift might be summarized, without too much damage, as one from the historical to the cultural. What had begun in the late eighteenth century as a quest to sort out the relationship between Native Americans and history ended by the end of the nineteenth century with largely ahistorical theories of social development.

Having looked then at how the historical dimensions of Native American linguistic, archaeological and anthropological research receded in importance during these years, we will end with a consideration of the place of Indians in nineteenth-century historical writing itself, concluding the story of the discipline's emergence that we began in chapter 1. As we will see, Indians were written out of the American historical narrative altogether. And yet at the same time, as we will also see, their absence was itself central to the construction of that narrative.

Native Americans and the Romance of History

In 1828, Jared Sparks reviewed books by Henry Schoolcraft and Henry Rawle in the pages of the *North American Review*. In this lengthy essay he had ample space for another attack on John Heckewelder for sympathizing too much with the Indians about whom he wrote. There was in Heckewelder's work "a spirit of credulity" which Sparks could not forgive. That spirit, Sparks went on, was "irreconcilable with the cautious deliberation of an historian."[3]

Condescending though his tone was, Sparks was in a position to make a distinction between historians and others, like Heckewelder, who professed to chronicle Indian history. A year earlier he had begun the task of editing the George Washington papers—a task that would prove a landmark of documentary history—and ten years after this essay appeared, Sparks assumed the McLean Professorship of ancient and modern history at Harvard University, thus becoming the first professor of history at an American institution. Sparks had a personal and professional stake in distinguishing what he did from what people like Heckewelder did.

Yet, the fact that Sparks should have reviewed both Schoolcraft and Rawle, and used that review to comment on Heckewelder besides, reminds us that the lines that came to separate history from ethnology and literature were just then being drawn. Sparks stands at the head of a line of historians who would shape the modern practice of history, help establish it as an autonomous discipline, and work to define what would be considered history proper and what would not be. Sharing its origins with ethnography as a literary genre, one "whose 'borders' were open to other forms of literature," in critic Stephen Bann's words, history developed in the early nineteenth century to be "the paradigmatic form of knowledge to which all others aspired."

That the modern practice of history grew as part of a set of impulses we call "Romanticism" has by now been well established by historians. According to Bann, Clio, muse of history, presided over the whole of the Romantic period, having "inevitably" superseded some of the other muses.[4] There is, of course, a long and rich scholarly debate over just what one means by Romanticism, and it is not my intention to sort it out here. We can borrow from the still-useful definition offered by literary critic Northrop Frye and define the romance as located between myth and naturalism, a place where myth is displaced in a human direction and where events themselves are conventionalized in an ideal direction. Furthermore, the narrative course of the romance can be charted as an ascent from lower to higher, where a hero, often on a personal quest, seeks and finds redemption and with it a happy ending. As Hayden White has elaborated: "It is a drama of the triumph of good over evil, of virtue over vice, of light over darkness, and of the ultimate transcendence of man over the world in which he was imprisoned by the Fall."[5]

The historians associated with the discipline's incipient period in the

United States—Sparks, George Bancroft, Francis Parkman, John Lothrop Motley, and William Prescott—are all almost invariably called "Romantic," and their work characterized as "romances." Some years ago, historian David Levin wrote of this era: "The historian was a romantic man of letters."[6] Though they wrote about different regions, different eras, and different events, they each shared the same larger project: to refashion the story of America as one of progress—romantic progress at that. Each believed that history revealed unmistakable patterns of human progress, and each believed in a kind of American exceptionalism, which saw that progress as rooted in this soil. These Romantic historians, as Levin puts it, "recorded the operation of a natural law, 'the inexorable law of Freedom and Progress.' " Or in Motley's words, as he addressed the New York Historical Society in 1868: "It is of Human Progress that I speak tonight. It is of Progress that I find a startling result when I survey the spectacle which the American Present displays....The law is Progress; the result Democracy."[7] In this sense, each wrote romantic history.

In telling the story of the New World as the progressive fulfillment of an almost providential mandate, American historians of the mid-nineteenth century did not merely reflect a larger cultural attitude. After all, these historians began to publish at a moment, as we have already discussed, when a cyclical theory of historical motion still lingered in certain quarters. Sparks began editing George Washington's papers the year after Cooper's *The Last of the Mohicans* appeared. And while Hayden White is surely right that a historian can achieve authority only with a public already predisposed to the particular rhetorical strategy she has employed,[8] I think it is reciprocally true that America's romantic historians helped to drive the shift away from the gloomy historical outlook of Cooper and Thomas Cole, and helped to reify progress as the American credo.

Native Americans, needless to say, had no place in the romance of American history. Here, then, lies the real source of the almost palpable irritation that one can still sense in Sparks's comments about Heckewelder. Sparks was offended not so much as a historian, but as a believer in this romantic history of America in which Indians could not register as actors or even as sympathetic figures.

The four historians chiefly associated with the romantic tradition of American historical writing—Bancroft, Prescott, Motley and Parkman—were staggeringly, humblingly prolific. Taken together, their histories run to thousands of pages. Part of their shared romanticism, as Robert Berkhofer has noted, was that none of them espoused the noble savage ideal when they dealt with Native Americans.[9] Of the four, however, Sparks's student Francis Parkman interests us primarily. In addition to being, along with Bancroft, the best-known of these four, his work most intersects with the questions we have been considering.

Born in 1823, Parkman enrolled at Harvard in 1840, and became one of Sparks's first students. When he graduated in 1844, after some time spent in Europe on tour, he composed an oration titled, fittingly enough, "Romance in America." In it, he began with a familiar theme of American cultural discourse: "The tourist in Europe finds the scenes of Nature polished by the hand of art" but "the American traveler is less fortunate."

But Parkman extended this commonplace critique of the American landscape and its lack of history to American history itself. That same traveler might "pause over the battle-fields of Saratoga or Bennington" but he will find "none of the romantic charm" of European sites. The great events of European history demonstrated great displays "of chivalry or of headlong passion," while the great event of American history—the Revolution—had been driven by "cool reason, not passion." He went on almost to complain about the nature of the Revolutionary War by elaborating on this comparison:

> When Napoleon placed his brother on the throne of Spain, the Spanish peasant sprang to the gun and the dagger and leaped on the invader with the blind fury of a tiger. The men of New England heard that they were taxed, called a meeting and voted resistance. Philanthropists may rejoice over the calm deliberation of such proceedings, but the poet has deep reason to lament.[10]

Independence declared by accountants.

There was romance in American history, Parkman told his fellow graduates, and it could be glimpsed in "the passes of our northern mountains" and in "the black depths of the woods, and listening to the plunge of the hidden torrent." Encounters with the American wilderness, with all its sublimity, brought back for our traveler "the stories of his nursery of Indian wars and massacres. A fearful romance invests all around him, for he associates it with those scenes of horror. And surely the early days of no nation could afford truer elements of romance."[11]

The romance here operates at two levels. Most conventionally, the opposition between passion and reason, between wilderness and a tamed landscape are familiar juxtapositions of romanticism. At the same time, however, those "scenes of horror" suggest the kind of struggles against nature, and the Indians as nature's agents, central to the identity of the romantic hero. Those kinds of struggles, rather than the dull fight against the British, strike Parkman as truly romantic because his audience also knew that the hero won his fight. The wilderness of New England had been tamed and conquered by New Englanders with a real sense of mission and daring. After all, their progeny, those overtaxed farmers, could only have met to vote for war because their romantic ancestors had triumphed in those earlier, more primal struggles.

Not content simply to lament that America no longer had the capacity for romance, Parkman left Boston to find it. In 1846, having spent his boyhood summers exactly like the imaginary traveler in his graduation oration, "in the forests chiefly between Maine and Canada," he journeyed west both to look for the history of that romantic encounter, and, as his biographer Wilbur Jacobs describes it, to recreate himself as that romantic hero. As he wrote to his parents from Missouri, "One season on the prairies will teach a man more than a half a dozen years in the settlements. There is no place on earth where he is thrown more completely on his own resources."[12] This trip provided the basis for Parkman's *The Oregon Trail,* which appeared in 1849, and his firsthand experience with both the territory and the people who inhabited it gave the book an added legitimacy.

Parkman is probably best remembered for his pioneering studies of the French empire in the New World and for his ideas about the triumph of Anglo-American Protestantism over French Catholicism as a motive force in that history. As he described it in a note to his fellow historian George Bancroft, "Your object is the opposite of mine. You trace the development of American independence, while I shall try to show the fall of French absolutism."[13] Perhaps we can see something significant in Parkman's focus. Rather than examine the events leading to independence, for him altogether without romantic passion, he chose instead to study that period when the romantic encounter with nature played itself out more obviously. As he recalled to Pierre Margry in 1878, through writing history, "I realized that these two preferences, books and the woods, could be reconciled, could even help one another, in the field of Franco-American history."[14]

When he went west, Parkman carried James Fenimore Cooper as part of his imaginative baggage. He admired Cooper's novels and his literary style. In particular, Parkman liked the "breathing men" that Cooper had created of his characters and the way nature played such a central role in the stories. Yet, as we discussed in the previous chapter, Cooper did not provide the literary emplotment for the romance that Parkman would come to write. Cooper's sense of history was closer to tragic than romantic. What enabled Parkman to shake the literary influence of Cooper, I believe, what

Frontispiece for Francis Parkman, *The California and Oregon Trail* (1849). This image, though not drawn by Parkman himself, conveyed to readers a pretty good sense of what the historian thought about Native Americans. Courtesy of the Library Company of Philadelphia.

allowed him to draw from the American experience of wilderness encounter the stuff of romance, was Parkman's treatment of Native Americans.

We have already seen in chapter 5 that Parkman's enthusiasm for Cooper's characters did not extend to his Indians, whom Parkman found "either superficially or falsely drawn." Early in his literary career, Parkman seems to have had ambitions of writing a full-scale history of the Native Americans, presumably to redress some of the errors he found in Cooper and elsewhere. He claimed in a letter to Orasmus Holmes in 1849 that "for some time past, I have entertained the plan of writing, at some future period, a general history of the Indians." He remembered this plan late in his life when he wrote to the abbé Henri-Raymond Casgrain. "I had a taste for the woods and the Indians. . . . At one time I thought of writing the history of the Indians," he told the Abbé, "but on reflection I preferred the French colonies."[15]

In fact, his brief experience with Native Americans—experience that Cooper, of course, did not have—seems to have left Parkman with thoroughly racist, if altogether mainstream, attitudes toward them. (Interestingly, his ugly portrayal of Indians has no counterpart in the writings of Bancroft or Prescott).[16] Writing to his friend Ephraim Squier to congratulate him on the publication of his own researches, Parkman wrote jocularly: it is "a document for which by the way, I owe you a grudge, as it kindled in me a burning desire to get among fevers and volcanoes, niggers, Indians and other outcasts of humanity, a restless fit which is apt to seize me at intervals and which you have unmercifully aggravated." In the midst of an 1875 review, he paused for "a word touching our recent Indian policy. To suppose that presents, blandishments, and kind treatment . . . can restrain these banditti from molesting travelers and settlers is a mistake. . . . The chief enemies of peace in the Indian country are the philanthropist, the politician, and the border ruffian."[17]

Parkman addressed himself to the question of the Indian squarely in the second major publication of his career, although perhaps not as squarely as he had originally intended. *The Conspiracy of Pontiac* came out in 1851 in two volumes.[18] As he prepared the book in his head, Parkman wrote to Lyman Draper, explaining, "I mean to write the history of the Indian War of '63–'64, in all its bearing, and especially as connected with the famous Ottawa chief *Pontiac*." In fact, Parkman went on, "my first idea was to make something like a biography of him," but he ultimately rejected that idea because "you know how meagre is the information that one gets concerning the life of an Indian chief."[19]

Historians are notoriously bad at explaining why things did not happen. With that said, however, it is worth speculating about Parkman's failure to produce a big volume on the history of Native America or even a biography of Pontiac. Biographies of Indian chiefs had been a popular genre in the early nineteenth century, as Lee Clark Mitchell reminds us, analogous to the enthusiasm for studio portraits like Charles Bird King's. At one level, we should take Parkman at his word. Like his teacher Jared Sparks to whom Parkman dedicated *Pontiac,* Parkman was a man of documents, and when he reminded Draper about the "meagre information" to be had regarding the lives of Indians, Parkman echoed many others who were, in this very period, defining the practice of history as an entirely documentary enterprise. As Brantz Mayer put it in the same year that *Pontiac* appeared, "Indian history, and especially Indian Biography must always resemble the pictorial sketches of the Indians themselves, who, by a few rude etchings on a rock, a few bold dashes on the skin of a buffalo, or scratches on the bark of a birch-tree, record the outline memoranda which may serve to recall an event though they can only commemorate a character by inferences."[20] Those who left no documentary trace, even significant figures like Pontiac, could never be the subject of a major historical book. They resided, therefore, outside the boundaries of history.

Similarly, in Parkman's admission that he could not undertake his original biography project, we can hear the foreshadowing of Otis Mason and the echo of C. S. Rafinesque, and their delineation of the place of biography in history. For Mason and other anthropologists, biography, with all that it implied of individuality and agency, belonged as a subset of history; anthropologists had no interest in or use for biographies of the people they studied because those people existed at the more abstract level of cultural generalization. In 1845, Parkman had already anticipated this divorce between biography and anthropology in the study of Native Americans.

Finally, it bears repeating, one suspects that beyond the documentary difficulties, Parkman did not pursue either a general history of Native Americans or a biography of Pontiac because neither, in the end, would have satisfied his romantic sensibilities. He conceived of both these projects early in his career, perhaps while he was still working out just how to tell the romance of American history he longed to tell. Indians clearly fascinated him, but in the end he rejected them as inappropriate subjects for history. They were foils for the Anglo-Americans, hurdles to be cleared in the marching of Anglo-American progress. What replaces Indian civilization—and French for that matter—is not simply another society doomed to rise and fall, but a better society, a more advanced civilization moving toward perfection.[21]

Ostensibly, the two-volume study Parkman did produce traces the frontier conflict between the confederacy of native groups led by Pontiac against the English settlers and military who moved into the areas previously occupied by the French. Those volumes stand as the first installment in Parkman's life work, which was chronicling the clash of French and English in the New World. He began, as it were, at the end, with the French defeated and the English left fighting Native groups. His work is filled with battles, forest scenes, and metaphors even thicker than the forest vegetation.

Yet before the reader even gets to the narrative of these events, Parkman spends the first chapter of *Pontiac* in an extraordinary—and undocumented, one might add ironically—attack on the Indian too much sentimentalized in American writing. This "Introductory" begins with a tribe-by-tribe sketch of groups who inhabited the Great Lakes region, including the Iroquois, Hurons, and Ojibwa. At the end of the chapter, however, Parkman turns away from specific tribes and toward the Indian in general. "Of the Indian character," he writes, "much has been written foolishly, and credulously believed." True, Parkman acknowledges, "his own inscrutable reserve" might make the Indian seem at first mysterious. "Yet to the eye of rational observation there is nothing unintelligible about him."

The rational observations Parkman then makes for his readers are thoroughly familiar: "He is full . . . of contradiction," Parkman tells us; "ambition, revenge, envy, jealousy, are his ruling passions," he goes on. While he does have "a wild love of liberty, an utter intolerance of control," and a "reverence to the sages and heroes of his tribe," these admirable traits "are overcast by much that is dark, cold, and sinister, by sleepless distrust, and rankling jealousy." He keeps his emotions behind a "veil of an iron self-control," but this "shallow mastery" serves only "to give dignity to public deliberation, and harmony to social life."

"His intellect," Parkman continues in case there might be any ambiguity, "is as peculiar as his moral organization." In all "savages the powers of perception preponderate over those of reason and analysis; but this is especially the case with the Indian." His intellectual curiosity, "abundantly active within its own narrow circle," is otherwise a "torpor" which cannot be roused. "The absence of reflection," Parkman says, "makes him grossly improvident, and unfits him for pursuing any complicated scheme of war or policy."

Having made these "rational observations," Parkman brings them all together in ominous conclusion: "Some races of men seem molded in wax, soft and melting. . . . Some races, like some metals, combine the greatest flexibility with the greatest strength. But the Indian is hewn out of a rock. You cannot change the form without destruction of the substance." This being true, and for Parkman there is no doubt, then it follows that "he will not learn the arts of civilization, and he and his forest must perish together. The stern, unchanging features of his mind excite our admiration, from their very immutability; and we look with deep interest on the fate of this irreclaimable son of the wilderness, the child who will not be weaned from the breast of his rugged mother."[22]

In fact, of course, even this Indian whom Parkman has just described no longer existed. "The imprisoned lion in the showman's cage," he writes in a telling analogy, "differs not more widely from the lord of the desert, than the beggarly frequenter of frontier garrisons and dramshops differs from the proud denizen of the woods." Only "in his native wilds" should the Indian "be seen and studied. Thus to depict him is the aim of the ensuing History," Parkman writes as he brings this chapter to a close.

Parkman may have traded on his travels out west and his brief time among the Pawnee and Sioux to give this dissection of Indian character its authority, but as we have seen already, much here is entirely retread.

Parkman simply repeated much of the opinion already circulating in mid-nineteenth century America. By placing this at the very beginning of his historical narrative, by using it to set up the action of 1763–1765, Parkman has accomplished several things.

First, he has used this introductory chapter to dispatch Cooper's Indians and with them any vestige of the "noble savage" tradition that might still linger in the literary or historical imagination of his readers. But beyond any literary jousting in which Parkman might have been engaged, the first chapter serves as something of an admonition to his readers not to sentimentalize the Indian characters who will traverse the coming pages. After all, whatever nobility might be exhibited by Indians is "overcast by much that is dark," even in a great leader like Pontiac. By deprecating all Indians in this way, Parkman reminds his readers from the outset that his real historical actors are French, English, and ultimately American.

Indians are at the center of the events Parkman recounts in *Pontiac*— indeed, they initiate the action that leads ultimately to their defeat. But their function in the book is precisely to rouse the English to complete the triumph that had begun with the defeat of the French. In this sense, Indians serve as elaborate plot complications, "involuntary agents of progress," as David Levin has called them.[23] This, in turn, may help explain the way Parkman treated the title character of his drama. Although it may be unfair to evaluate his historical accuracy from a distance of more than one hundred and fifty years, it does seem to be the case that Parkman largely invented the conspiracy he attributes to Pontiac. It is surely true that Pontiac led an attack against Fort Detroit, but the evidence Parkman cites that he tried to organize a larger confederacy against the British simply has not been substantiated by modern scholars.[24]

Perhaps Parkman had the evidentiary goods here, and they have simply been lost to subsequent historians. Or perhaps Parkman needed a worthy villain against whom his romantic heroes could wage battle, and so he re-created Pontiac in that image. The book ends, after all, with Pontiac killed by another Indian bribed with a barrel of whiskey, an orgy of fratricidal Native violence, and with the English trampling "with unceasing footsteps over his forgotten grave."[25]

Here was the most important way Parkman distinguished himself from Cooper and all his ambivalence about the course of American empire. In Cooper's novels, as Susan Scheckel has observed, the Indians never quite die, thus complicating the narrative of Anglo-American triumph.[26] Cooper's *The Pioneers* also ends with a graveside scene in which Mohegan and

Major Effingham have been buried side by side. It drips with a maudlin sentimentality, and Parkman has replaced it with an entirely different scene—one where the white men almost literally dance on the grave of a dead Indian.[27]

Most significantly, however, was the somewhat clumsy metaphor Parkman used to characterize the Indian "race." By saying that they have been made out of rock, he really insisted that Indians were incapable of changing. Without saying so directly, by sculpting Indians in immutable stone he has underscored for his readers that Indians do not operate in the flow of history. Parkman's history, after all, charts progressive change over time. In sum, as Harry Henderson has put it, while Parkman "could *conceive* of North American Indian life as a *Gestalt,* he had difficulty in dramatizing it as a cultural entity."[28]

Unable to change in any progressive way, these static Indians have one historical fate: extinction. Parkman said as much in his 1851 introduction to *Pontiac,* claiming that the eighteenth-century Indians he chronicles have been replaced with beggars and drunks. Nearly forty years later, in 1887, Parkman looked back on his own experiences with Indians and concluded: "the condition of things [the *Oregon Trail*] describes belong[s] wholly to the past. The life which I saw and shared has ceased forever."[29]

Parkman probably did not pause over the small inconsistency of logic revealed here by the juxtaposition of these two quotes: in 1851, he claimed that the kind of Indians who participated in the uprising of 1763 had already disappeared. In 1887, he claimed to have seen just this sort of Indian in his own travels, but *now* they had all vanished. No matter. Having located Indians outside the discourse of history, Parkman could not conceive of them in any other terms but extinction, even if he himself was a bit fuzzy about exactly when that might have happened.

And needless to say, the story of inevitable, fated extinction could not be the central plot of any romantic history. American history could be a romance only because Native Americans had been removed, not so much from the story as from history itself.

As it happens, when Parkman wrote *Pontiac* he had another version of the story on his shelf, a version told almost one hundred years earlier. An anonymously published 1766 play treated some of the same events. It was entitled *Ponteach: Or the Savages of America. A Tragedy.*[30]

PROGRESS BECAME THE AMERICAN faith by the middle of the nineteenth century. The past revealed it, and the future promised more of it, or so most Americans believed. Most, but not all. In a lecture delivered some time in 1878, Ely Parker offered his presumably progressive audience a different view.

Parker was himself a Seneca Indian, born in western New York in 1828, and his extraordinary life consisted of negotiating his two identities as Native American and American. He received a classical education through a missionary school, and became an important Seneca diplomat in their negotiations over treaty rights and obligations with Washington. He became a civil engineer after attending Rensselaer Polytechnic Institute, worked on the Erie Canal, and wound up as a superintendent of government projects in Galena, Illinois, where he befriended Army veteran Ulysses S. Grant. He enlisted with the Union army, wrote the final terms of Lee's surrender as an aide to Grant, and retired as a brigadier general. With Grant in the White House, Parker became the chief architect of the Peace Policy, and was appointed the commissioner of Indian affairs, the first Native American to hold the post.

Before he left New York to embark on this remarkable career, however, he came to the notice of Lewis Henry Morgan, who helped arrange his education. In return, Parker played the role of interlocutor for Morgan as he prepared his study of the Iroquois. It probably does not overstate the case to say that without Parker, Morgan's *League of the Iroquois* would not have been possible, and without that seminal book, American anthropology might not have developed as it did. Morgan recognized as much when he dedicated the 1851 book to Parker, acknowledging in doing so that "the materials [ ] are the fruit of our joint researches."

Before his audience in 1878, Parker described history from his Seneca point of view. He started, fittingly enough, with chronology: "They measured time by the seasons. . . . They never attempted accounting for extraordinary natural phenomenon . . . but were content to attribute all such things to the good will or malevolence of [the spirits]." This way of understanding history had been recognized and, as we have seen, dismissed by Euro-Americans. But Parker went on in a more haunting vein: "Even nations die out and peoples are disintegrated, but some other organizations spring into existence and take their place in the great family of nations. . . . The world moves and lives as it were in large and endless cycles."[31]

With his feet in both the Native and Euro-American worlds, Parker understood, if only intuitively, the implications for Native Americans of conceiving of history as romantic progress. Viewing the world as "endless cycles," Parker knew, might be a better way for Native Americans to hold on to some sense of themselves and their past.

The Prehistoric Revolution

In 1851, the very same year Parkman's two volumes on *Pontiac* came out, Scottish archaeologist Daniel Wilson published *The Archaeology and Prehistoric Annals of Scotland* in Edinburgh. "It was in that work," Wilson wrote to Frederic Ward Putnam thirty years later, "that the word 'Prehistoric' made its first appearance."[32] With that modest-sounding admission Wilson laid claim to the invention of prehistory, which must stand as one of the most remarkable conceptual developments of the nineteenth century.

Wilson deserves credit for his invention, as does anyone who coins a new phrase and with it names an entire field of study. People had been reaching to conceptualize the past beyond history for at least a generation. In fact, in an 1832 essay otherwise devoted to the "Influence of Ardent Spirits on the Condition of the North American Indians," Henry Schoolcraft paused to attempt a periodization of Native American history. He arrived at three: "1) The Allegoric and Fabulous Age 2) The Ante-Historical Period 3) The Period of Actual History."[33] Schoolcraft did not elaborate in the essay on what might distinguish the fabulous from the ante-historical, but we should acknowledge the attempt to create categories and periods to organize the history of these people who had proved so elusive to historians. Schoolcraft's term "ante-historical" did not catch on, but it underscores that if Wilson had not invented the prehistoric, someone else surely would have.

As scholars became increasingly liberated from biblical chronologies, it became easier to imagine some human time before history. And with the evidence mounting that humans had indeed existed long before any classical or biblical text recorded them, the need to label that time became imperative. As John Baldwin put it somewhat testily in his 1869 book *Prehistoric Nations*, "the authority of what is falsely called 'biblical' chronology is no longer very potent. . . . In all these attempts to construct systems of 'biblical' chronology, nothing is more apparent than utter lack of scientific method and purpose." Thomas Wilson sounded a bit more condescending when he wrote in 1892: "During the past eighteen hundred years the Christian and consequently the civilized world had . . . lived on in the belief that man's appearance on earth dated no more than 4,000 years."[34]

Still, the extent to which, after 1851, the use of the term proliferated is genuinely remarkable. American scholars latched on to it almost immediately, and it became the categorical catch basin into which Indians were put. By 1883, the National Museum in Washington had created a Department of Prehistoric Archaeology, with Charles Rau as its curator.[35] A decade later, the department assembled a display of 2,500 prehistoric objects for the world's fair in Madrid in 1892, thus giving this concept a tangible, objective reality.

But, as we have seen with other conceptual imports from Europe, Wilson's notion of the prehistoric did not fit the American situation quite so neatly as it did the European. Wilson left Scotland to take a position at the University of Toronto in 1853. In 1862 he published his two-volume *Prehistoric Man* as his attempt to apply his conception of prehistory to America.

In the eleven years between his book on Scotland and his book dealing with North America, Wilson recognized that the intellectual landscape had fundamentally changed: "It seems as if the whole comprehensive question of man's origin must be reopened. . . . Is [ ] civilization natural to man? Such questions involve the whole ethnological problem reopened by Lamarck, Agassiz, Darwin and others. Whence is man?" North America, which the Scot still referred to as the New World, only seemed to complicate these questions. "In all ways," he seemed to lament, "in its recoverable past, in its comprehensible present; in its conceivable future, the New World is a great mystery."[36]

Wilson also discovered, as several of the other scholars we have examined did, that applying European theories to the American continent could be problematic. "The age of bronze in the archaeological history of European civilization," Wilson pointed out, "symbolizes a transitional stage . . . through which the Old World passed in its progress." However, "the bronze period of the New World is the highest stage of its self-developed civilization." (Frenchman Louis Figuier had a similar problem trying to sort out the Stone, Bronze, and Iron ages in America, suggesting that "in the history of primitive man in North America we shall have to invent another age of special character; this is the *Age of Copper*.")[37]

Wilson's solution to these dilemmas involved a version of the "ethnographic analogy" we discussed in chapter 5. The present in the New World could be seen as the past in the Old World. "Turning from the history of the old world's infancy," Wilson wrote, "to the modern scenes of the new world, we seem to return to primeval times, and to witness anew the birth of human society." The primary interest, then, in studying the New World, at least for Wilson, lies in its illustration of the prehistory of Europe: "Guided by the disclosures of a New World just entering on the dawn of its historic life, may we not hope to read more clearly the traditions of ancient primitive history, and to recover new light wherewith to illuminate the Old World's prehistoric times?"[38] Though now a resident of the New World, Wilson saw the American prehistoric as of interest primarily because it could provide living illustration of Europe's now-vanished prehistoric ages.

Many agreed with Wilson on two propositions. First, all prehistoric societies looked approximately the same, progressed through the same stages, and demonstrated progress toward civilization. Second, modern Native Americans were prehistoric people, and thus studying them would provide insight into the long-vanished prehistory of the Old World. In an essay on "Early Man in America," W. Boyd Dawkins asserted that "the story of early man in America is a part of the greater story of the first appearance of man on the earth." He went on: "the hunter of the reindeer in the valley of the Delaware was the same kind of savage as the hunter of the reindeer on the banks of the Thames or the Seine." Stephen Peet agreed and believed that "we can find in the pre-historic records a description of the growth of society and the advancement of mankind which, we think, is applicable not only to this continent but to other continents as well." This use of ethnographic analogy to illuminate the past by looking at the present could be taken to the absurd by at least some Europeans. In 1889, Otis Mason, writing from the Congress of Prehistoric Archaeology and Anthropology in Paris, complained to George Brown Goode that the United States had been represented by Buffalo Bill's Wild West show: "On Monday the bill of fare was Buffalo Bill and his savages. We did not go to the wild west, but the wild west kindly came to the Ecole de France."[39]

For other Americans, however, American prehistory held just as much promise as ammunition in the cultural battles of independence still being fought against the Europeans. Here might be the way to demonstrate that the New World was not so new after all, and thus deserved more respect. As Peet put it at the beginning of his multivolume *Prehistoric America*: "America is called the New World, and so it is for it is newly discovered. Our claim, however, is that America is also an old world, and compares well with other countries in this respect."[40]

Thomas Wilson, who succeeded Charles Rau as curator of the Department of Prehistoric Archaeology, was quite upset that the study of prehistory "has not attained to that dignity and importance as a science as it has in Europe." This despite the fact that "the knowledge of prehistoric man began on this continent several hundred years before it did in Europe," since Europeans had actually encountered prehistoric people in the New World. Just as Americans saw themselves as perfectly positioned to pioneer the study of languages and of archaeology, so too the study of prehistory seemed another great scholarly opportunity lost to the Europeans. W. S. Blacket raised this nationalistic flag in more histrionic tones on the very first page of his 1884 book:

America is a great country. . . .Yet this great country, in the literature of the world, is destitute of history. In the historical antiquities of the human race, it is a blank—an absolute blank. . . . In books on ancient history America has no chapter. . . . Ancient America is a nonentity—an hiatus—a vast terra incognita, in the Geography of the Old World.[41]

Americans too felt acutely what Stephen Bann has called the nineteenth century's "desire for history"—or at least prehistory—and Mason recognized that "all Europe will ever know of [Native Americans] will be what we tell her."

That desire for history, as Bann and others have charted, grew alongside nineteenth-century nationalism. Nations needed history, after all, to establish their very legitimacy. The importance of prehistory for this project was to extend this nationalistic past, especially in northern European countries, to compete, as it were, with the classical past. Wilson claimed, in the second edition of *Prehistoric Annals*, that his purpose in writing the book had been "to rescue archaeological research from that limited range to which a too exclusive devotion to classical studies had given rise."[42] By linking his neologism with the word "annals," a word usually used in connection with historical writings, Wilson clearly intended his notion of prehistory to extend the conception of history backward in time and hoped that the former would be embraced by the latter. In the European context, this proved successful. Prehistory served as the category into which to put the archaeological evidence of the three ages. It represented a seamless connection between that past and the more recent, documented, historical past.

In the United States at least, matters did not turn out quite that way. When he turned his attentions to North America, Wilson believed that the "discovery" of prehistoric Americans, which began in 1492, admitted "into the great family of nations" those who, "isolated and apart, had through unnumbered generations enacted the drama of history."[43] Yet despite pleas like this to use prehistoric researches to expand the history of the North American continent to something like European dimensions—to include Indians as part of "the great family of nations"—those who studied American prehistory did so in a way that underscored the separation between Euro-Americans and Native, between those with history and those without.

The lack of chronology and the absence of any specificity of time distinguished prehistory from history, and in this sense prehistory reinforced the perception that Native Americans lived outside the flow of historical time. Rather, they developed through cultural stages. As Otis Mason put it, "when grade, or stage of culture, is the concept, the word 'prehistoric' does not refer to time at all."[44]

Further, the belief that Native Americans represented living examples of prehistory created some chronometric confusion, if not outright dissonance. Curator Wilson, echoing others we have just heard, wrote in an essay that "the white man on arriving beheld prehistoric man face to face."[45] Thrilling as the prospect of staring at the past must have been to people like Wilson, it posed a real dilemma for anyone who paused to think about it. Did these Indians cease to be "prehistoric"—before history—once Europeans arrived on the continent, bringing history with them? Could two different human clocks run simultaneously, one measuring historical time, the other marking stages of cultural development? If Western history, synonymous in this era with Western progress, was to triumph over the prehistoric, could Indians ever become part of that history? Social theorist George Fellows saw the problem in 1895: "If extermination can no longer be tolerated," he wrote in the *American Journal of Sociology*, "then the savage peoples must in the march of progress be brought closer to each other [so that] their development could proceed in the line of nature, but with the assistance of contact with those who had already made great advances."[46] On the one hand, development "in the line of nature"; on the other, the assistance of those moving in historical time.

In the last part of the nineteenth century, the answer to these questions was, essentially, no. Native Americans were being written out of the romantic narrative of American history at the very same moment when their study became the sole purview of a largely ahistorical anthropology. Their status as prehistoric—and many argued that they occupied the lowest rung of that particular ladder—demonstrated ipso facto their inability to be progressive, which meant, ipso facto, that they did not conform to the "law" of progressive history.

Finally, there might still be considerable debate among archaeologists and anthropologists about the relationship between present-day Indians and prehistoric peoples, but there was certainly no question about the relationship between Native Americans and Euro-Americans. "We of to-day," one writer put it, "have no filial interest in the man of Natchez [an important mid-century find]. He was no ancestor of ours nor have he and his descendant left traces along the dreary track of their existence to induce a desire to claim relationship with them. We are Americans."[47]

That writer was historian John Lothrop Motley.

While some archaeologists and anthropologists might believe, like

Thomas Wilson, that prehistoric artifacts "are at once the text of history as well as its illustrations," or, like Otis Mason, that prehistoric history is "a story written in things,"[48] those who owned the past by the mid-nineteenth century—not the winners so much as the writers—drew the line quite clearly. The history of prehistoric North America had no connection with the history of postcontact North America. Unlike in Europe, where the concept of prehistory enabled Britons or Danes to see the origins of their nationhood reaching back well past the era of recorded documents, prehistory in the United States helped wall off the history of Native Americans from the history of Euro-Americans.

Two clocks could surely not share the same continental mantelpiece, and this may help us complete the answer to the question of extinction we raised in chapter 1. As we saw, virtually everyone who studied the question concluded that Indians teetered on the brink of extinction—it became almost a leitmotif of nineteenth-century writings about Indians. But these writers and scholars were surely not so daft or blind as to have ignored that Indians were not dying out, literally, nor were they going to be exterminated, like the bison or the passenger pigeon.

Instead, I think, they observed and lamented the extinction of this prehistoric Indian. Trapped by the category of prehistory and its developmental stages, many white Americans, like Francis Parkman, could not conceive of Native Americans in any other terms. Unable to imagine Indians as within the boundaries of history, white Americans could not register the possibility of Native cultural change or adaptation. Indians were prehistoric; with the loss of their prehistoric characteristics, they simply ceased being Indians. And whatever humanitarian impulses might have been behind the laments of American writers on this topic, they mourned too their own loss of the opportunity to confront the past face to face.

In the New World context, the concept of prehistory helped ensure that American history quite literally began in 1492.

Native Americans and the Science of History

"History," announced John Wesley Powell, "is no longer a field for literary exploitation. It is fast becoming a science."

Although it may have been presumptuous for this geologist-turned-anthropologist to make such pronouncements about the state of historical scholarship, he largely echoed a consensus that the literary and the scientific lay at opposite ends of the intellectual spectrum—the former, hopelessly subjective, and feminine; the latter, objective, rigorous, and hardheaded. Whereas in 1853, Samuel Goodrich could write "history at the present day is regarded as a very important brand of polite literature," in 1890, the same year that Powell wrote, Justin Winsor sneered, "The treatment of the historical narrative by a mere *litterateur* is almost as bad as that by a mere philosopher." When Carl Becker entered graduate school in history in 1896 he observed that, "the old union between history and literature is now broken in all the growing colleges." Powell, then, only expressed the confident sense that history, like so much else in late-nineteenth-century American life, had become "scientific." The scientist replaced the man of letters writing history, and as historian James Rhodes put it in 1899, "even as a chemist and physicist, we talk of practice in the laboratory."[49]

More than anyone else, Herbert Baxter Adams tried to make American history in this scientific image. Adams's story is familiar to most students of history's history. After graduating from Amherst College at the top of his class, Adams went to Germany, where he joined a growing number of American students who sought in Germany the cutting edge of higher education. He attended several universities, he took his doctorate from Heidelberg in 1876, and returned to the United States immediately to accept a postdoctoral fellowship at the newly created Johns Hopkins University. He remained there until his death in 1901, moving through the academic ranks to become a full professor.[50]

With his German Ph.D. and his position at the nation's first modern research university, Adams was in the vanguard of academic professionalization, and he shaped the development of the profession in the last quarter of the nineteenth century in two critical ways. First, he played a central role in establishing the American Historical Association, which came into being in 1884 complete with a federal charter, which Adams had arranged. Proper disciplines needed disciplinary organizations, and Adams ensured that historians, no less than chemists or physicists, would have one. Second, he brought to Hopkins the German seminar methods of historical study, training a generation of American historians and placing them in colleges and universities around the country, where they would establish "colonies" of Hopkins, as Adams put it a bit imperially. In those seminars, students learned how to study history scientifically. "The Baltimore seminaries," he famously wrote, "are laboratories where books are treated like mineralogical specimens, passed from hand to hand, examined and tested."[51]

Adams had an agenda to go with his method. In Germany, he had become enamored of the Teutonic germ theory of historical development. Upon returning to the United States, he pursued these germs as they sprouted in local communities. This, Baxter believed, would explain how European institutions crossed the Atlantic and established themselves anew in America. He sent his students to examine local history to trace these lines of influence.

At one level, the scientists of the American historical profession reacted against their Romantic forebears. Positivism replaced the pictorial qualities of historical writing; cold fact replaced romantic presupposition. "In presenting situations," as John Higham has described these historical scientists, "they endeavored to stand apart, observing from the outside."[52] Unlike Parkman, Adams did not cast himself as his own romantic hero.

At another level, however, there remained a deep continuity between the Romantics and the scientists. The scientific historians might shy away from the use of providential explanations, as Dorothy Ross has noted, but they still told a story of national progress and triumph. The evidence, and the way that evidence was used by these new historians, might have changed, but the narrative of American history remained "a pattern of age-old, unchanging principle."[53] As if to acknowledge these continuities, Adams became the biographer of Jared Sparks. That turned out to be Adams's largest scholarly project.

On the wall of his seminar "lab" at Hopkins, Adams hung the aphorism he borrowed from English historian Edward Freeman: "History is Past Politics and Politics Present History." For Adams, history was really synonymous with the political history of the nation, and although his interest in institutional history may have extended to include the church, his chief interest, as Bert Loewenberg observed, lay with political institutions, "and then only selected political institutions."[54]

It hardly needs saying that Native Americans did not occupy much of Adams's attention. Indians, after all, contained no Teutonic germs, nor had they much to offer in the way of political institutions. But we should underscore that the kind of history Adams pursued—absent as it was of much consideration of Native Americans—became the ideal and the practice of that first generation of professionalized American historians. Adams himself made sure of it. This absence too the scientists shared with the romantics.

We should note as well what must surely be a historical coincidence, however pregnant it might be. Five years before Adams began his career at Hopkins, the United States Congress passed legislation forbidding the president to negotiate any new treaties with Indian groups. Treaties, after all, are concluded between sovereign nations, and after 1871 the Federal government no longer regarded Indian tribes as such. At the moment, then, when Adams and his scholarly progeny were making a science of studying the American nation, Congress made certain that there would only be one rec-

The historian as scientist. Johns Hopkins University professor Herbert Baxter Adams sitting (center) in his famous seminar room, surrounded by the history department's class of 1890. If "history is past politics," then Indians had no real history. Courtesy of the Ferdinand Hamburger Archives, John Hopkins University.

ognized nation within the borders of the United States. Just as those without written records could have no history, so too those without a nation could not be part of history's march.

Finally, and ironically, Adams went to work at Hopkins just as Powell took charge of the Bureau of American Ethnology. We have already examined Powell's drive to create a scientific study of humankind with Indians at its center. As a historian, Powell too was committed to notions of human progress. "The course of human events," he wrote in the first issue of the *American Anthropologist,* as if addressing himself to Cooper and Cole, "is not an eternal round."[55] Yet, though the new science of history grew up simultaneously with the new science of anthropology, these two sciences seem not to have informed one another. As a result, Native Americans, who by the late nineteenth century were being treated as objects of anthropological science, did not find a place in the new science of history.

From Romance to Comedy: Frederick Jackson Turner's Frontier

On a very hot day in July 1893, one of Herbert Baxter Adams's former students from the Hopkins seminars took to the lectern to deliver an essay before the American Historical Association in Chicago. And the rest, as they say, is history—or at least the history of the historical profession.

Frederick Jackson Turner delivered "The Significance of the Frontier in American History" as the fifth paper on what must have been a long day at the historian's conference. Adams, for one, was impressed by his former student. Adams devoted about half a page to the lecture in his summary of the Chicago meeting for the AHA's annual report, though he did not give it quite as much billing as Charles Homer Haskins's paper on the Eleventh Amendment.[56] Nonetheless, Turner's essay attracted much attention after he presented it, and it has since become probably the single most influential, most debated piece of writing about American history. Only a few years after 1893, Charles Beard could already write that the essay had a "more profound influence on thought about American history than any other essay or volume written on the subject."[57]

Although Turner paid a certain deference to his teacher sitting in the audience with his insistence that "the germ theory of politics has been sufficiently demonstrated," in fact, Turner used the essay as a way of breaking from the ideas that had loomed large in his graduate training. "Our early history," he went on, "is the study of European germs developing in an American environment." But, he said immediately after this, "too exclusive attention has been paid by institutional students to the Germanic origins, too little to the American factors." American history, as Turner told the assembled historians was "not simply the development of Germanic germs."[58]

"The Significance of the Frontier in American History" was—in many ways still is—irresistible. Turner managed to answer how America became America, how Americans became Americans, by providing an altogether American answer: the process of settling the frontier, Turner posited, turned heterogeneous Europeans into something new. "The fact is," Turner announced, "that here is a new product that is American." No need for providential mechanisms, or for the influence of the Old World, the frontier was a pure process of America, and through its workings came American democracy. "Thus," Turner went on, "the advance of the frontier has meant a steady movement away from the influence of Europe, a steady growth of independence on American lines."[59] "The Significance of the Frontier in American History" stands as a kind of declaration of independence for the American historical profession, and for American historical consciousness.

For many historians, the modern historical profession begins with Turner. Richard Hofstadter, for example, saw Turner among a select few of his generation who formulated "the pivotal ideas of the first half of the twentieth century." Given the enormous space Turner occupies in the development of modern historiography, it has been easy to overlook the observation David Noble has made that Turner's role in the historical profession "was that of a messenger of defeat."[60]

Turner began the essay with that now famous passage from the census of 1890 tersely declaring the frontier closed. He then spent much of the reminder of his talk expounding on his thesis that "the existence of an area of free land, its continuous recession, and the advance of American settlement westward, explain American development." Turner hinted at this sense of endings and defeat toward the end of the essay when he announced in the very last line that with the disappearance of a frontier, so "has closed the first period of American history."[61] The question of what would happen to American development now that the frontier was gone must have hung in the heavy air, at least for some, in July 1893.

Turner, then, imagined himself presenting a summing up, a grand synthesis to explain how America had developed the way it had from the arrival of the Puritans—he tackled this specifically in his 1914 essay "The First Official Frontier of the Massachusetts Bay"—until the fateful census of 1890. But "The Significance of the Frontier in American History" represented another kind of culmination as well. While this epochal essay might have set the terms of historical debate through much of the twentieth century, we should also see it as having grown out of the debates over the place of Native Americans in American history we have examined already.

When Turner himself looked back on the origins of his essay from a distance of nearly thirty years, he found it almost overdetermined. Writing to Constance Skinner in response to some biographical inquiries, he mused: "Is it strange that I saw the frontier as a real thing and experienced its changes? My people were pioneers from the beginning of the seventeenth century. . . . My mother's ancestors were preachers! Is it strange that I preached of the frontier?" He also wrote the essay, so he claimed, with a certain midwestern pride: "The Frontier paper was a programme, and in some degree a protest against eastern neglect at the time, of institutional study of the West."[62]

His recent biographer, Allen Bogue, believes we must understand Turner's "social background" if we are to understand the essay and its place in Turner's career. Bogue argues that the essay reflected everything from "family and environmental influences, friendly professional guidance, intellectual preparation, personal and institutional ambitions," to "his love for [his wife] Caroline." Bogue also notes that intimations of Turner's thesis had been floating around for some while. Take, for example, the inaugural address Albert Gallatin gave when he assumed the presidency of the New York Historical Society in 1843:

> A few emigrants to a land inhabited only by Savage Tribes . . . found it absolutely necessary to establish some regulations, some form of Government among themselves. United by a community of interest, with so striking inequality amongst themselves, and soon brought to the same level by the situation in which they were placed, their first regulations must necessarily have been founded on the principle of equal rights.[63]

At some level, then, the frontier thesis was waiting for its champion to come along.

Before Turner could be that champion, however, the discussions surrounding Native Americans had to reach their own culmination. Indians had to be cleared from the frontier of historical discourse in order to make way for Turner's frontier. As we look for the intellectual origins of "The Significance of the Frontier in American History," we can see that it stands as the nineteenth century's last, best word on the relationship between Native Americans and history.

To begin with, Indians are absent, or nearly so, from Turner's essay. In fact, even as sympathetic a biographer as Bogue acknowledges that Indians or even Indian policy never interested Turner all that much.[64] At the same time, it does seem clear that Turner kept up with much of the current work in anthropology and ethnography. His bookshelves in his Cambridge, Massachusetts, house held nearly two dozen *Bulletins* from the Bureau of Ethnology, four volumes of their *Annual Reports,* several volumes of the *Ohio Archaeological and Historical Quarterly,* along with other miscellaneous works on Indians. Further, in his History 17a course, he devoted some time to lecturing about Indians, including topics like their numbers and location in different parts of the continent, their agricultural practices, and their political organization.[65]

Yet, whatever time he gave to Indians in his undergraduate lectures notwithstanding, and despite what seems the obvious importance of Native Americans to the study of the frontier, Indians did not play much role in what Turner called the frontier "process." In History 17a, he told his students

blandly that "at each stage of the advance of the frontier, some relations occurred with the Indians." In New England, the Indians created an "obstacle
so that expansion was not unchecked."[66] Thus, when Indians do turn up in
Turner's writings, as Kerwin Lee Klein has put it nicely, "they own no verbs
of their own."[67]

Turner might not have cared much about primitive Indians, but prim-
itiveness concerned him deeply. In perhaps the most famous passage of the
frontier essay, Turner describes a process of cultural degeneration:

> The wilderness masters the colonist; It finds him a European in dress, in-
> dustries, tools, modes of travel, and thought. It takes him from the railroad car
> and puts him in the birch canoe. It strips off the garments of civilization and
> arrays him in the hunting shirt and moccasin. It puts him in the log cabin of the
> Cherokee and Iroquois and runs an Indian palisade around him. Before long
> he has gone to planting Indian corn and plowing with a sharp stick; he shouts
> the war cry and takes the scalp in orthodox Indian fashion. In short, at the
> frontier the environment is at first too strong for the man. He must accept the
> conditions which it furnishes, or perish, and so he fits himself into the Indian
> clearings and follows the Indian trails.

Here, Turner has taken head-on one of the chief dangers of frontier life and
one of the enduring tropes of American literary life: going native. Turner,
however, quickly turns this potential hazard of frontier life into an important virtue. The frontier put incipient Americans "in continuous touch with
the simplicity of primitive society," which furnishes "the forces dominating
the American character." In this sense, the "return to primitive conditions"
constituted a "perennial rebirth" and created a "fluidity" in American life.
"American social development," Turner argued, "has been continually beginning over again on the frontier."[68] In passages like these, Turner has borrowed the theme of regeneration through unpolluted nature central in so
much romantic writing.

But Turner has also made Indianness the condition to which Europeans descended in order to begin their ascent and transformation into
Americans. Indianness, though not Indians themselves. Turner quite scru-
pulously avoids suggesting that these frontier Europeans interacted directly
with Indians. Rather, they live in "the log cabin of the Cherokee and Iroquois," plant Indian corn, and follow Indian trails. Thus, when Turner
defines the frontier as "the outer edge of the wave—the meeting point between savagery and civilization," he does not mean that European civilization and Indian savagery intersect there, but rather that it is here that civi-

lized Europeans confront their own capacity to be savage. More than that, the frontier is where Europeans must become savage if Americans are ever to emerge.

Turner has accomplished two things of importance for our story here. First, he has addressed the debate about whether cultural degeneration could occur. In the anthropological discussion about Indians, backsliding on the course of social evolution seemed problematic. None other than John Wesley Powell, for one, had concluded that "retrogression in culture proper is rarely, perhaps never exhibited on any large scale."[69] For Europeans, however, Turner assured his audience that degeneration and then "rebirth" were not only possible, but essential.

Second, he has redeemed the reputation of those pioneers and frontiersmen whom some had condemned for contaminating pure and unspoiled Indians in the first place. This had been, at least for some in the nineteenth century, one of the most troublesome and vexing things about Indian-white relations. Whenever Indians came into contact with Euro-Americans on the frontier, they came away the worse for it. John Heckewelder said as much in 1819. He claimed to describe "the original character of the Indians" as they all were "but fifty or sixty years back," but now that character could not be found "within the precincts of any part of their territory bordering on the settlements of the white people!" In a conceptualization of cultural frontiers I have not encountered anywhere else, Henry Schoolcraft saw the French as responsible for brandy; the English for rum; and Americans for bringing whiskey to the Indians. "Under this triple curse," Schoolcraft wrote, "they have maintained an existence in the face of a white population. But it has been an *existence* merely." Isaac McCoy, who campaigned for a more humane Indian policy in the Jacksonian era, saw the "degradation" and "wretchedness" of the Indians as the result of their "natural comforts" being ruined by "proximity to that of the civilized." Thomas McKenney was a bit more sarcastic. He found the Indians to be quite admirable people when "not yet imbued with the vices of civilization."[70]

To explain this apparent conundrum, some writers insisted that the whites Indians encountered on the frontier constituted the very roughest, most ill-mannered Americans, those who revealed by their choice to live on the frontier that they were incapable of succeeding in polite society—the white squatters in Cooper's *The Prairie* come to mind. This then was the real tragedy of the frontier encounter: those who should have been the agents of civilization turned out to be nothing but drunken "border ruffians," and they took the Indians down with them. This was Heckewelder's refrain, as we saw in the last chapter, and many picked it up after him.

Turner's thesis recast these ruffians and their role in history entirely. Far from being the "worst sort," these trappers and traders constituted the very vanguard of American civilization. Whatever might have happened to the Indians was, for Turner, epiphenomenal to the frontier "process."

What interested Turner was how the frontier stripped Europeanness away and thus cleared the space for Americanness to arise. He sought to explain how a single national identity could be created from multiple European identities. After all, the frontier, as Turner knew personally, attracted Germans, Scots, French, Irish, Scandinavians, who all became, at least in Turner's view, Americans. In this sense, if we return again to literary analysis, Turner's essay replaced "romance" with "comedy" as the narrative strategy for telling American history.

Borrowing again from Northrop Frye, we can define comedy as a plot in which disparate elements are thrown together, clash initially, but resolve their antagonisms and create a new harmonious unity at the end. This, for Turner, was the American story. It could only be thus, however, if Native Americans were dropped from the plot almost entirely. They, after all, played no role in Turner's harmonious resolution. Parkman had dropped them already by removing the element of tragedy so that America could be a romance. He did so at a time when Native Americans themselves still constituted a very real presence in American life. By the time Turner took that romance and made it comedy, Indians might constitute a part of the American memory, but not of its history.[71]

Finally, Turner quoted the Italian economist Achille Loria later in his address. "America," Loria says, "has the key to the historical enigma which Europe has sought for centuries in vain, and the land which has no history reveals luminously the course of universal history." Turner agreed and added, "The United States lies like a huge page in the history of society. Line by line as we read this continental page from West to East we find the record of social evolution." Turner went on to sketch the stages of that social evolution: "It begins with the Indian and the hunter; it goes on to tell of the disintegration of savagery by the entrance of the trader, the pathfinder of civilization; we read the annals of the pastoral stage in ranch life; the exploitation of the soil by the raising of unrotated crops of corn and wheat in sparsely settled farming communities; the intensive culture of the denser farm settlement; and finally the manufacturing organization with city and factory system."[72]

This should, I trust, sound remarkably familiar, echoing as it does the convictions of the prehistorians that America offered a glimpse into the prehistory of all societies. But what Turner has deftly done, whether intentionally or not, is to root that universality of social evolution entirely within white experience. We have already discussed the way in which the use of prehistory differed in Europe and in the United States—in Europe, it served to extend a sense of national history backward, while in the United States it served as a categorical repository for Native American history distinct and set apart from that of white America. What made the study of American prehistory intriguing for many was the light it might cast on the prehistory of other places. Turner sidestepped this altogether by offering a vision of history in which America still held the key to "universal history," but one in which Indians played no important part. Turner's frontier thesis represented the quintessential American solution to the problem of American history, defined without much attention to Native America at all.

This, though, is where the intellectual conversation about Indians had been heading across the nineteenth century. As the nation's intellectual life began to take shape, as lines were drawn to define disciplinary boundaries, and as a distinctively American historical consciousness formed, the questions of Indian history receded or were pushed from the center stage of our intellectual life. For American historians launched on their new professional endeavor, the solution to the problem of the relationship between Native Americans and history was to stop asking the question. After all, the same year that saw the closing of the frontier also saw the massacre at Wounded Knee, the last major episode of violence visited upon Native Americans by federal troops. Turner might have mentioned this in his 1893 address, but he chose not to. As far as most Americans were concerned, by the 1890s Indians had ceased to be a problem, historical or otherwise.

Gone from the nation's history, Indians assumed instead a starring role in the nation's mythology, from the circus spectacles of Buffalo Bill's Wild West shows of the late nineteenth century to the Hollywood westerns of the twentieth. Ironic in a way, since as we saw at the beginning of this book, Native Americans' own understanding of their history was largely dismissed as "myth" early in the nineteenth century. By the end of the century, Euro-Americans clearly hungered for myths about Native Americans, but they wanted them of their own making. They wanted Native Americans as a source of entertainment, not history.

HENRY ADAMS WROTE OF Lewis Henry Morgan's magnum opus *Ancient Society* that it must become "the foundation of all future work in American historical science." Remarkable praise from a man who would himself, among other things, help establish the historical profession in the

United States for a book usually regarded as a part of the foundation of American anthropology. In fact, Francis Parkman too counted himself among Morgan's biggest fans. Adams's applause serves to remind us that in the middle years of the nineteenth century, as the practice of American history was still taking shape, the boundaries around American history might have been drawn widely enough to include Native America as well. To congratulate him on the publication of his *Crania Americana*, for example, George Combe wrote to Samuel Morton late in 1839, informing him: "I have asked Mr. Bancroft, the Author of the History of the United States, to consult it in regard to the character of the Indians, about whom he is composing a chapter."[73] By the end of the century, with the study of Native Americans located squarely in the discipline of anthropology, George Fellows asserted that anthropology "is absolutely essential to any comprehensive studies in history."[74]

Justin Winsor, Harvard's librarian and a distinguished historian in his own right, made such an attempt at a comprehensive history of America with the eight-volume *Narrative and Critical History* he edited. Volume one of that history covered "Aboriginal America." In truth, only two of the six chapters in this book dealt with North American Indians—chapter 5, "The Red Indian of North America in Contact with the French and English" (Winsor, after all, was a friend and admirer of Parkman's) and chapter 7, "The Prehistoric Archaeology of North America." The former, written by George Ellis, dealt largely with the violence between native groups and whites, demonstrating that "the Indians generally practiced an indiscriminate slaughter," and the latter, written by Henry W. Haynes, concerned itself almost entirely with debates over the antiquity of humans in the New World. Charles Abbott's Trenton Gravels feature prominently in that discussion. Still, Winsor's *History* made the attempt to include some consideration of Native Americans as part of a larger history.

Many did not even make the attempt. Daniel Brinton, the nation's first professor of anthropology, if idiosyncratically so, complained about historians: "how few have even attempted to avail themselves of the myriad of sidelights which ethnology can throw upon the motives and manners of a people." Thirty years earlier, Parkman, even while corresponding with Morgan, already understood the divide that was growing between history and anthropology. Although he admitted to Morgan in 1865, "I have always felt much interest in the ethnological aspect of the subject," he went on, "my examinations have been made with an historical, not an ethnological, object."[75]

Most of the questions about Native Americans posed by scholars and investigators at the dawn of the nation had been answered by the dawn of the new millennium, though countless more have been raised and drive research by anthropologists, archaeologists, linguists, folklorists, and others. We generally acknowledge that Indians descended from groups of wanderers who crossed the Bering Straits relatively recently, at least in terms of the human species. The Mound Builders have been laid to rest and replaced by cultural groups defined with more exactitude. Advances in archaeological technique have even made it possible to create rough chronologies of America's prehistoric peoples, a development that would surely have dazzled that first generation of prehistorians.

Still, we should avoid feeling too smug. Much of what we think we know about the original inhabitants of the continent remains contingent and theoretical. New finds, and the reevaluation of old ones, continue to threaten to upset what we think we know. We may dismiss some of the answers our nineteenth-century scholarly forebears came up with, but we ought to acknowledge just how difficult some of these questions were and remain.

History too has changed profoundly. The narrative of America is no longer told as a simple romance or a triumphant comedy. Most of us anyway have not returned to a cyclical conception of history's motion, but tragedy and declension are now a part of how most of us understand our nation's past. Native American history too has carved out its own space within the discipline, and within the academy, insistently reminding us that the people who have always been on the verge of extinction have not, in fact, gone away. What's more, they do have a history worth telling.

Yet one thing, I think, remains stubbornly the same. The story of America still begins with the arrival of Europeans, at least to judge by most of our survey courses and textbooks. Although scholars, say, of medieval English history might divide their field into pre-Norman and post-Norman periods, they would surely acknowledge continuities across that divide of conquest. But in America 1492 still stands as a historical rupture so complete and total that for the most part all that came before, and much of Native history that happened after, stands outside standard historical narratives. Nearly one hundred years after Parkman admitted to Morgan that he pursued history, not ethnology, archaeologist Glyn Daniel, sounding almost bemused, could still write: "Historians are taking a long time to integrate prehistory into their general view of man."[76] Certainly in the conception of American history that situation has been slow to change. I give the last word, then, to Stephen Peet, whose 1895 quandary we have considered before:

But the strange thing about American history is that it dates its beginnings with a very modern event—the Discovery of Columbus—and confines its history mainly to the white race. The question is whether this shall continue to be so. If the archaeologists have brought about such results elsewhere, may they not break through barriers which surround them here and carry back our history, so that it may compare with that of other nations?[77]

That question remains.

Chapter One

1. Lewis, *W. E. B. DuBois*, p. 72.
2. Drake, *Indian History for Young Folks*, pp. 5, 13.
3. McKenney, *Memoirs*, p. 229; Tocqueville, *Democracy in America*, pp. 317–318.
4. Wallace, *Jefferson and the Indians*, p. 50.
5. Ibid., p. 19.
6. *Writings of Thomas Jefferson*, 5:390.
7. See Wallace, *Jefferson and the Indians*, pp. 11, 205, 218.
8. *Events in Indian History*, p. 9.
9. See Fitzpatrick, *History's Memory*, chap.3.
10. R. S. H. "Indian Women," pp. 401–402.
11. Drake, *Biography and History of the Indians*, p. 33.
12. Conn, *Museums and American Intellectual Life*, chap.1.
13. Higham, "The Reorientation of American Culture in the 1890s," in *Writing American History*.
14. Toqueville, *Democracy in America*, pp. 28–29.
15. McCoy, *Indian Reform*, p. 9.
16. Bidney, "Idea of the Savage," p. 322.
17. There were, of course, all kinds of differences between the various religious groups proselytizing among Indians. As Edward Gray has noted, for the Puritans, unlike the Jesuits, "the first objective was not to administer the sacraments, but to make the Indians self-sufficient enquirers after grace." Gray, *New World Babel*, p. 50.
18. Pagden, *Fall of Natural Man*, pp. 2, 19.
19. Barton, "An Essay towards a Natural History of the North American Indians." The hand-written essay is undated.
20. See Adair, *History of the American Indians*.
21. Barton, "Natural History of the North American Indians."
22. Jennings, ed., *Ancient North Americans*, p. 25.
23. Atwater, "Eloquence of the North American Indians," p. 205.
24. Noah, *Discourse on . . . Lost Tribes of Israel*, pp. 4, 11, 36.

25. McKenney, *Memoirs*, 2:11; *History of the Indians of North and South America by the Author of Peter Parley's Tales*, p. 10.

26. Atwater, "Eloquence of the North American Indians," p. 199.

27. McKenney, *Memoirs*, 2:14.

28. Barton , *New Views*, p. iv.

29. McKenney, *Memoirs*, 2:15; Forry, "The Mosaic Account of the Unity of the Human Race," p. 30.

30. "Is the African and Caucasian of Common Origin?" pp. 243–245.

31. See, for example, Stanton, *The Leopard's Spots*, and Gould, *The Mismeasure of Man*.

32. Pickering, *Races of Man*, p. 10.

33. Nott, "Unity of the Human Race," pp. 1–57; Nott, *Two Lectures*, p. 7; "Is the African and Caucasian of Common Origin?" p. 243.

34. Noah, *Discourse on . . . Lost Tribes of Israel*, p. 31; Forry, "Unity of the Human Race," p. 80; Southall, *Recent Origin of Man*, p. 72.

35. Humphrey, "Indian Rights and Our Duties," pp. 19–20.

36. Noah, *Discourse on . . . Lost Tribes of Israel*, p. 33.

37. I should note that polygenesis survived well past Darwin. In a savagely racist screed published in 1891, for example, a southern writer found monogenesis a theory "so offensive to our natural instincts, and . . . so absurd, and preposterous, that it never could have been entertained by intelligent minds, but from the apprehension that belief in it was required by the Bible." *Caucasian Anthropology*, p. 26. For more on this topic, see Stocking, "Polygenesist Thought in Post-Darwinian Anthropology," in *Culture and Evolution*, pp. 42–68. Curtis Hinsley has pointed out that the defense of monogenesism "lay at the religious core" of American anthropology well into the twentieth century. See Hinsley, *The Smithsonian and the American Indian*, p. 22.

38. McKenney, *Memoirs*, 2:61.

39. Adair, *History of the American Indians*, p. 10.

40. Heckewelder, "An Account," p. 327; Schoolcraft, *Notes on the Iroquois*, p. 358.

41. Schoolcraft, "Discourse," pp. 8–9.

42. Bradford, *American Antiquities*, p. 9; Regis, *Describing America*, p. 37.

43. Wissler, "American Indian and the American Philosophical Society," p. 189; Regis, *Describing America*, p. 25.

44. Frost, *Indian Wars*, p. 4; Hayden, *Contributions to Ethnography and Philology*, pp. 234–235.

45. *Copway's American Indian* 1 (1851).

46. Bellin, *Demon of the Continent*, p. 134.

47. Gossman, *Between History and Literature*, p. 227.

48. Nott, *Two Lectures*, p. 68; see Anderson, *Imagined Communities*, p. 149.

49. Drake, *Biography and History of the Indians*, p. 29.

50. Pagden, *Fall of Natural Man*, p. 200.

51. Bartlett, *Progress of Ethnology*, p. 4.

52. McKenney, *Memoirs*, p. 34; Edwin James, "Contributions towards a History of Indian Languages"; Morgan to Stone, June 10, 1844, New York Historical Society.

53. Kemp, *Estrangement of the Past*, p. vi.

54. "Origins of the American Antiquarian Society," p. 30.

55. For this discussion I have drawn particularly from Persons, "Cyclical Theory of History," pp. 147–163; Ross, "Historical Consciousness," pp. 909–928; and Miles, "The Young American Nation," pp. 259–274.

56. Cooper to Louis Legrand Noble, January 6, 1849, in *Letters and Journals of James Fenimore Cooper*, 5:396–400.

57. For more on *The Course of Empire*, see Miller, "Thomas Cole and Jacksonian America," pp. 65–92; and Miller, *Empire of the Eye*; Powell, *Thomas Cole*; and Truettner and Wallach, eds., *Thomas Cole*. Quotes from Wallach, "Thomas Cole: Landscape and the Course of American Empire," in *Thomas Cole: Landscape Into History*, p. 95.

58. See especially Miller, "Thomas Cole and Jacksonian America."

59. It was not until 1954 that the American Anthropological Association acknowledged officially that the assimilation of Native America into Euro-America was perhaps not "inevitable."

60. Sheehan, *Seeds of Extinction*, pp. 4–5.

61. Bliss, "Drake's Indian History," p. 301; "American Indians," pp. 333, 337; Pidgeon, *Traditions of De-Coo-Dah*, p. 21.

62. Cole quoted in Powell, *Thomas Cole*, p. 64.

63. Pearce makes a related point in his classic work *The Savages of America*. See especially p. 160. David Bidney dates this shift to 1795, after which point he says "Americans come to believe that the savages in their midst could have no share in the progress of their civilization." Bidney, "Idea of the Savage," p. 325.

64. Marienstras, "The Common Man's Indian: The Image of the Indian as a Promoter of National Identity in the Early National Era," in Hoxie et al., eds., *Native Americans and the Early Republic*, pp. 261–262; Deloria, *Playing Indian*, p. 37.

65. Bartlett, *Progress of Ethnology*, p. 7.

66. Baldwin, *Ancient America*, pp. 58–59.

67. Fabian, *Time and the Other*, p. 144.

68. "Removal of the Indians," pp. 64, 107.

69. Bradford, *American Antiquities*, p. 9.

Chapter Two

1. DuPonceau, "History of the Celebrated Treaty," 3:147.

2. Faust, "Race, Gender, and Confederate Nationalism," p. 297.

3. Peirce, *Arts and Sciences Abridged*, p. 48.

4. Goodrich, *History of All Nations*, pp. 10, 16; Rafinesque, *American Nations*, pp. 76–77.

5. Burnham and Giese, "History Painting: How It Works," in *Redefining American History Painting*, p. 6; Reynolds, *Discourses on Art*, p. 244.

6. Levin, *History as Romantic Art*, pp. 12, 19.

7. Galt, *Life and Works of Benjamin West*, p. 13; Galt, *Progress of Genius*, p. 56.

8. Peale to West, July 4, 1808, Historical Society of Pennsylvania, Titian Peale Collection 745.

9. Galt, *Life and Studies of Benjamin West*, p. 70.

10. See Galt, *Life and Studies of Benjamin West*, p. 45–50.

11. The only competition *Penn's Treaty* might have had for this place in the American imagination was from the dramatic painting of Pocahontas rescuing John Smith from execution that Chapman did for the Capitol Rotunda, but as Robert Tilton has noted in his thorough study of the Pocahontas myth, "Chapman's effort never captured the imagination of either the public or the American artistic community." Tilton, *Pocahontas*, p. 122.

12. Galt, *Life and Studies of Benjamin West* (1816), pp. 28–29.

13. Abrams, "Benjamin West's Documentation," p. 65.

14. For the best reading of the composition of the painting see Abrams, "Benjamin West's Documentation," pp. 60, 69.

15. Published as "Historical Notes," pp. 334–338.

16. Benjamin West to William West, July 12, 1775, in *Pennsylvania Magazine of History and Biography* 32 (1908): 14.

17. Cited in Landis, "Benjamin West and the Royal Academy," p. 248.

18. Abrams, *Valiant Hero*, p. 195. For more on the relationship between Pennsylvanians and Native Americans, see Richter, "Onas, the Long Knife," in Hoxie et al., eds., *Native Americans*, pp. 125–161.

19. Hale, "Heckewelder's Indian History," pp. 161–162; DuPonceau, "Memoir on the History of the Celebrated Treaty," p. 147.

20. Frost, *American Speaker*, pp. 129–130.

21. See Conningham, *Currier & Ives Prints, An Illustrated Check List*.

22. In this discussion, I have relied entirely on the extraordinary research of Ellen Starr Brinton on the subject. See Brinton, "Benjamin West's Painting of Penn's Treaty," pp. 99–166.

23. I have made this argument elsewhere. See Steven Conn, "Narrative Trauma."

24. "The Indians in American Art," p. 28. Grand manner compositional conventions did have a longer life in the form of lithographs, prints, and other mass-produced, commercially available images. Indians did indeed populate many of these, although largely as detail and ornament. For example, in John McCrea's colored engraving *First in Peace* (1867), Indians turn up as part of the large crowd of figures waiting to greet Washington as he arrives in New York City.

25. See "American Indians look for recognition from Pa."

26. There is not a great deal known about King's biography. For this brief sketch I have relied on Robert J. Moore, *Native Americans, A Portrait*; and Cosentino, *Paintings of Charles Bird King*.

27. Dunlap, *History of the Rise and Progress of the Arts and Designs*, 2:261.

28. See Wiet, "McKenney-Hall Prints," p. 12.

29. Trollope, *Domestic Manners of the Americans*, pp. 220–221.

30. Murray, "Painting the Indians," pp. 6–12; quoted in Wainwright, *Philadelphia in the Romantic Age of Lithography*, p. 50.

31. Smithsonian *Journal of the Regents*, 1857, p. 82; Schimmel, "Inventing the Indian," in Truettner, ed., *The West as America*, p. 149. Schimmel goes on to say that "Real Indians never inhabited the paintings of white artists," (p. 186); and while it is absolutely true that representations of Indians were the imaginative creations of their painters,

Schimmel's statement seems to me to elide the fact that this is true of all painting. She seems to suggest that there were "real" Indians to be painted, whose realness she is in some better position to evaluate, and that American painters chose not to. This strikes me as a vast oversimplification of the complicated problems of representation that have been described by many scholars.

32. Quoted in Murray, "Painting the Indians," p. 10.

33. McKenney and Hall, *Indian Tribes of North America*, 3:95.

34. See Halttunen, *Confidence Men and Painted Women*. See also Trachtenberg, *Reading American Photographs*, pp. 27–28.

35. Quoted in Murray, "Painting the Indians," p. 10.

36. Felton and Sparks, "McKenney and Hall's *History of the North American Indians*," p. 148.

37. Ibid., p. 138.

38. This letter is quoted in full in McKenney and Hall, *Indian Tribes of North America*, 1:xxix–xxxii.

39. The most exhaustive study of Catlin remains Brian Dippie's *Catlin and His Contemporaries: The Politics of Patronage*. Dippie situates Catlin within many contexts and treats many of the other figures who had an interest in Indian studies in the mid-century. The book is, however, a celebratory treatment of the painter, using Henry Schoolcraft as a foil against which to portray Catlin as essentially heroic.

40. William Truettner doubts that this story—repeated by subsequent biographers—is in fact true. See his *A Natural Man Observed: A Study of Catlin's Indian Gallery.*

41. Dunlap, *History of the Rise and Progress of the Arts and Designs*, 2:378.

42. Schoolcraft, "The Red Man of America," p. 286.

43. "Catlin's North American Indians," p. 44.

44. *Catlin's North American Indian Portfolio*, p. 4.

45. Quoted in Schoolcraft, "The Red Man of America," p. 287.

46. *Catlin's North American Indian Portfolio*, p. 4.

47. Truettner, *Natural Man Observed*, p. 126.

48. See Donaldson, *George Catlin Indian Gallery*, p. 718; and Truettner, *Natural Man Observed*, pp. 61–68.

49. "Catlin's North American Indians," p. 44; Donaldson, *George Catlin Indian Gallery*, p. 747; Youmans, *Pioneers of Science in America*, p. 336.

50. Truettner, *Natural Man Observed*, pp. 66–67; Catlin, *Last Rambles*, esp. chap. 9.

51. Quoted in Truettner, *Natural Man Observed*, p. 13.

52. Quoted in Truettner, *Natural Man Observed*, pp. 12, 13.

53. *Catlin's North American Indian Portfolio*, p. 3; see Truettner, *Natural Man Observed*, p. 117; Catlin to Webster, April 4, 1852 quoted in Dippie, *Catlin and His Contemporaries*, p. 97.

54. Donaldson, *George Catlin Indian Gallery*, pp. 742, 745.

55. Quoted in ibid., p. 719; quoted in "Sketch of George Catlin," p. 404.

56. Quoted in Donaldson, *George Catlin Indian Gallery*, p. 719.

57. See ibid., p. 719; *Catlin's North American Indian Portfolio* , p. 4.

58. Johnes, *Philological Proofs*, p. 156.

59. "Catlin's North American Indians," pp. 44–45; "Vindication of the United States," pp. 202–204.

60. Catlin to Harper, ca. 1870. Newberry Library, Edward Ayer Papers, Box 2, Folder 146. Brian Dippie stresses that Catlin was a great champion of the Indian cause, especially as he grew older and the situation in Native America grew more dire.

61. Donaldson, *George Catlin Indian Gallery,* pp. 736–739.

62. Andrew Walker and I have written about this issue in more detail. See Conn and Walker, "The History in the Art: Painting the Civil War."

63. Quoted in Hendricks, *Albert Bierstadt,* pp. 141, 144.

64. Quoted ibid., p. 144; *New York Times,* February 22, 1864.

65. Quoted in Hendricks, *Albert Bierstadt,* p. 291.

66. Quoted ibid., p. 291.

67. For more on Brush's biography, see Bowditch, *George de Forest Brush;* see also *A Catalogue of an Exhibition of Paintings and Drawings by George de Forest Brush.*

68. Brush, "An Artist among the Indians," pp. 55–57.

69. Nemerov, "Doing the 'Old America': The Image of the American West, 1880–1920," in Truettner, ed., *The West as America,* pp. 285–343.

70. Burbank, *Burbank among the Indians,* pp. 7–9.

71. Gallati, "Blurring the Lines between Likeness and Type," in Wolfe, ed., *American Indian Portraits,* p. 30.

72. Dippie, "Representing the Other," in Edwards, ed., *Anthropology and Photography,* p. 136.

73. The best recent treatment of Curtis's production of *The North American Indian* is Gidley, *Edward S. Curtis and the North American Indian, Incorporated.* I have relied on this book heavily for my discussion of Curtis.

74. Quoted in Adam, *Edward Sheriff Curtis,* p. 31.

75. Curtis to Edward Ayer, April 28, 1907. Newberry Library, Edward Ayer Collection, Box 1, Folder 12; quoted in Gidley, *Edward S. Curtis and the North American Indian, Incorporated,* p. 44.

76. Gordon, "Review," p. 436.

77. Ayer to Managers of the North American Indian Fund, January 25, 1921. Newberry Library, Edward Ayer Collection, Box 2, Folder 26.

78. Gordon, "Review," p. 440.

79. Gidley, *Edward S. Curtis and the North American Indian, Incorporated,* pp. 276–277.

80. Trachtenberg is building on the ideas of Roland Barthes. See Trachtenberg, *Reading American Photographs,* p. 5.

81. See Gidley, *Edward S. Curtis and the North American Indian, Incorporated,* especially chap. 9.

Chapter Three

1. He did have a name, of course. Actor Iron Eyes Cody, a Cherokee-Cree Indian, played the part of the "crying Indian" for this spot produced by the Ad Council for the Keep America Beautiful Campaign.

2. Alexie, "What You Pawn I Will Redeem," p. 169.

3. It probably does not overstate the case to say that most of what we know about Amerindian languages comes from the work of anthropologists, working with native speakers.

4. Kah-ge-ga-goh-bouh, "The American Indian," pp. 633–634.

5. See Gray, *New World Babel*, p. 83.

6. Smith, "The Interest in Language and Languages in Colonial and Federal America," pp. 29–46.

7. Quoted in Andreson, *Linguistics in America*, 82–84.

8. Edwards, *Observations on the Language of the Muhhekanaew Indians*, pp. 15–16.

9. Jefferson, *Notes on the State of Virginia*, p. 102.

10. Ibid., p. 62.

11. B. T. C., "Indian Eloquence," pp. 277–278.

12. Ibid., pp. 62–63.

13. Lauzon, "Savage Eloquence," pp. 123–157. As Lauzon notes, numbers of prominent British colonials "all agreed that the native American languages were somehow poetic and eloquent"; Adair, *History of the American Indians*, p. 11.

14. See Eastman, "The Indian Censures the White Man: 'Indian Eloquence' and American Reading Audiences in the Early Republic"; Bliss, "Drake's Indian History," p. 332; Frost, *Book of Good Examples*, p. 254; Stone, *Life and Times of Sa-go-ye-wat-ha, or Red Jacket*, pp. vii, 103, 129; Irving, *Indian Sketches*, 2:294.

15. Humphrey, "Indian Rights and Our Duties," pp. 5–9; McKenney, *Memoirs*, 2:88.

16. "American Indians," pp. 335–336; Atwater, "Eloquence of the North American Indians," pp. 211–212.

17. "The North American Indians," pp. 345–346.

18. DuPonceau to Jefferson, February 17, 1817, American Philosophical Society, Historical and Literary Committee, Letterbook, vol. 1.

19. I have borrowed this brief biographical information from Robins, "DuPonceau and Early Nineteenth Century Linguistics," in Aarsleff, Kelly, and Niederehe, eds., *Papers in the History of Linguistics*, p. 435.

20. DuPonceau, "Report on Philology," October 17, 1836, American Philosophical Society Archives; DuPonceau to Butrick, September 7, 1818, American Philosophical Society, Historical and Literary Committee, Letterbook, vol. 2; DuPonceau to Jefferson, February 17, 1817, American Philosophical Society, Historical and Literary Committee, Letterbook, vol. 2.

21. DuPonceau to Heckewelder, August 3, 1816, American Philosophical Society, Historical and Literary Committee, Letterbook, vol. 1; see Gray, *New World Babel*, p. 7; DuPonceau to Heckewelder, September 19, 1816, American Philosophical Society, Historical and Literary Committee, Letterbook, vol. 1.

22. DuPonceau to Heckewelder, September 19, 1816, American Philosophical Society, Historical and Literary Committee, Letterbook, vol. 1.

23. DuPonceau to Jefferson, December 11, 1817, American Philosophical Society, Historical and Literary Committee, Letterbook, vol. 1.

24. Schoolcraft, "History and Languages of the North American Tribes," p. 43; Pickering, "Indian Languages," *Encyclopedia Americana*, 6:581–582.

25. Gray, *New World Babel*, p. 141; see Wallace, *Jefferson and the Indians*.

26. DuPonceau to Jefferson, February 17, 1817, American Philosophical Society, Historical and Literary Committee, Letterbook, vol. 1.

27. Pickering, "Languages of the American Indians," p. 183.

28. Ibid., p. 182; Johnes, *Philological Proofs*, pp. 2–3.

29. DuPonceau to Jefferson, February 17, 1817, American Philosophical Society, Historical and Literary Committee, Letterbook, vol. 1; see DuPonceau to Gallatin, March 12, 1835, New York Historical Society, Gallatin Papers. As it turns out, some Native languages are polysynthetic, but not all. Thanks to Dell Hymes for pointing this out.

30. For this gloss, I have relied heavily on Gray, *New World Babel*, esp. pp. 6, 110–113.

31. Schoolcraft, "Mr. Schoolcraft's Address before the New York Historical Society," p. 23; Schoolcraft, "Plan for American Ethnological Investigation," p. 913.

32. "Indian Eloquence," pp. 385–390.

33. Quoted in Gustafson, *Eloquence is Power*, p. xiii.

34. Anderson, *Imagined Communities*, pp. 36, 133.

35. DuPonceau to Gallatin, March 12, 1835, New York Historical Society, Gallatin Papers.

36. Atwater, "Eloquence of the North American Indians," pp. 213–214.

37. Eastman, "The Indian Censures the White Man," pp. 20, 38.

38. "Reports of the Commissioner of Indian Affairs, 1855–58," p. 60.

39. Irving, *Indian Sketches*, p. 21.

40. Catlin, *Life among the Indians*, p. 335. The book appeared in the United States in 1861; my copy, much to my surprise, turns out to be a reprint of the English edition, which appeared posthumously.

41. Tracy, "Indian Eloquence," pp. 543–545; "Cooper's Indians," p. 266.

42. Mayer, "Tah-Gah-Jute or, Logan and Captain Michael Cresap," p. 61.

43. DuPonceau to Jefferson, September 12, 1820, American Philosophical Society, Historical and Literary Committee, Letterbook, vol. 2.

44. Pickering, "Languages of the American Indians," p. 179.

45. Wallace, *Jefferson and the Indians*, p. 144; Pickering quoted in Andresen, *Linguistics in America*, p. 123.

46. DuPonceau, "Report on Philology"; Freeman, "Race and Language," p. 719; Schoolcraft, "History and Languages of the North American Tribes," pp. 34–40. Stephen Alter has made this observation: "Philology of all kinds was distinguished by its historical emphasis, its concern with linguistic and literary change over time." Alter, *Darwinism and the Linguistic Image*, p. 2.

47. Schoolcraft, "Mr. Schoolcraft's Address before the New York Historical Society, 'Incentives to the Study of the Ancient Period of American History,' " p. 33.

48. James, "Contributions towards a History of Indian Languages."

49. DuPonceau to Albert Gallatin, March 12, 1835, New York Historical Society, Gallatin Papers.

50. Gallatin, "Synopsis of the Indian Tribes of North America," pp. 155–158.

51. Ibid., pp. vii–viii, 6. He reiterated this point to Secretary of War W. L. Macy in 1846: "All the American languages, as far as they have been investigated, though differing in many respects have strongly marked common characters." Gallatin to Macy, March 17, 1846, in *Writings of Albert Gallatin*, 2:627.

52. Gallatin, "Synopsis of the Indian Tribes of North America," p. 142.

53. Johnes, *Philological Proofs*, p. 172.

54. Ibid., p. xv.

55. "The Unity of Language and of Mankind," pp. 165, 179.

56. Andresen, *Linguistics in America*, p. 127.

57. Campbell, *American Indian Languages*, pp. 37, 41.

58. "The Unity of Language and of Mankind," pp. 470–471.

59. Whitney, "Darwinism and Language," pp. 83–84, 88.

60. Farrar, "Philology and Darwinism," p. 528.

61. Ibid., p. 529; see Alter, *Darwinism and the Linguistic Image*, p. 2; Charlton Laird also makes a similar point in *Language in America*, p. 29.

62. Fiske, "The Genesis of Language," p. 312.

63. Pedersen, *The Discovery of Language*, p. 137; Laird, *Language in America*, p. 29.

64. Whitney, *The Life and Growth of Language*, pp. 259–263.

65. Fiske, "The Genesis of Language," p. 309; "Language and the Study of Language," p. 369; Whitney, *The Life and Growth of Language*, pp. 317–319.

66. "Language and the Study of Language," p. 370.

67. See most recently Worster, *A River Running West*.

68. McKenney to Gallatin, January 5, 1827, New York Historical Society, Gallatin Papers.

69. Powell, *Introduction to the Study of Indian Languages*, pp. v–vi; Whitney to Powell, October 6, 1884, National Anthropological Archives, Records of the Bureau of American Ethnology, Box 82.

70. Campbell, *American Indian Languages*, p. 27.

71. Powell, "Indian Linguistic Families," pp. 8–9.

72. Powell, "Whence Came the American Indians," p. 684.

73. John Wesley Powell, "Problems of American Archaeology," p. 647.

74. For a nice rundown of these figures, see Hinsley, *The Smithsonian and the American Indian*.

75. Powell, *Introduction to the Study of Indian Languages*, p. vi.

76. Quoted in Holder, ed., *Introduction to Handbook of American Indian Languages*, p. vi; Laird, *Language in America*, p. 30.

77. Hymes, "Notes toward a History of Linguistic Anthropology," in *Essays in the History of Linguistic Anthropology*, p. 19.

78. Goddard, "The Present Condition of Our Knowledge of North American Languages," pp. 560, 592.

79. See Andresen, *Linguistics in America*, pp. 176, 188.

80. Brinton, "American Languages and Why We Should Study Them," p. 32; White, "Indian Peoples and the Natural World: Asking the Right Questions," in Fixico, ed., *Rethinking American Indian History*, p. 94.

81. For a brief mention of this, see Holmes, "The World's Fair Congress of Anthropology," p. 429.

82. See Baker, "Daniel G. Brinton's Success on the Road to Obscurity, 1890–1899," pp. 394–395. Baker's article stands as the best, most recent assessment of Brinton's career. Regna Darnell has also written extensively about Brinton.

83. See Baker, "Daniel G. Brinton's Success on the Road to Obscurity, 1890–1899," p. 413; Powell, *Indian Linguistic Families,* pp. 35–36.

84. Baker, "Daniel G. Brinton's Success on the Road to Obscurity, 1890–1899," p. 417, n. 8.

85. Some of these issues would be revived in the twentieth century by anthropologists and folklorists, but not, for the most part, by historians or literary scholars until the second half of the twentieth century.

86. Daniel Brinton, *Essays of an Americanist,* p. 46.

87. Brinton, "American Languages and Why We Should Study Them," pp. 24, 33.

88. Ibid., p. 35; Brinton, *Aboriginal Authors and Their Productions,* p. 66.

89. Brinton, "American Languages and Why We Should Study Them," pp. 33–35.

90. Ibid., p. 16.

91. Brinton, *Aboriginal Authors and Their Productions,* pp. 10–11, 13.

92. See "The Library of Aboriginal American Literature," prospectus in the University of Pennsylvania Museum Library, p. 1.

93. Scheckel, *The Insistence of the Indian,* p. 16.

94. Bellin, *The Demon of the Continent,* p. 158.

95. Brinton, *Aboriginal Authors and Their Productions,* p. 43.

96. Brinton, *Essays of an Americanist,* p. 304.

97. Quoted in Campbell, *American Indian Languages,* p. 26.

98. DuPonceau to Williams, December 17, 1817, American Philosophical Society, Historical Committee, Letterbook, vol. 2.

Chapter Four

1. Brinkerhoff, quoted in Barnhart, "In Search of the Mound Builders," p. 131.

2. "History and Languages of the North American Tribes," p. 35.

3. Hinsley, "Digging for Identity," p. 47.

4. Moorehead, "Archaeology."

5. See Jefferson, *Notes on the State of Virginia,* pp. 97–100.

6. "Origins of the American Antiquarian Society," p. 18

7. For more on the early history of the American Antiquarian Society, see Joyce, "Antiquarians and Archaeologists," p. 302–307.

8. Moorehead, "Archaeology."

9. Atwater, "Description of the Antiquities Discovered in the State of Ohio and Other Western States," p. 219.

10. See "Origins of the North American Indians," p. 168; Short, "Antiquities of Ohio," pp. 179–181.

11. Atwater, "Description of the Antiquities Discovered in the State of Ohio and Other Western States," p. 195.

12. Rafinesque to Atwater, July 12, 1820, Newberry Library, Edward Ayer Collection, Mss. folder 253–254.

13. Atwater, "Description of the Antiquities Discovered in the State of Ohio and Other Western States," p. 209.

14. Ibid., pp. 195, 205–206, 213.

15. Ibid., p. 251.

16. Bradford, *American Antiquities and Researches into the Origin and History of the Red Race*, pp. 71, 167.

17. *History of the Indians of North and South America by the Author of Peter Parley's Tales*, p. 10.

18. See Flannery, "Who Came First?" pp. 51–53.

19. A very truncated version of this book appeared as "Aboriginal Monuments of the Mississippi Valley," in the *Transactions of the American Ethnological Society* 1 (1845–48). Squier and Davis had originally offered their work to the Ethnological Society for publication, but as it grew longer and more elaborate, the society simply could not afford to pay for the printing. The prose is sufficiently different in each version that I shall quote from both.

20. Squier and Davis, *Ancient Monuments of the Mississippi Valley*, p. xxxiii.

21. Frank Hamilton Cushing to Isaac Hayes, January 20, 1899, American Philosophical Society Archives.

22. Squier, "Aboriginal Monuments of the Mississippi Valley," p. 206.

23. For more on the popularity of geology in the nineteenth century, see Bedell, *The Anatomy of Nature*, chap. 1; Anstead to John Evans, March 30, 1861, American Philosophical Society, Misc. Mss. Collection.

24. Squier, "Aboriginal Monuments of the Mississippi Valley," pp. 158, 163.

25. Ibid., pp. 134–135; Bruce Trigger has noted that the Smithsonian's Joseph Henry played a key role in promoting the "scientific" work of Squier and Davis, helping to establish their methods as the legitimate way of doing archaeological work. See Trigger, *History of Archaeological Thought*, p. 108.

26. Lubbock, "North American Archaeology," p. 319.

27. Gallatin, "A Synopsis of the Indian Tribes of North America," 2:155.

28. Stephen Williams and I disagree on this point. He writes, "From 1870 until nearly the turn of the century, there was a tremendously strong interest in North American archaeology" (Williams, *Fantastic Archaeology*, p. 71). His statement here is unfootnoted so I don't have a good sense of the evidence upon which he bases this claim. My own research indicates that, although interest in North American archaeology certainly didn't vanish, it did wane especially in the emerging institutional worlds of museums and universities.

29. Quoted in Joyce, "Antiquarians and Archaeologists," pp. 312–313.

30. Jefferson, *Notes on the State of Virginia*, p. 97.

31. "Progress of Ethnology in the United States," *Literary World*, 3:663.

32. For a good debunking of Pidgeon's work, see Silverberg, *The Mound Builders;* and Williams, *Fantastic Archaeology.*

33. Pidgeon, *Traditions of De-Coo-Dah and Antiquarian Researches*, pp. 5–12.

34. See "Indian Idols in Iowa," p. 285; see also unidentified newsclipping, American Philosophical Society, Samuel Kneeland Papers.

35. Baldwin, *Ancient America,* p. 34; Bradford, *American Antiquities and Researches into the Origin and History of the Red Race,* p. 435.

36. Kehoe, *The Land of Prehistory,* p. xi, Hinsley, "Revising and Revisioning the History of Archaeology," pp. 79–80.

37. Hinsley, "Digging for Identity," in Mihesuah, ed., *Repatriation Reader,* p. 42.

38. Baldwin, *Ancient America,* p. 33; Pidgeon, *Traditions of De-Coo-Dah,* p. 19.

39. Lubbock, *The Origin of Civilization and the Primitive Condition of Man,* p. iv.

40. Quoted in Carpenter, "The Role of Archaeology in the 19th Century Controversy between Developmentalism and Degeneration," p. 14. Lubbock and fellow antiquarian John Tylor became known as among the foremost of English "progressionists."

41. Kehoe, *The Land of Prehistory,* p. xii; Trigger, "Archaeology and the Image of the American Indian," p. 665.

42. Bradford, *American Antiquities and Researches into the Origin and History of the Red Race,* pp. 172–173.

43. Samuel Kneeland to de Guichainville, December 29, 1885, American Philosophical Society.

44. Trigger, "Archaeology and the Image of the American Indian," p. 664.

45. Peet, "The Mound Builders," pp. 185, 188; and "The Difference between Indian and Mound-Builder Relics," *American Antiquarian,* p. 272.

46. Hallowell, "The Beginnings of Anthropology in America," in de Laguna, ed., *Selected Papers from the American Anthropologist, 1888–1920,* p. 63.

47. Peet, "Some Problems in Connection with the Stone Age," p. 280.

48. Undated, unidentified lecture, Harvard University Archives, Putnam Papers, HUG 1717.2.5.

49. Peet, "A Comparison between the Archaeology of Europe and American," p. 211.

50. Trigger, *A History of Archaeological Thought,* p. 73.

51. Wissler, "The American Indian and the American Philosophical Society," p. 195.

52. Putnam, "Periods of Prehistoric Man," undated, Harvard University Archives, Putnam Papers, HUG 1717.2.5.

53. Peet, "A Comparison between the Archaeology of Europe and American," p. 216, 222; Peet, "Some Problems in Connection with the Stone Age," p. 286.

54. Peet, "Some Problems in Connection with the Stone Age," p. 294.

55. Of course, in the twentieth century archaeologists did develop sophisticated and successful techniques to recover just what people grew and ate.

56. Wilson to Putnam, January 28, 1888, Harvard University Archives, Putnam Papers, HUG 1717.2.1.

57. See Harvard University, Peabody Museum Archives, Director's Records, Box 5.

58. Putnam to Jesup, January 12, 1898, Harvard University Archives, Putnam Papers, HUG 1717.10.

59. In fact, the question of whether or not humans inhabited the continent during the last ice age was only settled to widespread satisfaction in 1926 when the near-complete skeleton of a giant, now extinct, bison was unearthed in New Mexico with a beautifully flaked spear point lodged between its ribs.

60. Baldwin, *Ancient America*, p. 181.

61. Orne to Putnam, February 7, 1890, Harvard University Archives, Putnam Papers, HUG 1717.2.1.

62. Southall, *The Epoch of the Mammoth*, p. viii; Southall, *The Recent Origin of Man*, pp. 56–57.

63. Southall, *The Recent Origin of Man*, pp. 18, 43; Southall, *The Epoch of the Mammoth*, pp. 290, 383.

64. John Henslow to Daniel Nihill, February 14, 1861, American Philosophical Society Archives.

65. See Kehoe, *The Land of Prehistory*, p. 40.

66. Abbott, "Indications of the Indians of North America," p. 67.

67. Peet, "A Comparison between the Archaeology of Europe and America," p. 222.

68. Peet, "Some Problems in Connection with the Stone Age," p. 294; Gero, "Producing History, Controlling the Past: The Case of the New England Beehives," in Wylie and Pinsky, eds., *Critical Traditions in Contemporary Archaeology*, p. 96.

69. See Trigger, "Archaeology and the Image of the American Indian," pp. 662–664 for more on this.

70. Peet, "The Beginnings of History," pp. 273–274.

71. For a thorough account of this, see Kuklick, *Puritans in Babylon*, esp. ch. 1.

72. Kuklick, *Puritans in Babylon*, p. 24.

73. Southall, *The Recent Origin of Man*, see pp. 20–23.

74. Bieder also makes this point in *Science Encounters the Indian, 1820–1880*, p. 143.

75. Kuklick, *Puritans in Babylon*, p. 103.

76. Boas, "Ethnology at the Exposition," pp. 607–609.

77. For more on this see Kuklick, *Puritans in Babylon*, chap. 5.

78. My research on this topic is largely anecdotal and by no means thorough, but my sense is that even today, art history departments don't generally reserve faculty slots for experts in Native American art except at a handful of places. Likewise, though language study in this country began with the study of Indian languages, there are no departments in American universities devoted to teaching them, as there are with, say, Slavic, Romance and classical languages. See Andresen, *Linguistics in America*, esp. pp. 176–188. Increasing numbers of history departments now have experts in Native American history on their faculties, yet while many of them incorporate archaeology into their researches, few, I believe, are actually field workers. Finally, of course, several important museums employ archaeologists on their staff and continue to sponsor fieldwork. Still, on the whole, archaeologists working in the American field didn't make the leap into the new world of the research university one hundred years ago, except into departments of anthropology.

79. See Brinton to Stevenson, July 11, 1894, University Museum Archive, Administrative Records, Director's Office, Box 3.

80. Culin to Brock, March 19, 1902, University Museum Archives, Director's Files, Box 5.

81. Brock to Stevenson, January 25, 1902, University Museum Archives, Director's Files, Box 5.

82. See, for example, Williams, *Fantastic Archaeology,* p. 76.

83. Kneeland to De Guichainville, January 27, 1886, and October 20, 1886, American Philosophical Society Archives.

84. Untitled circular in Director's Files, University Museum Archives, Box 2.

85. Quoted in Mark, *Four Anthropologists,* p. 29.

86. Norton, "The First American Classical Archaeologist," p. 4.

87. Powell, "Problems of American Archaeology," p. 652.

88. Quoted by Hinsley, "Revising and Revisioning the History of Archaeology," in Christenson, ed., *Tracing Archaeology's Past,* p. 84.

Chapter Five

1. Winsor, *Narrative and Critical History of America,* p. 411.

2. Hymes, "The Use of Anthropology: Critical, Political, Personal," in *Reinventing Anthropology,* p. 3.

3. Rafinesque, *The American Nations,* 1:55.

4. For more on Cooper's Russian reception, see Angela Brintlinger, "The Persian Frontier: Griboedov as Orientalist and Literary Hero," *Canadian Slavonic Papers* (Sept.–Dec. 2003). I have stolen this wonderful line about Cooper from Slotkin, *The Fatal Frontier,* p. 81.

5. Cooper to de Broglie, March 22, 1827; Cooper to Gosselin, April 1827, in *Letters and Journals of James Fenimore Cooper,* 1:199, 211–212.

6. "Cooper's Novels and Travels," p. 11; Parkman, "James Fenimore Cooper," p. 150; Sparks, "Heckewelder on the American Indians," pp. 357–403.

7. Heckewelder, "An Account of the History, Manners, and Customs of the Indian Nations," pp. 24, 152, 148, 142–143, 88.

8. Ibid., p. 332.

9. Ibid., pp. 7–8, 343.

10. Ibid., p. 4.

11. See for example, Steele, "Cooper and Clio," pp. 121–135. Slotkin, for one, points out that having studied Heckewelder quite closely, Cooper then took considerable literary license with the material. See Slotkin, *The Fatal Frontier,* p. 94.

12. Heckewelder, "An Account of the History, Manners, and Customs of the Indian Nations," pp. 7–8, 25.

13. Cooper, *Notions of the Americans,* p. 277.

14. Cooper to Bancroft, June 4, 1839, in *Letters of Journals of James Fenimore Cooper,* 3:383–385.

15. Mizruchi, *The Power of Historical Knowledge,* p. 11; Kelly, *Plotting America's Past,* p. vii; "Catlin on the North American Indians," p. 415.

16. See Martin, "From History to Requiem," in Peck, ed., *New Essays on the Last of the Mohicans,* p. 47; Schnell, "The For[e]gone Conclusion," pp. 332–340; Miller, "Thomas Cole and Jacksonian America," p. 80. Richard Slotkin stresses the violent nature of Cooper's view of history, and he sees Cooper as central to the creation of the frontier "myth." See Slotkin, *The Fatal Frontier,* chap. 5.

17. Schnell, "The For[e]gone Conclusion," pp. 333, 340; Axelrad, *History and*

Utopia, p. 2. Louis Rubin makes a similar point in "The Romance of the Colonial Frontier," in Kennedy and Fogel, ed., *American Letters and the Historical Consciousness*, p. 116.

18. DuPonceau, "Report to the Committee on Ethnography," October 17, 1836, American Philosophical Society Archives.

19. The Oxford English Dictionary lists an 1847 use of the word "ethnology" in the *Proceedings of the American Philosophical Society*. I think there must almost certainly be an earlier American use of the term.

20. Clifford, "On Ethnographic Authority," in *The Predicament of Culture*, p. 25.

21. Ibid., pp. 30–32.

22. Irving, *Sketches Taken during an Expedition to the Pawnee Tribes*, pp. 18–19, 41.

23. Ibid., pp. 77–78.

24. *Dictionary of American Biography*, s.v. "Irving, John."

25. Dunbar, "The Pawnee Indians: Their History and Ethnology," pp. 241–281; Dunbar, "The Pawnee Indians," pp. 321–342.

26. Dunbar, "The Pawnee Indians: Their History and Ethnology," p. 256.

27. Quoted in Tilton, *Pocahontas*, p. 88.

28. Cooke, "Cooper's Indians," pp. 264–267.

29. Davis, "Anthropology and Ethnology," p. 394.

30. Gallatin to Macy, March 17, 1846, in *The Writings of Albert Gallatin*, 2:625.

31. There are of course still ethnographers and ethnologists who call themselves such working today. My point however is that by and large most of these are considered to be working within the anthropological field.

32. *Transactions of the American Ethnological Society*, 1:iii, ix.

33. Ibid., 1:ix; E. G. S., "American Ethnology," p. 386; "Transactions of the American Ethnological Society," p. 50.

34. Bartlett, *The Progress of Ethnology*; E. G. S., "American Ethnology," p. 386.

35. *Transactions of the American Ethnological Society*, 2:viii.

36. E. G. S., "American Ethnology," p. 385.

37. Quoted in Davis, "Anthropology and Ethnology," p. 396.

38. Bieder, *Science Encounters the Indian, 1820–1880*, p. 3.

39. E. G. S., "American Ethnology," p. 386.

40. Ruschenberger to Morton, March 3, 1833, American Philosophical Society, Morton Papers.

41. Morton, "Dr. Morton's Craniological Collection," 2:218.

42. Stephen J. Gould claims to have examined the skulls in 1977 and details how Morton jury-rigged the results. See Stephen J. Gould, *The Mismeasure of Man*, pp. 51–72. Whatever one thinks of Morton, his collection remains a remarkable assemblage and a tremendous resource for anatomical studies. Now housed in the University of Pennsylvania's museum, the Morton Collection may be broken up because of claims under the Native American Graves Protection and Repatriation Act (NAGPRA).

43. Hrdlicka to Edward Nolan, May 2, 1911, American Philosophical Society, Morton Papers; Doornek to Morton, June 28, 1835, American Philosophical Society, Morton Papers.

44. E. G. S., "American Ethnology," p. 395.

45. Morton, "Dr. Morton's Craniological Collection," pp. 219.

46. One of those who did proclaim this position publicly was Louis Agassiz, perhaps the preeminent naturalist of the day. Agassiz was thrilled with Morton's empirical research—and told him so in letters and during his visit to Philadelphia. Agassiz seems to have come to polygenesis largely on aesthetic grounds, so revolted was he by the mere presence of black people. Morton gave him the data to support this position. For more on this, see Stephen J. Gould, *The Mismeasure of Man*, chap. 2; and Reginald Horsman, "Scientific Racism and the American Indian in the Mid-Nineteenth Century," pp. 152–168.

47. E. G. S., "American Ethnology," p. 392.

48. Morton, "Dr. Morton's Craniological Collection," pp. 218–219.

49. See Bieder and Tax, "From Ethnologists to Anthropologists," in Murra, ed., *American Anthropology*; Squier, no title, *Journal of the Anthropological Institute of New York* 1 (1871–1872): 16.

50. I risk overgeneralizing here. "Ethnology" and "ethnography" did not simply disappear either as terms or as practices. For example, the American Ethnological Society did revive in the twentieth century and continues to publish *American Ethnologist*. But in the main, "anthropology" became the term of art.

51. Squier, no title, *Journal of the Anthropological Institute of New York* 1 (1871–1872): 3.

52. Ibid., 1:16.

53. Bieder and Tax, "From Ethnologists to Anthropologists," p. 15.

54. Broca, "The Progress of Anthropology in Europe and America," 1:24–41.

55. Clifford, "On Ethnographic Authority," p. 28.

56. Browne, *The Classification of Mankind by the Hair and Wool of their Heads*; Peet, "The Three Fold Division of the Human Race," pp. 171–172.

57. Wright, *Anthropology; or the Science of Man*, p. 93. I don't want to suggest that "ethnology" became coterminous only with race—"anthropology," as a term, sufficed perfectly well for Caucasian, the pseudonym of the Reverend William H. Campbell, author of *Anthropology for the People*. A viciously racist book written by a southerner, its purpose was to provide, according to the subtitle, "a refutation of the theory of the Adamic origin of all races." Published in 1891, this book simply appropriated the new term to fight an old fight.

58. Powell to Boas, December 15, 1887, American Philosophical Society, Boas Papers, Powell Folders.

59. McGee, "Plan for BAE Operations, 7/99–6/00," National Anthropological Archive, Records of the Bureau of American Ethnology/Smithsonian Institution Correspondence, Box 1.

60. Mason, "What Is Anthropology?" p. 4.

61. Hale, "Man and Language," p. 16.

62. "The American Indian and the American Philosophical Society," pp. 190–193. Wissler also believed that Powell's 1891 handbook "is still the accepted one."

63. Boas to Powell, June 2, 1887, National Anthropological Archive, Records of the Bureau of American Ethnology, Correspondence Box 54; Boas to Powell, November 28, 1888, American Philosophical Society, Boas Papers, Powell Folders.

64. Powell, "The Course of Human Progress," p. 220; Powell, "The Problems of American Archaeology," pp. 650–651; Powell, "The Three Methods of Evolution," reprinted in Daniel, ed. *Darwinism Comes to America*, p. 116–119.

65. Powell, "Sketch of Lewis H. Morgan," p. 117.

66. Murphree, "The Evolutionary Anthropologists," pp. 290, 299.

67. Bieder, *Science Encounters the Indian, 1820–1880*, p. 194; Lowie, *The History of Ethnological Theory*, p. 56. See also Resek, *Lewis Henry Morgan*, esp. p. 156.

68. See Kuper, *The Invention of Primitive Society*, p. 42.

69. Resek, *Lewis Henry Morgan*, p. 134.

70. Hinsley, *The Smithsonian and the American Indian*, p. 29; Campbell, *American Indian Languages*, p. 58.

71. Hinsley, *The Smithsonian and the American Indian*, p. 29.

72. Powell, "The Course of Human Progress," p. 220; quoted in Hinsley, *The Smithsonian and the American Indian*, p. 161.

73. Whitney, "The Value of Linguistic Science to Ethnology," pp. 44–52.

74. Trigger, *History of Archaeological Thought*, p. 125.

75. Achelis, "The Science of Ethnology," p. 2313.

76. For an important general discussion of this topic, see Collier and Tschopik, "The Role of Museums in American Anthropology," pp. 768–779.

77. Agassiz to Cary, March 23, 1863, Harvard University, Peabody Museum Archives, Director's Records, Box 5.

78. See *First Annual Report of the Trustees of the Peabody Museum*, pp. 25–26.

79. *Fifth Annual Report of the Trustees of the Peabody Museum*, p. 26.

80. Putnam to Morgan, April 8, 1880, Putnam Papers, HUG 11717.2.1, Harvard University Archives.

81. *Tenth Annual Report of the Trustees of the Peabody Museum*, p. 7; unidentified lecture, 1882, Harvard University Archives, Putnam Papers, HUG 11717.2.5; Putnam to Morgan, April 8, 1880, Harvard University Archives, Putnam Papers, HUG 11717.2.1.

82. *Fourteenth Annual Report of the Trustees of the Peabody Museum*, p. 7; *Eighteenth & Nineteenth Annual Reports of the Trustees of the Peabody Museum*, pp. 481–482.

83. See, for example, *Guide to the Peabody Museum of Harvard University* (1898).

84. *Fourteenth Annual Report of the Trustees of the Peabody Museum*, p. 25; for an account of the early years of the Peabody and of Harvard's anthropology department, see Hinsley, "The Museum Origins of Harvard Anthropology," in Elliott and Rossiter eds., *Science at Harvard University*, pp. 121–145.

85. Putnam to Jesup, November, 1894, and June, 21, 1894, Putnam Papers, HUG 1717.10, Harvard University Archives.

86. The episode is related in Rydell, *All the World's a Fair*, p. 63. Quotes taken from there.

87. Speech, November 28, 1891, Field Museum Archives.

88. Putnam to Boas, May 14, 1894, Boas Papers, American Philosophical Society.

89. Putnam to Jesup, April 6, 1896, Harvard University Archives, HUG 1717.10.

90. Putnam to Bowditch, March 4, 1892, Harvard University Archives, Putnam Papers, HUG 11717.2.1.

91. In 1911, the Smithsonian transferred all the Indian objects it had been accumulating since the 1850s to the newly created National Museum of Natural History.

92. Undated speech, Harvard University Archives, Putnam Papers, HUG 11717.2.5.

93. Putnam to Bowditch, March 4, 1892, Harvard University Archives, Putnam Papers, HUG 11717.2.1.

94. Goode, "Museum-History and Museums of History," in *Origins of Natural Science in America*, pp. 311–312.

95. See Conn, *Museums and American Intellectual Life,* chap. 3.

96. *Bulletin of the Free Museum of Science and Art,* June, 1899, p. 71.

97. Putnam to Eliot, December 21, 1889, Harvard University, Peabody Museum Archives, Director's Records, Box 5.

98. Mason, Annual Report, Smithsonian Institution Archives, RU 158, Box 4.

99. Achelis, "The Science of Ethnology," p. 2314.

100. Putnam to Jesup, January 12, 1898, Harvard University Archives, Putnam Papers, HUG 1717.10.

101. Dixon, "Anthropology, 1866–1929," in Morison, ed. *The Development of Harvard University Since the Inauguration of President Eliot, 1869–1929,* p. 202; Hinsley, "The Museum Origins of Harvard Anthropology, 1866–1915," p. 121.

102. Guide to the Peabody Museum of Harvard University, 1898, pp. 26–27.

103. Hinsley, *The Smithsonian and the American Indian,* p. 265. Of course, important work continued to come from the BAE throughout the twentieth century.

104. It has already been told by several scholars, including Regna Darnell and George Stocking.

105. Boas to Walcott, January 30, 1918, American Philosophical Society, Boas Papers.

106. Darnell, *Invisible Genealogies,* p. 41.

107. Ibid.

108. Mark, *Four Anthropologists,* pp. 54–55.

109. David Jenkins, "Object Lessons and Ethnographic Displays," p. 256; Boas quoted in Hinsley, *The Smithsonian and the American Indian,* p. 98. As Annie Coombs has written, even as more anthropologists became disenchanted with the crude evolutionary theories of culture at the turn of the twentieth century, those theories still largely governed the way ethnographic material was presented to the public in museum displays. See Coombs, "Ethnography and the Formation of National and Cultural Identities," in Hiller, ed. *The Myth of Primitivism,* p. 197.

110. Boas, "Ethnology at the Exposition," p. 609.

111. Clifford, "On Ethnographic Authority," in *The Predicament of Culture,* p. 32.

112. Mason, "Sketch of North American Anthropology in 1879," p. 345; "What Is Anthropology?" p. 4.

113. Lowie, *The History of Ethnological Theory,* pp. 3–4.

Chapter Six

1. Alvord to Peet, January 28, 1908, Beloit College Archives, Peet Papers. The references to Holmes come from a 1906 letter also at Beloit. See Holmes to Peet, November 22, 1906.

2. Wilson to Goode, April 28, 1890, Smithsonian Institution Archives, RU 201, Box 13.

3. Sparks, no title, *North American Review* 20 (1828): 367.

4. Bann, *Romanticism and the Rise of History*, p. 15.

5. Frye, *Anatomy of Criticism*, pp. 136–137; White, *Metahistory*, p. 9; see also Ross, "Grand Narrative in American Historical Writing: From Romance to Uncertainty," esp. pp. 651–653.

6. Levin, *History as Romantic Art*, p. 7.

7. Ibid., p. 31; Motley, *Historic Progress and American Democracy*, p. 6.

8. White, *Metahistory*, pp. 429–430.

9. Berkhofer, *The White Man's Indian*, p. 95.

10. Quoted in Jacobs, *Francis Parkman*, pp. 171–173.

11. Ibid., pp. 171–173.

12. Quoted in ibid., p. 6; Parkman to Underwood, September 11, 1887, *Parkman Letters*, 3:208.

13. Parkman to Bancroft, October 18, 1878, *Parkman Letters*, 2:117

14. Parkman to Margry, December 6, 1878, ibid., 2:124

15. Parkman to Holmes, May 6, 1849, ibid., 1:61; Parkman to Casgrain, October 23, 1887, ibid., 2:213.

16. Historian Francis Jennings has accused Parkman of promoting "an ideology of divisiveness and hate based on racism, bigotry, misogyny, authoritarianism, chauvinism, and upper-class arrogance," which strikes me as both true and unfairly anachronistic in equal measure. Jennings, *Empire of Fortune*, p. 480. See also, Levin, *History as Romantic Art*, p. 137.

17. Parkman to Squier, April 2, 1850, *Parkman Letters*, 1:68; Parkman, "Native Races of the Pacific States," pp. 43–44.

18. *Pontiac* has proved remarkably enduring—the University of Nebraska Press came out with a new edition of the work in 1994.

19. Parkman to Draper, December 23, 1845, *Parkman Letters*, 1:31.

20. Mitchell, *Witnesses to a Vanishing American*, p. 161; Mayer, "Tah-Gah-Jute or Logan and Captain Michael Cresap."

21. See Salamon, "Two Nineteenth-Century Views of History," p. 156.

22. Parkman, *The Conspiracy of Pontiac*, 1:39–45.

23. Levin, *History as Romantic Art*, p. 139.

24. Sheehan, "Looking Back: Parkman's Pontiac," p. 58.

25. Parkman, *The Conspiracy of Pontiac*, 2:313.

26. Scheckel, *The Insistence of the Indian*, pp. 39–40.

27. I should note here that my reading of this differs from that of Susan Mizruchi, who sees Parkman's treatment of Pontiac as a "refusal to accommodate the national amnesia about the American Indian." Mizruchi, *The Power of Knowledge*, p. 51.

28. Henderson, *Versions of the Past*, p. 33.

29. Parkman to Underwood, September 17, 1887, *Parkman Letters*, 2:208.

30. See Parkman to Draper, July 19, 1851, ibid., 1:84.

31. Parker, "Notes for a Lecture," Newberry Library, Ayer Papers, Mss folder 674.

32. Wilson to Putnam, December 27, 1881, Harvard University Archives, Putnam Papers, HUG 1717.2.1.

33. Schoolcraft, "Influence of Ardent Spirits on the Condition of the North American Indians," pp. 19–20.

34. Baldwin, *Prehistoric Nations*, pp. 26–27; Wilson, "Importance of the Science and of the Department of Prehistoric Anthropology," p. 681.

35. In 1897, the departments of ethnology, oriental antiquities, prehistoric anthropology, and arts and industries at the National Museum were merged into one comprehensive Department of Anthropology.

36. Wilson, *Prehistoric Man*, pp. vii, 3, 17.

37. Ibid., p. 280; Figuier, *Primitive Man*, p. 336.

38. Wilson, *Prehistoric Man*, pp. 36, 43.

39. Dawkins, "Early Man in America," pp. 338, 348; Peet, "Autochthonous Origin of the American Civilization," p. 314; Mason to Goode, August 31, 1889, Smithsonian Institution Archives, Unites States National Museum Correspondence, RU 201, Box 12. This view of the "prehistoric" nature of Native American "savages" lasted well into the twentieth century. Glyn Daniel, a distinguished British archaeologist, believed that "in studying American cultural origins we are engaged in what is almost a controlled laboratory experiment. That is why American prehistory is so important to the prehistorian working in Europe or the Near East or India." He wrote that in 1962. Daniel, *The Idea of Prehistory*, p. 99.

40. Louis Agassiz also volleyed forth in this vein in an essay for the *Atlantic* entitled, "America the Old World."

41. Peet, *Prehistoric America*, 1:1; Wilson, "Importance of the Science and of the Department of Prehistoric Anthropology," pp. 682–683; Blacket, *Researches into the Lost Histories of America*, p. 1.

42. Wilson, *Prehistoric Annals of Scotland*, p. xiii.

43. Wilson, *Prehistoric Man*, 2:155.

44. Mason, untitled, undated manuscript, National Anthropological Archives, Records of the BAE, Correspondence 1888–1906, Box 36A. See also Carpenter, "The Role of Archaeology in the 19th Century Controversy between Developmentalism and Degeneration," p. 15.

45. Wilson, "Importance of the Science and of the Department of Prehistoric Anthropology," p. 682.

46. Fellows, "The Relation of Anthropology to the Study of History," p. 47.

47. Motley, *Historic Progress*, p. 12.

48. Wilson, Annual Report, 1890–91, Smithsonian Institution Archives, RU 158, Box 4; Otis Mason, "The Border-land between the Historian and the Archaeologist," National Anthropological Archives, Department of Anthropology, Division of Ethnology, Box 37.

49. Powell, "Problems of American Archaeology," p. 650; Goodrich, *A History of All Nations*, p. 9; Winsor, "The Perils of Historical Narrative," p. 296; Becker quoted in Higham, "The Construction of American History," p. 113; Rhodes quoted in Holt, *Historical Scholarship in the United States*, p. 17.

50. For details about Adams's career in Germany, see Cunningham, "The German Historical World of Herbert Baxter Adams," pp. 261–275.

51. Quoted in Holt, *Historical Scholarship in the United States*, p. 17.

52. Higham, "The Construction of American History," p. 113.

53. Ross, "Historical Consciousness in Nineteenth Century America," p. 921.

54. Loewenberg, *American History in American Thought*, p. 372; see also Tyrell, "Making Nations/Making States," p. 1031.

55. Powell, "From Barbarism to Civilization," p. 97.

56. See Bogue, *Frederick Jackson Turner*, p. 99.

57. Beard quoted in Bogue, p. 117.

58. Turner, "The Significance of the Frontier in American History," in *The Frontier in American History*, pp. 2–4.

59. Turner, "The Significance of the Frontier in American History," p. 4.

60. Hofstadter quoted in Bogue, *Frederick Jackson Turner*, p. 117; Noble, *The End of American History*, p. 18.

61. Turner, "The Significance of the Frontier in American History," pp. 1, 38.

62. Turner to Constance Skinner, March 15, 1922, State Historical Society of Wisconsin, Turner Papers, Box 3.

63. Gallatin, *Inaugural Address*, pp. 11–12.

64. Bogue, *Frederick Jackson Turner*, p. 55.

65. See "Inventory," State Historical Society of Wisconsin, Turner Papers, Box 3; Lecture Notes, ibid., Box 4.

66. Lecture Notes, State Historical Society of Wisconsin, Turner Papers, Box 4.

67. Klein, *Frontiers of Historical Imagination*, p. 142.

68. Turner, "The Significance of the Frontier in American History," pp. 2–4.

69. Powell, "From Barbarism to Civilization," p. 99.

70. Heckewelder, "An Account" p. 331; Schoolcraft, *Influence of Ardent Spirits on the Condition of the North American Indians*, p. 7; McCoy, *Remarks on the Practicability of Indian Reform*, pp. 3–4; McKenney, *Memoirs, Official and Personal*, p. 234.

71. For more on this see Klein, *Frontiers of Historical Imagination*, especially Book I. I disagree with Klein on Turner's use of the Indians as part of the comedic strategy, but his analysis is powerful and worth considering.

72. Turner, "The Significance of the Frontier in American History," p. 11.

73. Combe to Morton, December 23, 1839, American Philosophical Society, Morton Papers.

74. Adams quoted in Resek, *Lewis Henry Morgan*, pp. 41–42; Fellows, "The Relation of Anthropology to the Study of History," p. 48.

75. Brinton, "The Aims of Anthropology," p. 64; Parkman to Morgan, September 24, 1865, *Parkman Letters*, 1:190.

76. Daniel, *The Idea of Prehistory*, p. 34.

77. Peet, "The Beginnings of History," p. 273.

BIBLIOGRAPHY

Archival Sources
American Philosophical Society, Boas Papers; Historical and Literary Committee,
    Letterbooks; Morton Papers
Beloit College Archives, Peet Papers
Harvard University Archives
National Anthropological Archive, Records of the Bureau of American Ethnology/
    Smithsonian Institution, Correspondence
Newberry Library, Edward Ayer Collection
New York Historical Society, Gallatin Papers
Peabody Museum Archives, Harvard University
Smithsonian Institution Archives
University of Pennsylvania Museum Archives, Director's Files
Wisconsin State Historical Society

Books
Aarsleff, Hans, Louis G. Kelly, and Hans-Josef Niederehe, eds. *Papers in the History of
    Linguistics.* Amsterdam/Philadelphia: John Benjamins Publishing Company, 1987.
Abrams, Ann Uhry. *The Valiant Hero: Benjamin West and Grand-Style History Painting.*
    Washington, D.C.: Smithsonian Institution Press, 1985.
Adair, James. *The History of the American Indians.* London: Edward and Charles Dilly,
    1775.
Adam, Hans Christian. *Edward Sheriff Curtis.* New York: Taschen, 1999.
Alter, Stephen. *Darwinism and the Linguistic Image: Language, Race, and Natural Theol-
    ogy in the Nineteenth Century.* Baltimore: Johns Hopkins University Press, 1999.
Anderson, Benedict. *Imagined Communities: Reflections on the Origin and Spread of Na-
    tionalism.* New York: Verso, 1991.
Andreson, Julie Tetel. *Linguistics in America, 1769–1924: A Critical History.* London:
    Routledge, 1990.
Annual Reports of the Trustees of the Peabody Museum (1868–1887).
Axelrad, Allan. *History and Utopia: A Study of the World View of James Fenimore Cooper.*
    Norwood, Pa.: Norwood Editions, 1978.

253

Baldwin, J. D. *Ancient America*. New York: Harper & Brothers, 1872.

———. *Pre-historic Nations*. New York: Harper & Brothers, 1873.

Bann, Stephen. *Romanticism and the Rise of History*. New York: Twayne, 1995.

Bartlett, John Russell. *The Progress of Ethnology*. New York: Bartlett & Welford, 1847.

Barton, Benjamin Smith. *New Views of the Origin of the Tribes and Nations of America*. Philadelphia: n.p., 1797.

Beach, W. W., ed. *The Indian Miscellany*. Albany: J. Munsell, 1877.

Bedell, Rebecca. *The Anatomy of Nature: Geology and American Landscape Painting, 1825–1875*. Princeton: Princeton University Press, 2001.

Bellin, Joshua David. *The Demon of the Continent: Indians and the Shaping of American Literature*. Philadelphia: University of Pennsylvania Press, 2001.

Berkhofer, Robert. *The White Man's Indian: Images of the American Indian from Columbus to the Present*. New York: Vintage Books, 1978.

Bieder, Robert. *Science Encounters the Indian, 1820–1880: The Early Years of American Ethnology*. Norman: University of Oklahoma Press, 1986.

Blacket, W. S. *Researches into the Lost Histories of America*. Philadelphia: J. B. Lippincott & Co., 1884.

Boas, Franz. *Handbook of American Indian Languages*; J. W. Powell, *Indian Linguistic Families of America North of Mexico*. Edited by Preston Holder. Lincoln: University of Nebraska Press, 1966.

Bogue, Allen G. *Frederick Jackson Turner: Strange Roads Going Down*. Norman: University of Oklahoma Press, 1998.

Bowditch, Nancy Douglas. *George de Forest Brush: Recollections of a Joyous Painter*. Peterborough, N.H.: Noone House, 1970.

Bradford, Alexander. *American Antiquities and Researches into the Origin and History of the Red Race*. New York: Wiley & Putnam, 1843.

Brinton, Daniel. *Aboriginal Authors and Their Productions*. Philadelphia: n.p., 1883.

———. *Essays of an Americanist*. Philadelphia: Porter & Coates, 1890.

Browne, Peter. *The Classification of Mankind by the Hair and Wool of Their Heads*. Philadelphia: J. H. Jones, 1852.

Brush, George de Forest. *A Catalogue of an Exhibition of Paintings and Drawings by George de Forest Brush*. New York: American Academy of Arts and Letters, 1933.

Bulletin of the Archaeological Institute of America (1883).

Burbank, E. A. *Burbank among the Indians*. Caldwell, Idaho: The Caxton Printers, 1944.

Burnham, Patricia, and Lucretia Hoover Giese, eds. *Redefining American History Painting*. Cambridge: Cambridge University Press, 1995.

A Cabinet of Curiosities: Five Episodes in the Evolution of American Museums. Charlottesville: University of Virginia Press, 1967.

Campbell, Lyle. *American Indian Languages: The Historical Linguistics of Native America*. Oxford: Oxford University Press, 1997.

Campbell, Rev. William [Caucasian, pseud.]. *Anthropology for the People: A Refutation of the Theory of the Adamic Origin of All Races*. Richmond, Va.: Everett Waddey, 1891.

Carr, Helen. *Inventing the American Primitive*. Cork: Cork University Press, 1996.

Catlin, George. *Catlin's North American Indian Portfolio*. London: n.p., 1844.

————. *Last Rambles amongst the Indians of the Rocky Mountains and the Andes.* London: Gall and Inglis, n.d.

————. *Letters and Notes on the Manners, Customs and Condition of the North American Indians.* 1841. Reprint, New York: Dover, 1973.

————. *Life among the Indians.* 1875. Reprint, New York: Random House, 1996.

Child, Lydia Marie. *Hobomok & Other Writings on Indians.* Edited by Carolyn Karcher. New Brunswick, N.J.: Rutgers University Press, 1986.

Christenson, Andrew L., ed. *Tracing Archaeology's Past: The Historiography of Archaeology.* Carbondale : Southern Illinois University Press, 1989.

Cmiel, Kenneth. *Democratic Eloquence: The Fight over Popular Speech in Nineteenth-Century America.* New York: William Morrow, 1990.

Conn, Steven. *Museums and American Intellectual Life, 1876–1926.* Chicago: University of Chicago Press, 1998.

Conningham, Frederic A. *Currier & Ives Prints, An Illustrated Check List.* New York: Crown Publishers, Inc. 1970.

Cooper, James Fenimore. *The Letters and Journals of James Fenimore Cooper.* Edited by James Franklin Beard. 6 vols. Cambridge: Harvard University Press, Belknap Press, 1960–1968.

————. *Notions of the Americans.* New York: Frederick Ungar Publishing Co., 1963.

Cosentino, Andrew F. *The Paintings of Charles Bird King (1785–1862).* Washington, D.C.: Smithsonian Institution Press, 1977.

Daniel, Glyn. *The Idea of Prehistory.* London: C. A. Watts & Co., 1962.

Darnell, Regna. *Daniel Garrison Brinton: "The Fearless Critic" of Philadelphia.* Philadelphia: University of Pennsylvania Publications in Anthropology, #3, 1988.

————. *Invisible Genealogies: A History of Americanist Anthropology.* Lincoln: University of Nebraska Press, 2001.

Degler, Carl. *In Search of Human Nature: The Decline and Revival of Darwinism in American Social Thought.* Oxford: Oxford University Press, 1991.

Deloria, Philip. *Playing Indian.* New Haven: Yale University Press, 1998.

Dilworth, Leah. *Imagining Indians in the Southwest: Persistent Visions of a Primitive Past.* Washington, D.C.: Smithsonian Institution Press, 1996.

Dinneen, Francis P., and E. F. Konrad Koerner, eds. *North American Contributions to the History of Linguistics.* Philadelphia: John Benjamins Publishing Company, 1990.

Dippie, Brian. *Catlin and His Contemporaries: The Politics of Patronage.* Lincoln: University of Nebraska Press, 1990.

Donaldson, Thomas. *The George Catlin Indian Gallery in the U.S. National Museum.* Washington, D.C.: Government Printing Office, 1887.

Drake, Francis. *Indian History for Young Folks.* New York: Harper & Brothers, 1885.

Drake, Samuel. *Biography and History of the Indians of North America.* Boston: Benjamin & Murray & Co., 1851.

Dunlap, William. *History of the Rise and Progress of the Arts and Designs in the United States.* 2 vols. New York: George P. Scott & Co., 1834.

Edwards, Elizabeth. *Anthropology and Photography, 1860–1920.* New Haven: Yale University Press, 1992.

Edwards, Jonathan. *Observations on the Language of the Muhhekanwew Indians.* New Haven: Josiah Meigs, 1788.

Elliott, Clark A., and Margaret Rossiter, eds. *Science at Harvard University.* Bethlehem, Pa.: Lehigh University Press, 1992.

Encyclopedia Americana. Philadelphia: Desilver, Thomas & Co., 1836.

Events in Indian History. Lancaster, Pa.: G. Hills & Co., 1841.

Fabian, Johannes. *Time and the Other: How Anthropology Makes Its Object.* New York: Columbia University Press, 1983.

Fewkes, J. Walter, ed. *A Journal of American Ethnology and Archaeology.* Boston: Houghton, Mifflin and Company, 1891.

Fitzpatrick, Ellen. *History's Memory: Writing America's Past, 1880–1980.* Cambridge: Harvard University Press, 2002.

Fixico, Donald, ed. *Rethinking American Indian History.* Albuquerque: University of New Mexico Press, 1997.

Foster, J. W. *Pre-Historic Races of the United States of America.* Chicago: S. C. Griggs and Company, 1873.

Frost, John. *The American Speaker.* Philadelphia: Thomas, Cowperthwaite & Co., 1838.

———. *The Book of Good Examples,* Philadelphia: G. S. Appleton & Co., 1847.

———. *Indian Wars of the United States.* Philadelphia: Jos. B. Smith & Co., 1855.

Frye, Northrop. *Anatomy of Criticism.* Princeton: Princeton University Press, 1957.

Gallatin, Albert. *Inaugural Address.* New York: James Wright, 1843.

———. *The Writings of Albert Gallatin.* Edited by Henry Adams. 3 vols. Philadelphia: Lippincott & Co., 1879.

Galt, John. *The Life and Studies of Benjamin West.* Philadelphia: Moses Thomas, 1816.

———. *The Life and Works of Benjamin West.* London: T. Codell & W. Davies, 1820.

———. *The Progress of Genius, or Authentic Memoirs of the Early Life of Benjamin West.* Boston: Leonard C. Bowles, 1832.

Gidley, Mick. *Edward S. Curtis and the North American Indian, Incorporated.* Cambridge: Cambridge University Press, 1998.

Goode, George Brown, ed. *The Smithsonian Institution, 1846–1896.* Washington D.C., 1897.

Goodrich, Samuel G. *A History of All Nations.* Auburn: Derby and Miller, 1853.

Gossman, Lionel. *Between History and Literature.* Cambridge: Harvard University Press, 1990.

Gould, Stephen J. *The Mismeasure of Man.* New York: W. W. Norton & Company, 1981.

Gray, Edward. *New World Babel: Languages and Nations in Early America.* Princeton: Princeton University Press, 1999.

Gruber, Jacob, ed. *The Philadelphia Anthropological Society.* Philadelphia: Temple University Press, 1967.

Gustafson, Sandra M. *Eloquence Is Power: Oratory & Performance in Early America.* Chapel Hill: University of North Carolina Press, Omohundro Institute, 2001.

Halttunen, Karen. *Confidence Men and Painted Women: A Study of Middle-Class Culture in America, 1830–1870.* New Haven: Yale University Press, 1982.

Hauptman, Laurence M. *Tribes and Tribulations: Misconceptions about American Indians and their Histories.* Albuquerque: University of New Mexico Press, 1995.

Haven, Samuel. *The Archaeology of the United States*. Introduction by Gordon Willey. New York: AMS Press, Peabody Museum, 1973.

Hayden, F. V. *Contributions to the Ethnography and Philology of the Indian Tribes of the Missouri Valley*. Philadelphia: C. Sherman & Sons, 1862.

Hegeman, Susan. *Patterns for America: Modernism and the Concept of Culture*. Princeton: Princeton University Press, 1999.

Henderson, Harry B. *Versions of the Past: The Historical Imagination in American Fiction*. New York: Oxford University Press, 1974.

Hendricks, Gordon. *Albert Bierstadt: Painter of the American West*. New York: H. N. Abrams, in association with the Amon Carter Museum of Western Art, 1974. Reprint, New York: Harrison House, distributed by Crown Publishers, 1988.

Higham, John. *Writing American History: Essays on Modern Scholarship*. Bloomington: Indiana University Press, 1970.

Hiller, Susan, ed. *The Myth of Primitivism*. London: Routledge, 1991.

Hinsley, Curtis M. *The Smithsonian and the American Indian: Making a Moral Anthropology in Victorian America*. Washington, D.C.: Smithsonian Institution Press, 1981.

History of the Indians of North and South America by the Author of Peter Parley's Tales. Boston: Rand and Mann, 1849.

Holder, Preston, ed. *Introduction to Handbook of American Indian Languages*. [Includes Franz Boas, *Handbook of American Indian Languages*, and J. W. Powell, *Indian Linguistic Families of America North of Mexico*.] Lincoln: University of Nebraska Press, 1966.

Holt, W. Stull. *Historical Scholarship in the United States*. Seattle: University of Washington Press, 1967.

Horan, James D. *The McKenney-Hall Portrait Gallery of American Indians*. New York: Crown Publishers, Inc., 1972.

Hoxie, Frederick, et al., eds. *Native Americans and the Early Republic*. Charlottesville: University of Virginia Press, for the U.S. Capitol Historical Society, 1999.

Huhndorf, Shari M. *Going Native: Indians in the American Cultural Imagination*. Ithaca, N.Y.: Cornell University Press, 2001.

Hymes, Dell H. *Essays in the History of Linguistic Anthropology*. Philadelphia: John Benjamins Publishing Company, 1983.

———, ed. *Reinventing Anthropology*. New York: Vintage Books, 1974.

Irving, John T. *Indian Sketches Taken during an Expedition to the Pawnee Tribes*. 2 vols. Philadelphia: Carey, Lea and Blanchard, 1835.

Jackson, Henry. *Benjamin West: His Life and Work*. Philadelphia: John C. Winston Co., 1900.

Jacobs, Wilbur. *Francis Parkman: Historian as Hero*. Austin: University of Texas Press, 1991.

Jefferson, Thomas. *Notes on the State of Virginia*. Edited by William Peden. Chapel Hill: University of North Carolina Press, Institute of Early American History and Culture, 1955.

———. *The Writings of Thomas Jefferson*. Edited by Albert Bergh. 20 vols. in 10. Washington, D.C.: Thomas Jefferson Memorial Association, 1907.

Jennings, Francis. *Empire of Fortune: Crowns, Colonies, and Tribes in the Seven Years War in America*. New York: Norton, 1988.

Jennings, Jesse, ed. *Ancient North Americans.* New York: W. H. Freeman, 1983.

Johnes, Arthur James. *Philological Proofs of the Original Unity and Recent Origin of the Human Race.* London: J.R. Smith, 1846.

Karp, Ivan, and Steven D. Lavine, *Exhibiting Cultures: The Poetics and Politics of Museum Display.* Washington, D.C.: Smithsonian Institution Press, 1991.

Kehoe, Alice Beck. *The Land of Prehistory: A Critical History of American Archaeology.* London: Routledge, 1998.

Kelly, William. *Plotting America's Past: Fenimore Cooper and the Leatherstocking Tales.* Carbondale: Southern Illinois University Press, 1983.

Kemp, Anthony. *The Estrangement of the Past: A Study in the Origins of Modern Historical Consciousness.* Oxford: Oxford University Press, 1991.

Kennedy, J. Gerald, and Daniel Mark Fogel, eds. *American Letters and the Historical Consciousness.* Baton Rouge: Louisiana State University Press, 1987.

King, Richard C. *Colonial Discourses, Collective Memories, and the Exhibition of Native American Cultures and Histories in the Contemporary United States.* New York: Garland Press, 1998.

Klein, Kerwin Lee. *Frontiers of Historical Imagination: Narrating the European Conquest of Native America,* Berkeley: University of California Press, 1997.

Kohlstedt, Sally. *Origins of Natural Science in America: The Essays of George Brown Goode.* Washington, D.C.: Smithsonian Institution Press, 1991.

Kramer, Michael. *Imagining Language in America: From the Revolution to the Civil War.* Princeton: Princeton University Press, 1992.

Kuklick, Bruce. *Puritans in Babylon: The Ancient Near East and American Intellectual Life, 1880–1930.* Princeton: Princeton University Press, 1996.

Kuper, Adam. *The Invention of Primitive Society: Transformations of an Illusion.* London: Routledge, 1988.

Kupperman, Karen, ed. *America in the European Consciousness, 1493–1750.* Chapel Hill: University of North Carolina Press, Institute for Early American Study, 1995.

Laguna, Frederica de, ed. *Selected Papers from the American Anthropologist, 1888–1920.* Evanston, Ill.: Row, Peterson & Company, 1960.

Laird, Charlton. *Language in America.* Englewood Cliffs, N.J.: Prentice Hall, 1970.

Levin, David. *History as Romantic Art: Bancroft, Prescott, Motley and Parkman.* Palo Alto: Stanford University Press, 1959.

Lewis, David Levering. *W. E. B. Du Bois: Biography of a Race.* New York: Henry Holt, 1993.

Limerick, Patricia Nelson. *The Legacy of Conquest: The Unbroken Past of the American West.* New York: Norton, 1987.

Lowie, Robert. *The History of Ethnological Theory.* New York: Holt, Rinehart and Winston, 1937.

Lubbock, John. *The Origin of Civilization and the Primitive Condition of Man.* New York: D. Appleton and Company, 1874.

———. *Prehistoric Times.* 7th ed. New York: Henry Holt and Company, 1913.

Mark, Joan. *Four Anthropologists: An American Science in its Early Years.* New York: Science History Publications, 1980.

Martin, Calvin, ed. *The American Indian and the Problem of History.* Oxford: Oxford University Press, 1987.

McCabe, James. *The Illustrated History of the Centennial Exhibition.* Philadelphia: National Publishing Company, 1876.

McCoy, Isaac. *Remarks on the Practicability of Indian Reform.* New York: Gray and Bunce, 1829.

Mcgee, W. J., and Cyrus Thomas. *Prehistoric North America.* Philadelphia: George Barrie & Sons, 1905.

McKenney, Thomas, and James Hall. *History of the Indian Tribes of North America.* Philadelphia: D. Rice and A. N. Hart, 1849–1854.

———. *Memoirs, Official and Personal.* 2 vols. in 1. New York: Paine and Burgess, 1846.

McKenney, Thomas, and James Hall. *The Indian Tribes of North America.* Edited by Frederick Webb Hodge and David Bushnell. Edinburgh: John Grant, 1934.

Meek, Ronald. *Social Science and the Ignoble Savage.* Cambridge: Cambridge University Press, 1976.

Michaelson, Scott. *The Limits of Multiculturalism: Interrogating the Origins of American Anthropology.* Minneapolis: University of Minnesota Press, 1999.

Micklethwait, David. *Noah Webster and the American Dictionary.* Jefferson City, N.C.: McFarland & Company, Inc., 2000.

Mihesuah, Devon, ed. *Repatriation Reader: Who Owns American Indian Remains?* Lincoln: University of Nebraska Press, 2000.

Miller, Angela. *The Empire of the Eye.* Ithaca, N.Y.: Cornell University Press, 1993.

Mitchell, Lee Clark. *Witnesses to a Vanishing America: The Nineteenth-Century Response.* Princeton: Princeton University Press, 1981.

Mizruchi, Susan L. *The Power of Knowledge: Narrating the Past in Hawthorne, James, and Dreiser.* Princeton: Princeton University Press, 1988.

Moore, Robert J. *Native Americans, A Portrait: The Art and Travels of Charles Bird King, George Catlin, and Karl Bodmer.* New York: Stewart, Tabori & Chang, 1997.

Morison, Samuel Eliot, ed. *The Development of Harvard University Since the Inauguration of President Eliot, 1869–1929.* Cambridge: Harvard University Press, 1930.

Motella, Arthur P., et al., eds. *A Scientist in American Life: Essays and Lectures of Joseph Henry.* Washington, D.C.: Smithsonian Institution Press, 1980.

Motley, John Lothrop. *Historic Progress and American Democracy.* New York: Charles Scribner and Co., 1869.

Murra, John. *American Anthropology: The Early Years.* St. Paul, Minn.: West Publishing Co., 1976.

Nadaillac, Jean-François-Albert du Pouget, marquis de. *Pre-historic America.* New York: G. P. Putnam's Sons, 1884.

Noah, M. M. *Discourse on the Evidence of the American Indians Being Descendants of the Lost Tribes of Israel.* New York: James Van Norden, 1837.

Noble, David. *The End of American History: Democracy, Capitalism, and the Metaphor of Two Worlds in Anglo-American Historical Writing, 1880–1980.* Minneapolis: University of Minnesota Press, 1985.

Nobles, Gregory H. *American Frontiers: Cultural Encounters and Continental Conquest.* New York: Hill and Wang, 1997.

Nott, Josiah. *Two Lectures on the Connection between the Biblical and Physical History of Man.* New York: Bartlett & Welford, 1849.

Oleson, Alexandra, and John Voss, eds. *The Organization of Knowledge in Modern America, 1860–1920.* Baltimore: Johns Hopkins University Press, 1979.

Pagden, Anthony. *The Fall of Natural Man: The American Indian and the Origins of Comparative Ethnology.* Cambridge: Cambridge University Press, 1982.

Parkman, Francis. *The Conspiracy of Pontiac and the Indian War after the Conquest of Canada.* 9th ed. Boston: Little, Brown and Company, 1891.

———. *Letters of Francis Parkman.* Edited by Wilbur Jacobs. Norman: University of Oklahoma Press, 1960.

Pearce, Roy Harvey. *The Savages of America: A Study of the Indian and the Idea of Civilization.* Baltimore: Johns Hopkins University Press, 1953.

Peck, H. Daniel, ed. *New Essays on the Last of the Mohicans.* Cambridge: Cambridge University Press, 1992.

Pedersen, Holger. *The Discovery of Language: Linguistic Science in the Nineteenth Century.* Bloomington: Indiana University Press, 1931.

Peet, Stephen D. *Prehistoric America.* 3 vols. Chicago: Office of the American Antiquarian, 1892–1899.

Peirce, Charles. *The Arts and Sciences Abridged: With a Selection of Pieces, from Celebrated Modern Authors, Calculated to Improve the Manners and Refine the Taste of Youth: Particularly Designed and Arranged for the Use of Schools.* Portsmouth, N.H., 1811.

Pickering, Charles. *The Races of Man.* Boston: Charles C. Little and James Brown, 1848.

Pidgeon, William. *Traditions of De-Coo-Dah and Antiquarian Researches.* New York: Horace Thayer, 1858.

Porter, Charlotte. *The Eagle's Nest: Natural History and American Ideas, 1812–1842.* University Park: University of Alabama Press, 1986.

Powell, Earl. *Thomas Cole.* New York: Harry Abrams, Inc., 1990.

Powell, John Wesley. *Indian Linguistic Families of America North of Mexico; Franz Boas, Handbook of American Indian Languages.* Edited by Preston Holder. Lincoln: University of Nebraska Press, 1966.

———. *Introduction to the Study of Indian Languages.* Washington, D.C.: Government Printing Office, 1877.

———. *Introduction to the Study of Indian Languages.* 2d ed. Washington, D.C.: Government Printing Office, 1880.

Rafinesque, C. S. *Ancient Monuments of North and South America.* Philadelphia: n.p., 1838.

Regis, Pamela. *Describing America: Bartram, Jefferson, Crevecouer, and the Influence of Natural History.* Northern Illinois University Press, 1992.

Resek, Carl. *Lewis Henry Morgan: American Scholar.* Chicago: University of Chicago Press, 1960.

Reuben, Julie A. *The Making of the Modern University: Intellectual Transformation and the Marginalization of Morality.* Chicago: University of Chicago Press, 1996.

Reynolds, Joshua. *Discourses on Art.* Edited by Robert Wark. San Marino, Cal.: Huntington Library, 1959.

Rivinus, E. F., and E. M. Youssef. *Spencer Baird of the Smithsonian.* Washington, D.C.: Smithsonian Institution Press, 1992.

Rosenberg, Charles. *No Other Gods: On Science and American Social Thought.* Baltimore: Johns Hopkins University Press, 1961.

Ross, Dorothy, ed. *Modernist Impulses in the Human Sciences, 1870–1930.* Baltimore: Johns Hopkins University Press, 1994.

Rydell, Robert. *All the World's a Fair.* Chicago: University of Chicago Press, 1984.

Salamon, Lynda. "Two Nineteenth-Century Views of History: James Fenimore Cooper and Francis Parkman." Ph.D. diss., University of Maryland, 1989.

Scheckel, Susan. *The Insistence of the Indian: Race and Nationalism in Nineteenth-Century American Culture.* Princeton: Princeton University Press, 1998.

Schoolcraft, Henry. *Discourse Delivered on the Anniversary of the Historical Society of Michigan.* Detroit: Geo. L. Whitney, 1830.

———. *Mr. Schoolcraft's Address before the New York Historical Society: "Incentives to the Study of the Ancient Period of American History."* New York: n.p., 1847.

———. *Notes on the Iroquois; or Contributions to American History, Antiquities, and General Ethnology.* Albany: Erastus H. Pease & Co., 1847.

Sheehan, Bernard. *Seeds of Extinction: Jeffersonian Philanthropy and the American Indian.* Chapel Hill: University of North Carolina Press, Institute for Early American Study, 1973.

Silverberg, Robert. *The Mound Builders.* 1970. Reprint, Athens: Ohio University Press, 1986.

Silverstein, Michael, ed. *Whitney on Language.* Cambridge: MIT Press, 1971.

Simpson, David. *The Politics of American English, 1776–1850.* Oxford: Oxford University Press, 1985.

Slotkin, Richard. *The Fatal Frontier: The Myth of the Frontier in the Age of Industrialization, 1800–1890.* Norman: University of Oklahoma Press, 1985.

Smith, Sherry L. *Reimagining Indians: Native Americans through Anglo Eyes, 1880–1940.* Oxford: Oxford University Press, 2000.

Snead, James E. *Ruins and Rivals: The Making of Southwest Archaeology.* Tucson: University of Arizona Press, 2001.

Southall, James. *The Epoch of the Mammoth.* Philadelphia: J. B. Lippincott & Co., 1878.

———. *The Recent Origin of Man.* Philadelphia: J. B. Lippincott & Co., 1875.

Squier, E. G., and E. H. Davis. *Ancient Monuments of the Mississippi Valley.* New York: Barlett & Welford, 1848.

Stanton, William. *The Leopard's Spots: Scientific Attitudes toward Race in America, 1815–59.* Chicago: University of Chicago Press, 1960.

Stocking, George. *The Ethnographer's Magic.* Madison: University of Wisconsin Press, 1992.

———. *Race, Culture and Evolution: Essays in the History of Anthropology.* New York: Free Press, 1968.

———. *Victorian Anthropology.* New York: Free Press, 1987.

———, ed. *Objects and Others: Essays in Museums and Material Culture.* Madison: University of Wisconsin Press, 1985.

Stone, William. *The Life and Times of Sa-go-ye-wat-ha, or Red Jacket.* Albany: J. Munsell, 1866.

———. *Uncas and Miantonomah: A Historical Discourse.* New York: Dayton & Newman, 1842.

Tilton, Robert. *Pocahontas: The Evolution of an American Narrative.* Cambridge: Cambridge University Press, 1994.

Tiro, Karim. *Words and Deeds: Natives, Europeans and Writing in Eastern North America, 1500–1850.* Philadelphia: Rosenbach Museum and Library, 1997.

Tocqueville, Alexis de. *Democracy in America.* Garden City, N.Y.: Anchor Books, 1969.

Trachtenberg, Alan. *Reading American Photographs: Images as History, Mathew Brady to Walker Evans.* New York: Hill and Wang, 1989.

Trigger, Bruce. *A History of Archaeological Thought.* Cambridge: Cambridge University Press, 1989.

Truettner, William H. *A Natural Man Observed: A Study of Catlin's Indian Gallery.* Washington, D.C.: Smithsonian Institution Press, 1979.

————, ed. *The West as America: Reinterpreting Images of the Frontier, 1820–1920.* Washington, D.C.: Smithsonian Institution Press, National Museum of American Art, 1991.

Truettner, William H., and Alan Wallach, eds. *Thomas Cole: Landscape into History.* New Haven: Yale University Press, 1994.

Tylor, Edward. *Anthropology.* 1881. Reprint, New York: Appleton and Company, 1903.

Valentine, Lisa Philips, and Regna Darnell, eds. *Theorizing the Americanist Tradition.* Toronto: University of Toronto Press, 1999.

Voget, Fred. *A History of Ethnology.* New York: Holt, Rinehart and Winston, 1975.

Wainwright, Nicholas B. *Philadelphia in the Romantic Age of Lithography.* Philadelphia: Historical Society of Pennsylvania, 1958.

Wallace, Anthony F. C. *Jefferson and the Indians: The Tragic Fate of the First Americans.* Cambridge: Harvard University Press, Belknap Press, 1999.

White, Hayden. *Metahistory.* Baltimore: Johns Hopkins University Press, 1973.

Whitney, William Dwight. *The Life and Growth of Language.* 1875. Reprint, New York: Appleton & Company, 1898.

Willey, Gordon, and Jeremy Sabloff. *A History of American Archaeology.* 3d ed. New York: W. H. Freeman and Company, 1993.

Williams, Stephen. *Fantastic Archaeology: The Wild Side of North American Prehistory.* Philadelphia: University of Pennsylvania Press, 1991.

Wilshire, Bruce. *The Primal Roots of American Philosophy: Pragmatism, Phenomenology and Native American Thought.* University Park: Pennsylvania State University Press, 2000.

Wilson, Daniel. *Prehistoric Annals of Scotland.* 2d ed. London: Macmillan and Co., 1863.

————. *Prehistoric Man.* Cambridge: Macmillan and Co., 1862.

Wilson, Thomas. *Catalogue of the Display from the Department of Prehistoric Anthropology, United States National Museum.* Washington, D.C.: Government Printing Office, 1895.

Winchell, Alexander. *Preadamites; or a Demonstration of the Existence of Man Before Adam.* Chicago: S. C. Griggs and Company, 1880.

Winsor, Justin, ed. *Narrative and Critical History of America.* New York: Houghton, Mifflin & Company, 1888.

Wolfe, M. Melissa. *American Indian Portraits: Elbridge Ayer Burbank in the West, 1897–1910.* Youngstown, Ohio: Butler Museum of Art, 2000.

Worster, Donald. *A River Running West: The Life of John Wesley Powell.* Oxford: Oxford University Press, 2001.

Wright, Henry C. *Anthropology; or the Science of Man.* Cincinnati: E. Shepard, 1850.

Wylie, Alison, and Valerie Pinsky, eds. *Critical Traditions in Contemporary Archaeology.* Cambridge: Cambridge University Press, 1989.

Youmans, William Jay. *Pioneers of Science in America.* New York: Appleton and Company, 1896.

Articles

Abbott, C. C. "Indications of the Indians of North America." *American Naturalist* (1876): 65–72.

Abrams, Ann Uhry. "Benjamin West's Documentation of Colonial History: *William Penn's Treaty with the Indians.*" *Art Bulletin* 64 (1982): 59–75.

Achelis, Thomas. "The Science of Ethnology." *Open Court* 4 (1890): 2312–2318.

Agassiz, Louis. "America the Old World." *Atlantic* 11 (1863): 373–382.

Alexander, Hartley Burr. "The Poetry of the American Indian." *Nation* 109 (1919): 757–759.

Alexie, Sherman. "What You Pawn I Will Redeem." *The New Yorker,* April 21 and 28, 2003, p. 169.

"American Indians." *Southern Literary Messenger* 6 (1840): 333–337.

"American Indians Look for Recognition from Pa." *Philadelphia Inquirer,* February 23, 2003.

"Are Our Colleges Doing Their Job?" *The World's Work* 13 (1906–1907): 8524–8526.

Atwater, Caleb. "Description of the Antiquities Discovered in the State of Ohio and Other Western States." *Archaeologia Americana* 1 (1820): 105–251.

———. "Eloquence of the North American Indians." *Magazine of American History* 5 (1880): 211–214. Originally published in 1846.

Baker, Lee. "Daniel G. Brinton's Success on the Road to Obscurity, 1890–1899." *Cultural Anthropology* 15 (2000): 394–423.

"Baldwin's Prehistoric Nations." *Nation* 8 (1869): 397–399.

Banforth, D. B., and A. C. Spaulding. "Human Behavior, Explanation, Archaeology, History, and Science." *Journal of Anthropological Archaeology* 1 (1982): 159–178.

Barnhart, Terry. "An American Menagerie: The Cabinet of Squier and Davis." *Timeline* (1985–1986): 2–17.

———. "In Search of the Mound Builders: The State Archaeological Association of Ohio, 1875–1885." *Ohio History* 107 (1998): 125–170.

Barnes, James. "Bancroft, Motley, Parkman and Prescott: A Study of Their Success as Historians." *Literature and History* 5 (1977): 55–72.

Bidney, David. "The Idea of the Savage in North American Ethnohistory." *Journal of the History of Ideas* 15 (1954): 322–327.

Bliss, L. "Drake's Indian History." *North American Review* 44 (1837): 301–334.

Boas, Franz. "Ethnology at the Exposition." *Cosmopolitan* 15 (1893): 607–609.

Bolt, Christine. "Return of the Native: Some Reflections on the History of American Indians." *Journal of American Studies* 8 (1974): 247–259.

Brinton, Daniel. "The Aims of Anthropology." *Popular Science Monthly* 48 (1895–1896): 59–72.

———. "American Languages and Why We Should Study Them." *Pennsylvania Magazine of History and Biography* 9 (1885): 15–35.

Brinton, Ellen Starr. "Benjamin West's Painting of Penn's Treaty with the Indians." *Bulletin of the Friends Historical Society* 30 (1941): 99–166.

Brush, George de Forest. "An Artist among the Indians." *Century* 8 (1885): 55–57.

B.T.C. "Indian Eloquence." *Port Folio*, 2d ser., 5 (1811): 277–278.

Carpenter, Edmund S. "The Role of Archaeology in the 19th Century Controversy between Developmentalism and Degeneration." *Pennsylvania Archaeologist* 20 (1950): 5–18.

Carr, Helen. "The Myth of Hiawatha." *Literature and History* 12 (1986): 58–78.

Cass, L. "Indians of North America." *North American Review* 22 (1826): 53–119.

"Catlin on the North American Indians." *Edinburgh Review* 74 (1841–1842): 415–430.

"Catlin's North American Indians." *United States Magazine and Democratic Review* 11 (1842): 44–52.

Coan, T. M. "Prehistoric Times." *Popular Science Monthly* 1 (1872): 101–112.

Collier, Donald, and Harry Tschopik. "The Role of Museums in American Anthropology." *American Anthropologist* 56 (1954): 768–779.

Conn, Steven. "Narrative Trauma and Civil War History Painting, or Why Are These Pictures So Terrible?" *History and Theory* (2002): 17–42.

Conn, Steven, and Andrew Walker. "The History in the Art: Painting the Civil War." *Museum Studies* 27 (2001): 60–81.

Cooke, John Esten. "Cooper's Indians." *Appleton's Journal* 12 (1874): 264–267.

"Cooper's Novels and Travels." *North American Review*, 46 (1838): 1–19.

Cunningham, Raymond. "The German Historical World of Herbert Baxter Adams: 1874–1876." *Journal of American History* 68 (1981): 261–275.

Curtis, E. S. "Vanishing Indian Types: The Tribes of the Southwest." *Scribner's* 39 (1906): 513–529.

Davis, J. Barnard. "Anthropology and Ethnology." *Anthropological Review* 6 (1868): 394–399.

Dawkins, W. Boyd. "Early Man in America." *North American Review* 137 (1883): 338–349.

Dexter, Ralph W. "Frederic Ward Putnam and the Development of Museums of Natural History and Anthropology in the United States." *Curator* 9 (1966): 151–155.

Dippie, Brian. "Representing the Other: The North American Indian," in *Anthropology and Photography, 1860–1920*, ed. Elizabeth Edwards, 132–136. New Haven: Yale University Press, 1992.

Distant, W. L. "North American Ethnology." *Nature* 21 (1879–1880): 247–248.

Dunbar, John. "The Pawnee Indians." *Magazine of American History* 5 (1880): 321–342.

DuPonceau, Stephen. "A Memoir on the History of the Celebrated Treaty." *Memoirs of the Historical Society of Pennsylvania* 3 (1834, 1836): 147–199.

———. "A Short Description of the Province of New Sweden." *Memoirs of the Historical Society of Pennsylvania* 3 (1834, 1836): 32–146.

Eastman, Carolyn. "The Indian Censures the White Man: 'Indian Eloquence' and American Reading Audiences in the Early Republic." Unpublished paper.

Edgerton, Franklin. "Notes on Early American Work in Linguistics." *Proceedings of the American Philosophical Society* 87 (1943): 25–34.

Errington, Joseph. "Colonial Linguistics." *Annual Review of Anthropology* 30 (2001): 19–39.

Evans, John. "Prehistoric Archaeology." *Nature* 1 (1869): 77–78.

Farrar, F. W. "Philology and Darwinism." *Nature* 1 (1870): 527–529.

Faust, Drew Gilpin. "Race, Gender, and Confederate Nationalism: William D. Washington's *Burial of Latane*." *Southern Review* 25 (1989): 297.

Fellows, George. "The Relation of Anthropology to the Study of History." *American Journal of Sociology* 1 (1895–1896): 41–49.

Felton, C. C., and J. Sparks. "McKenney and Hall's *History of the North American Indians*." *North American Review* 47 (1838): 134–148.

Fiske, John. "The Genesis of Language." *North American Review* 109 (1869): 305–367.

Flannery, Tim. "Who Came First?" *New York Review of Books*, June 12, 2003, pp. 51–53.

Forbes, Jack D. "Frontiers in American History and the Role of the Frontier Historian." *Ethnohistory* 15 (1968): 203–235.

Forry, Samuel. "The Mosaic Account of the Unity of the Human Race." *American Biblical Repository*, 2d ser., 10 (1843): 29–80.

Freeman, Edward. "Race and Language." *Contemporary Review* 29 (1876–1877): 711–741.

Gallati, Barbara Dayer. "Blurring the Lines between Likeness and Type," in *American Indian Portraits: Elbridge Ayer Burbank in the West, 1897–1910*, ed. Melissa Wolfe. Youngstown, Ohio: Butler Museum of Art, 2000.

Gallatin, Albert. "Synopsis of the Indian Tribes of North America." *Archaeologia Americana* 2 (1836): 155–158.

Gibbon, John. "Civilization amongst the Indians." *Penn Monthly Magazine* 5 (1874): 300–304.

Gildersleeve, B. L. "University Work in America and Classical Philology." *Princeton Review* (Jan.–June 1879): 511–536.

Goddard, Pliny Earle. "The Present Condition of Our Knowledge of North American Languages." *American Anthropologist* 16 (1914): 555–601.

Goodman, Roy, and Pierre Swiggers. "'To Collect and Preserve Such Information as May Be Obtained Concerning the Indian Languages': An Early Program for American Linguistics." *Orbis* 37 (1994): 221–233.

Gordon, George Byron. "Review." *American Anthropologist* 10 (1908): 436.

Hale, Horatio. "Indian Migrations as Evidenced by Language." *American Antiquarian* 5 (1883): 18–28; 108–124.

———. "Man and Language; or, The True Basis of Anthropology." *American Antiquarian* 17 (1893): 15–24.

Hale, N. "Heckewelder's Indian History." *North American Review* 9 (1819): 155–178.

Hall, G. Stanley. "Civilization and Savagery." *Proceedings of the Massachusetts Historical Society*, 2d ser., 17 (1903): 5–13.

Heckewelder, John. "An Account of the History, Manners, and Customs of the Indian Nations Who Once Inhabited Pennsylvania and the Neighboring States." *Transactions of the Historical and Literary Committee of the American Philosophical Society* 1 (1819): 3–347.

Hill, Jane H., and Kenneth C. Hill. "American Indian Languages." *American Anthropologist* 102 (2000): 161–163.

"Historical Notes." *Pennsylvania Magazine of History and Biography* 9 (1885): 334–338.

"History and Languages of the North American Tribes." *North American Review* 44 (1837): 34–59.

Holmes, W. H. "Areas of Cultural Characterization Tentatively Outlined as an Aid in the Study of Antiquities." *American Anthropologist* 16 (1914): 413–446.

———. "The World's Fair Congress of Anthropology." *American Anthropologist* 6 (1893): 423–434.

Horsman, Reginald. "Scientific Racism and the American Indian in the Mid-Nineteenth Century." *American Quarterly* 27 (1975): 152–168.

Howells, William Dean. "Mr. Parkman's Histories." *Atlantic Monthly* 34 (1874): 602–610.

Hudson, Charles. "James Adair as Anthropologist." *Ethnohistory* 24 (1977): 311–328.

Humphrey, Herman. "Indian Rights and Our Duties." N.p., 1831.

"Indian Eloquence." *Knickerbocker* 7 (1836): 385–390.

"Indian Extermination or Civilization." *Republic; a Monthly Magazine Devoted to the Dissemination of Political Information* 2 (1874): 308–316.

"The Indians in American Art." *The Crayon* 3 (1856): 28.

"Is the African and Caucasian of Common Origin?" *DeBow's Review* 9 (1850): 243–245.

"Is the Study of Language a Physical Science?" *North American Review* 73 (1851): 163–189.

"Jeffries Wyman." Memorial Meeting of the Boston Society of Natural History, October 7, 1874.

Jenkins, David. "Object Lessons and Ethnographic Displays: Museum Exhibition and the Making of American Anthropology." *Comparative Studies in Society and History* 36 (1994): 242–270.

Joyce, William. "Antiquarians and Archaeologists: The American Antiquarian Society, 1812–1912." *Proceedings of the American Antiquarian Society*, n.s., 91 (1981): 301–317.

Kah-ge-ga-goh-bouh. "The American Indian." *American Whig Review* 9 (1849): 691–697.

Kornfield, Eve. "Encountering 'the Other': American Intellectuals and the Indians in the 1790s." *William and Mary Quarterly* 52 (1995): 287–314.

Landis, Charles. "Benjamin West and the Royal Academy." *Pennsylvania Magazine of History and Biography* 50 (1926): 241–253.

"Language and Human Unity." *North American Review* 105 (1867): 214–241.

"Language and the Study of Language." *The Nation* 5 (1867): 369–370.

Lauzon, Matthew. "Savage Eloquence in America and the Linguistic Construction of a British Identity in the 18th Century." *Historiographia Linguistica* 23 (1996): 123–157.

Lubbock, John. "North American Archaeology." Smithsonian Institution *Annual Report* (1862): 318–336.

Marienstras, Elise. "The Common Man's Indian: The Image of the Indian as a Promoter of National Identity in the Early National Era," in *Native Americans and the Early Republic*, ed. Frederick Hoxie et al., 261–262. Charlottesville: University of Virginia Press, U.S. Capitol Historical Society, 1999.

Mark, Joan. "Frank Hamilton Cushing and an American Science of Anthropology." *Perspectives in American History* 10 (1976): 449–486.

Mason, Otis T. "Sketch of North American Anthropology in 1879." *American Naturalist* 14 (1880): 348–356.

———. "What Is Anthropology?" Lecture delivered March 18, 1882. Washington, D.C.: Judd & Detweiler, 1882.

Matile, G. A. "American Ethnology." *American Journal of Education* 17 (1867): 425–432.

Mayer, Brantz. "Tah-Gah-Jute or Logan and Captain Michael Cresap." Lecture delivered to the Maryland Historical Society, 1851.

McGee, W. J. "Fifty Years of American Science." *Atlantic Monthly* 82 (1898): 307–318.

Meline, M. M. "Ethnologic Studies among the North American Indians." *Catholic World* 33 (1881): 355–360.

Miles, Edwin. "The Young American Nation and the Classical World." *Journal of the History of Ideas* 35 (1974): 259–274.

Miller, Angela. "Thomas Cole and Jacksonian America: *The Course of Empire* as Political Allegory." *Prospects* 14 (1989): 65–92.

Moorehead, Warren K. "A Century of American Archaeology." *Popular Science News,* June 4, 1901.

Morgan, Lewis Henry. "Indian Migrations." *North American Review* 109 (1869): 391–442.

Murphree, Idus L. "The Evolutionary Anthropologists: The Progress of Mankind." *Proceedings of the American Philosophical Society* 105 (1961): 265–300.

Murray, Patricia. "Painting the Indians," *Providence Journal-Bulletin,* 17 Nov. 1991, pp. 6–12.

Nemerov, Alex. "Doing the 'Old America': The Image of the American West, 1880–1920," in *The West as America: Reinterpreting Images of the Frontier, 1820–1920,* ed. William Truettner. Washington, D.C.: Smithsonian Institution Press, National Museum of American Art, 1991.

"North American Indians." *Southern Literary Messenger* 6 (1840): 190–192.

"The North American Indians." *Westminster Review* 74 (1860): 333–354.

"The North American Indians." *Living Age* 139 (1878): 436–438.

Norton, Charles Eliot. "The First American Classical Archaeologist." *American Journal of Archaeology* 1 (1885): 3–9.

"Notes on the Extinct Tribes of North America." *Historical Magazine* 7 (1863): 175–177.

Nott, J. C. "Unity of the Human Race." *Southern Quarterly Review* 9 (1846): 1–57.

"On the Causes of the Depopulation of the American Indians." *Analectic Magazine* 7 (1816): 318–333.

"Origins of the American Antiquarian Society." *Archaeologia Americana* 1 (1820): 30.

"The Origins of the North American Indians." *Port Folio* 4 (1817) 168–170.

Parkman, Francis. "James Fenimore Cooper." *North American Review* 74 (1852): 147–161.

———. "Native Races of the Pacific States." *North American Review* 120 (1875): 34–47.

Peet, Stephen Dennison. "Autochthonous Origin of the American Civilization." *American Antiquarian* 11 (1889): 314–320.

———. "The Beginnings of History." *American Antiquarian* 17 (1895): 273–288.

———. "A Comparison between the Archaeology of Europe and America." *American Antiquarian* 1 (1879): 211–294.

———. "The Congress of Anthropology." *American Antiquarian* 15 (1893): 308–311.

———. "The Difference between Indian and Mound-Builder Relics." *American Antiquarian* 12 (1890): 251–272.

———. "The Mound Builders." *American Antiquarian* 2 (1880): 185–200.

———. "Some Problems in Connection with the Stone Age." *American Antiquarian* 9 (1887): 280–295.

———. "The Three Fold Division of the Human Race." *American Antiquarian* 7 (1885): 171–176.

———. "The Tribal Condition of the American Races." *American Antiquarian* 3 (1880–1881): 202–217.

Persons, Stowe. "The Cyclical Theory of History in Eighteenth Century America." *American Quarterly* 4 (1954): 147–163.

Pickering, James. "Indian Languages." *Encyclopedia Americana.* Vol. 6. Philadelphia: Desilver, Thomas & Co., 1836.

———. "Languages of the American Indians." *North American Review* 9 (1819): 179–187.

Piggott, Stuart. "Prehistory and the Romantic Movement." *Antiquity* 11 (1937): 31–38.

Powell, John Wesley. "The Course of Human Progress." *Science,* 11 (1888): 220–222.

———. "From Barbarism to Civilization." *American Anthropologist* 1 (1888): 97–123.

———. "Philology, or the Science of Activities Designed for Expression." (Washington, D.C.: Government Printing Office, 1903): cxxxix–clxx.

———. "Philosophic Bearings of Darwinism." Lecture to the Biological Society of America, May 12, 1882. Washington, D.C.: Judd & Detweiler, 1882.

———. "Problems of American Archaeology." *The Forum* 8 (1889–1890): 638–652.

———. "The Pueblo Indians." *Potter's American Monthly* 10 (1878).

———. "Sketch of Lewis H. Morgan." *Popular Science Monthly* 18 (1880–1881): 114–121.

———. "Whence Came the American Indians." *The Forum* 24 (1898): 676–688.

Putnam, F. W. "Archaeological and Ethnological Research in the United States." *Proceedings of the American Antiquarian Society* 14 (1902): 461–470.

"Removal of the Indians." *North American Review* 30 (1830): 62–121.

"Reports of the Commissioner of Indian Affairs, 1855–58." *North American Review* 90 (1860): 57–76.

Richter, Daniel. "Onas, the Long Knife: Pennsylvanians and Indians: 1783–1794," in *Native Americans and the Early Republic,* ed. Frederick Hoxie et al., 125–161. Charlottesville: University of Virginia Press, U.S. Capitol Historical Society, 1999.

Reed, Eugene. "The Ignoble Savage." *Modern Language Review* 59 (1964): 53–64.

Ross, Dorothy. "Grand Narrative in American Historical Writing: From Romance to Uncertainty." *American Historical Review* 100 (1995): 651–677.

———. "Historical Consciousness in Nineteenth Century America." *American Historical Review* 89 (1984): 909–928.

R. S. H. "Indian Women." *Literary World* 3 (1848): 401–402.

Schnell, Michael. "The For[e]gone Conclusion: The Leatherstocking Tales and Antebellum History." *American Transcendental Quarterly* 10 (1996): 331–348.

Schoolcraft, Henry Rowe. "History and Languages of the North American Tribes." *North American Review* 45 (1837): 34–59.

———. "Plan for American Ethnological Investigation." *Annual Report of the Smithsonian Institution* 1885: 907–914.

———. "The Red Man of America." *North American Review* 54 (1842): 283–299.

"Schoolcraft on the Indian Tribes." *North American Review* 77 (1853): 245–262.

Sheehan, Bernard. "Looking Back: Parkman's Pontiac." *Indiana Magazine of History* 92 (1996): 56–66.

Short, C. W. "Antiquities of Ohio." *Port Folio* 4 (1817): 179–181.

"Sketch of George Catlin." *Popular Science Monthly* 39 (1891): 402–409.

Smith, Raoul N. "The Interest in Language and Languages in Colonial and Federal America." *Proceedings of the American Philosophical Society* 123 (1979): 29–46.

Squier, E. G. "Aboriginal Monuments of the Mississippi Valley." *Transactions of the American Ethnological Society* 2 (1848).

———. "American Ethnology." *American Whig Review* 9 (1849): 385–398.

Sparks, J. "Heckewelder on the American Indians." *North American Review* 26 (1828): 357–403.

Starr, Frederick. "Anthropology at the Fair." *Popular Science Monthly* 43 (1893): 610–621.

Steele, Ian K. "Cooper and Clio: The Sources for 'A Narrative of 1757,' " *Canadian Review of American Studies* 20 (1989): 121–135.

Stocking, George. "Polygenesist Thought in Post-Darwinian Anthropology," in *Culture and Evolution: Essays in the History of Anthropology.* New York: Free Press, 1968.

Stone, William. "Archaeological Discovery." *Magazine of American History* 5 (1880): 34–36.

Sturtevant, William. "Patagonian Giants and Baroness Hyde de Neuville's Iroquois Drawings." *Ethnohistory* 27 (1980): 331–348.

Swanton, John R., and Roland B. Dixon. "Primitive American History." *American Anthropologist* 16 (1914): 376–412.

Thomas, Cyrus. "Curious Customs and Strange Freaks of the Moundbuilders." *American Anthropologist* 1 (1888): 353–355.

Tracy, William. "Indian Eloquence." *Appleton's Journal* 6 (1871): 543–545.

"Transactions of the American Ethnological Society." *United States Magazine and Democratic Review* 17 (1845): 50–62.

Trennert, Robert A. "Fairs, Expositions, and the Changing Image of Southwestern Indians, 1876–1904." *New Mexico Historical Review* (1987): 127–150.

———. "Popular Imagery and the American Indian: A Centennial View." *New Mexico Historical Review* 51 (1976): 215–232.

Trigger, Bruce. "Archaeology and the Image of the American Indian." *American Antiquity* 45 (1980): 662–676.

Truettner, William H. "Dressing the Part: Thomas Eakins's Portrait of Frank Hamilton Cushing." *American Art Journal* 17 (1985): 49–72.

Tylor, Edward. "American Aspects of Anthropology." *Popular Science Monthly* 26 (1884–1885): 152–168.

Tyrell, Ian. "Making Nations/Making States: American Historians in the Context of Empire." *Journal of American History* 86 (1999): 1015–1044.

"The Unity of Language and of Mankind." *North American Review* 73 (1851): 163–189.

"The Unity of the Human Race." *American Whig Review* 12 (1850): 567–586.

Vail, C. E. "Our Duty to the Future." *Science Monthly* 3 (1916): 585–595.

Vaughan, Alden T. "From White Man to Redskin: Changing Anglo-American Perceptions of the American Indian." *American Historical Review* 87 (1982): 917–953.

Veit, Richard. "A Case of Archaeological Amnesia: A Contextual Biography of Montroville Wilson Dickeson (1810–1882), Early American Archaeologist." *Archaeology of Eastern North America* 25 (1997): 97–123.

"Vindication of the United States." *Southern Literary Messenger* 11 (1845): 202–211.

Virchow, Rudolph. "The Problems of Anthropology." *Popular Science Monthly* 42 (1892–1893): 373–377

Watson, Rubie. "Opening the Museum: The Peabody Museum of Archaeology and Ethnology." *Symbols* (Fall 2001): 2–7.

Whitney, William Dwight. "Darwinism and Language." *North American Review* 119 (1874): 61–88.

———. "The Value of Linguistic Science." *New Englander* 26 (1867): 30–52.

Wiet, John Phillip. "McKenney-Hall Prints from the History of the Indian Tribes of North America." *Imprint* 5 (1980): 12–19.

Wilder, Burt. "Sketch of Dr. Jeffries Wyman." *Popular Science Monthly* 6 (Jan. 1875): 355–360.

"William Penn's First Treaty with the Indians." *Penny Magazine* 2 (1833): 403–406.

Wilson, Thomas. "Importance of the Science and of the Department of Prehistoric Anthropology." *American Naturalist* 26 (1892): 681–689.

Winsor, Justin. "The Perils of Historical Narrative." *Atlantic Monthly* 66 (1890): 289–297.

Wissler, Clark. "The American Indian and the American Philosophical Society." *Proceedings of the American Philosophical Society* 86 (1942): 189–204.

———. "Material Cultures of the North American Indians." *American Anthropologist* 16 (1914): 447–505.

Zegas, Judy Braun. "North American Indian Exhibit at the Centennial Exposition." *Curator* 19 (1976): 162–173.